Peter Seabrook's book of
THE GARDEN

CASSELL LTD
35 Red Lion Square, London WC1R 4SG
and at Sydney, Auckland, Toronto, Johannesburg
an affiliate of Macmillan Publishing Co. Inc.,
New York

Designed and produced for Cassell Ltd by
Intercontinental Book Productions
Berkshire House, Queen Street,
Maidenhead, Berkshire, SL6 1NF.
Copyright © 1979 Intercontinental Book Productions.

ISBN 0 304 30320 8
Printed by L.E.G O - Vicenza - Italy

Peter Seabrook's book of
THE GARDEN

Written by Peter Seabrook
Illustrated by Brian Edwards
Michael Strand and Sara Silcock
Edited by Peter McHoy

CASSELL
London

Contents

Introduction

Several objectives have been remembered throughout the construction of this book. The term construction is used purposely because the written word, drawings and photographs have all been carefully built around the basic ideas.

The new gardener could well be entering his garden gate for the first time with this book tucked under his arm. Step by step and using one chapter after another, there is help in the construction, reconstruction and renovation of common sized gardens.

Every effort has been made to include information on the practical details. Tips are included to help achieve greater success with less effort and less chance of disappointment.

The requirements of gardeners with very little outdoor soil, and those restricted to window-boxes and paved terrace or yard, have been included. Those people with a limited amount of time will also find their needs given consideration.

Information gathered from many parts of the Western gardening world, coupled with years of practical gardening experience have helped to provide detail which will be of interest to the dedicated and skilled gardener.

Thumbing through the pages you will see fine plants and excellent plant uses illustrated in superb full colour photographs.

There are also many pictures taken in ordinary domestic gardens and situations when practical tasks were carried out.

Many miles were travelled to find some of the very fine gardening examples and these are the perfection for which we all strive. Don't feel disappointed if your first sowing and planting fails to reach the quality of perfect specimens. We all have our disappointments and luckily in gardening many mistakes can be buried at the end of one year and a completely fresh start made in the next one.

There are more ways than one to carry out many gardening practices. While we tend to use rules of thumb, the scope for variation is unlimited. If one way works for you, fine, but don't be afraid to carry out small trials to see where the proven way can be further improved.

Small gardens mean closer spacing for many plants, if we are to fit in the range and variety of plants which interest us. Modern varieties are often bred to be more compact.

If you cover the soil with plant foliage, weed growth will be smothered. A good canopy of leaves is the natural form of things, and soil shaded from the sun is less likely to dry out and cake on the surface.

Cultivating plants gives pleasure at all stages to the grower and, in many cases, to the onlooker as well.

Garden Planning

It is always a problem to know where to start when you take over a garden. Often it is easier starting absolutely from scratch, even if more work is involved improving the soil. Established gardens really need watching for a full growing season to see just what treasures the garden contains. Start chopping into the soil with a spade and all too soon hidden bulbs come up clearly dissected. Old, and on first sight apparently neglected, trees and bushes can produce the finest flowers and fruits, proving them well worth attention and rejuvenation.

In a perfect world previous owners would no doubt leave behind a detailed plan with every planting named and labelled. Sadly few of us have the time for such perfection, but it is worth sketching out ideas and attempting to include the many requirements needed from the average home plot.

Most of us are in a tearing rush to get things growing in much the same way we need curtains up and rooms redecorated indoors. But gardening isn't easy to rush and the first burst of enthusiasm is best directed at preparing the soil for hedges, trees and lawns.

Hedges need to go in first to give the whole garden shelter as quickly as possible and perhaps some privacy. Trees take time to give shade and fill the site allocated to them and the sooner they are in the better. Don't skimp on the soil preparation, however, because once in there is no second chance to improve soil around deeply penetrating roots.

Levelling the garden and establishing the lawns comes next. It is quite easy to dig beds and borders out from the grassed area but not very easy to get good edges to lawns where the flower and vegetable beds were planted first.

Trees will give height and depth to the smallest garden and it is well worth checking through neighbourhood gardens to see which kinds are growing

A colourful low hedge, attractive wall plants, specimen tree, conifers, lawn and summer bedding are used in this attractive small garden plan.

well. This is a good idea for other plants too in due course.

Container-grown specimens are recommended not only for the option to plant all the year round, even in full leaf, but more for the ability to site for a few days where you propose to plant. Then you can really look at the positioning and move a plant a foot or two to get a nice positioning when viewed from house and garden.

Hard landscaping, the paving and the walling can follow in due course as long as an overall plan is in mind with path access to sheds, garages and clothes driers included.

UNDERSTANDING SOIL

There is a tremendous variation in soil types; invariably gardeners wish they had a different kind to suit a particular kind of plant. Even within one garden the soil types can vary from quite light sandy soil to heavy clay as a result of work during house construction.

Excepting those gardens where topsoil was cleared before the house was built and new topsoil brought in after building, there is little chance of changing the basic soil types. There are four main classifications: light sandy and stony soils, which are free-draining and very hungry; heavy clay soils, which are difficult to work but once mastered can be heavy yielding; chalky soils, which are also hungry and in which ericaceous plants which require acid conditions can't be grown; and fertile medium loams.

Very occasionally one is lucky enough to find a rich black silty or peaty soil which is very fertile. The peat soils apart, all types are improved by the addition of bulky organic

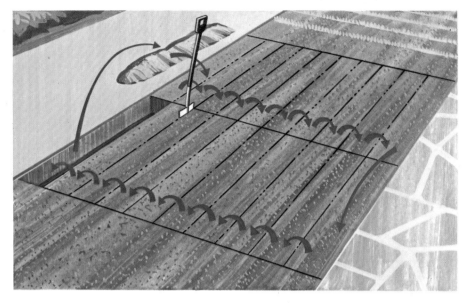

When single digging a large plot, the first trench of topsoil should be stacked as shown here; on a small plot, simply stack at the opposite end.

matter. It is important to distinguish between rotted down organic matter (garden compost, manure, spent mushroom compost and peat) which improve soil texture, and concentrated plant foods contained in fertilizers.

Generally the problem is getting sufficient organic matter. Even the heaviest clay soils and thinnest sandy soils will be easily worked and produce excellent plant growth if a 4–6 in. (10–15 cm) layer of organic matter is thoroughly incorporated.

Don't spread organic matter thinly over a large area. You never see the benefit this way. Really concentrate the application and spread thickly over a relatively small area before digging. Then when more rotted compost is available and more peat can be bought treat another patch and gradually improve the garden overall.

When buying peat and any other organic matter to improve soil always buy by volume, never by weight which is so much influenced by moisture content. Spent mushroom compost is often offered for garden soil improvement and this is fine as long as the soil is acid or neutral. Composts for mushroom growing usually contain some peat and chalk. The chalk will raise the pH and is therefore better not used excessively on alkaline soil.

Pulverized and composted bark is another organic material offered for soil improvement. I prefer to use this as a long-term mulch. The woody fibre resists weathering and lasts a long time. Dug into the ground it can draw too much nitrogen from the soil.

Organic matter in the soil helps light soil retain moisture, it improves the drainage in heavy soils, reduces the alkalinity of chalk soils and encourages the desired fibrous root growth.

By far the best method of incorporation is to mix well into the soil during autumn and winter digging. Spreading a good layer of compost over wet soil helps to keep the feet clean and makes the digging job much easier.

Mixing sand, ashes and other coarse material into heavy clay soils will improve drainage and make cultivation easier but don't over-do it. Equally, heavy clay soil brought in to mix with light sandy soils will improve the structure.

Whatever the soil type some form of annual cultivation is necessary in ornamental, fruit and vegetable gardens. Digging one spade's depth in autumn or winter is a good start.

Cultivation

There is no substitute for hand digging, and done in moderation, a small area at a time, it really is a most satisfying task. Use a spade which is comfortable for you, the handle smooth, the blade clean and shiny. Shiny blades are especially important when digging heavy, wet soil which sticks to everything.

Stony soils may on occasions be more easily dug with a fork but it is more difficult to get a level finish. Quite apart from the tool, I like to keep my footwear clean when digging. A scattering of peat or compost over wet surfaces helps here.

Single digging requires a good trench, the depth and width of a spade taken out first. On large plots divide in half and heap the soil from the trench across one half against the top of the other half. Just stack it at the other end of small plots.

Taking a 3–4 in. (7·5–10 cm) wide strip of soil at a time, cut out a clean

Do not remove large slices of soil when digging – 3–4 in. is about right.

Try to ensure that the soil is inverted, so that weeds are buried completely.

Heavy soils are best left in lumps, but in spring may be broken down.

slice of soil and invert it. When winter digging leave the large clods for the weather to break down. If you have to dig in spring then chop the surface down fine as you work back.

Watch what you are doing as the soil is inverted. Throw it over neatly so that surface weeds are thoroughly buried, rotted compost or peat well mixed in and the final surface left level across the plot. At the end of the plot fill in the trench with the soil heaped from the first trench.

Double digging involves cultivating to two spades' depth and is usually only needed where trees are being planted, hedges set out in poor soil and very thorough preparation is being made for exhibition flowers and vegetables.

Where you want to give a bit of extra-special treatment dig over the bottom of the trench when single digging. Cultivating the lower soil in this way is nearly as good as double digging.

Always pick out the roots of perennial weeds as you dig across. On heavy soils try to dig in drying weather conditions. Heavy rain can cake the surface on freshly turned wet soil and destroy the crumbly texture we are trying to produce. This is especially so with spring digging.

Where mechanical cultivators are used, rainfall immediately after chopping the soil fine and before the surface dries a little can be disastrous.

Alkalinity
Most plants require a neutral soil and apart from obvious white chalky soils the only sure way of finding the acidity or alkalinity of your soil is by chemical tests. There are cheap soil test kits available and if your soil registers below 6·5 pH (the term used to indicate an approximately neutral soil), then it is acid and lime must be added – ideally in early autumn.

If the soil is above 6·5 pH it is alkaline, and can be brought back to neutral by adding peat, which is naturally acid, by using acidic fertilizers such as sulphate of ammonia, or by adding powdered sulphur.

Soil Conditioners and Foods
Decaying organic matter, whether composted garden waste, rotted down leaves or peat, improves the soil for plants and encourages better root development, but it contains little plant food. Chemical fertilizers are one source of concentrated plant foods and

Regular digging, incorporating plenty of organic matter, will build up a good workable soil. Take out a good trench at the start.

well-rotted animal manures are the combination of organic matter and plant food.

Quite large quantities of organic matter are needed year after year to improve and retain a good tilth, with crumbly and easily worked soil.
· It is not possible for most gardeners to get plenty of bulky animal manure. Peat and garden compost is the alternative, backed up with concentrated chemical plant foods.

You will find it difficult to add too much organic matter to the garden but chemical fertilizers can be overdone, in extreme cases reducing plant growth.

One source of organic matter is 'green manure'. Here crops like lupin, mustard and even grass and clover mixtures are sown, then when well established dug into the soil. Annual lupin and clover has the advantage of adding nitrogen to the soil, and grass roots are very fibrous which improves soil structure.

Part of the green manure principle is included in garden cropping. Legume crops like Sweet Peas and beans enrich the soil by leaving behind extra nitrogenous plant food. The fibrous nature of leek roots will do much to break up heavy soil.

All of these are secondary however to the great quantity of soil-improving organic matter from composted garden waste.

Warmth, moisture and air are needed to rot down organic matter and if any one of these is absent the speed of breakdown is dramatically reduced. Shake up a great mixture of garden debris in mid-summer, damp it over and add a compost activator chemical to get a dramatic rise in temperature in days. This will quickly produce well-rotted material.

At other times of the year it will take longer and the easiest way is to have two heaps. Stake out a rectangle at least 5 ft × 3 ft (1·5 m × 1 m) using any convenient material for the sides. All non-weedy plant remains can be stacked in the bin. Once full to over-flowing I like to empty this out, ideally restacking in the second bin.

Mix soft green lawn mowings with tougher bean and flower stems as you refill. See that all the material is damp and dust over with a chemical compost maker to speed the rotting down. Cleanings from the rabbit cage and other animal cage cleanings are a good alternative for activation. This heap can then be left and the second one filled. Once the first is well rotted and dark brown it can be used either to dig in or mulch beds.

Some of the material on the top of the first heap may remain undecayed and this can be left behind to mix in with the material in the second bin. Using the warmth of summer to get compost

9

Lime is best applied in late autumn or during the winter, but as not all soils need lime it is best to test the soil first, using a special kit.

quickly well rotted provides material for autumn digging. Bins are then quickly refilled with fallen leaves and other crop remains.

Fertilizers

N.P.K. are the initials of nitrogen, phosphate and potash respectively, and these are the main soil-borne plant foods. They can be applied in natural organic form – usually more expensive – and as inorganic chemical fertilizers.

Nitrogen, the main food in organic fish manure and inorganic sulphate of ammonia, improves leafy growth. Use this to green-up lawns, to give a new vigorous boost to green leafy vegetables, and to encourage strong growth on blackcurrants and cucumbers.

Where plants have suffered from lack of water, hot sun and checks from cold, they can often be reinvigorated with nitrogenous fertilizers. They must not be used excessively in damp shaded conditions as they encourage leafy growth and susceptibility to disease.

Phosphate is the principal plant food in organic bonemeal and inorganic superphosphate. It encourages root development and helps seeds and fruit to mature. It is not generally used alone, although a dusting can be applied before raking down a seed bed.

Potash is very much the counterbalance to nitrogen. Where lack of sun gives excessive leaf growth and poor flowers, increasing the potash improves the growth.

Wood and bonfire ash is a good source of organic potash while sulphate of potash is the main inorganic source.

Compound fertilizers carefully mixed by the manufacturers are the easiest plant foods for gardeners to use. Good compounds like Growmore have a balanced formula, if anything with the emphasis on nitrogen. Most lawn fertilizers are high in nitrogen, while tomato and rose fertilizers are high in potash.

Apply general fertilizers at 2 oz per sq yd (60 g per sq m) early in spring, working it well into the soil. Never apply directly on or near the seed drill.

When transplanting woody subjects add all the peat and organic matter immediately, mixing it well into the soil, then topdress with fertilizers subsequently. This fertilizer is then slowly washed with rain to the developing roots.

It is a good idea to split the application to fruit and other trees, half in late summer to be taken up by the tree and held ready for the spring burst of growth. The second application in spring will improve summer growth. Well-fed plants are more resistant to frost damage.

Do not apply any general fertilizer in late autumn or winter as much will be washed out with winter rain.

While the general fertilizer applied in the initial soil preparation will do much of what is required, a little top-up material is helpful. Liquid fertilizer can be applied to runner beans, tomatoes, Sweet Peas and evergreen hedges for example. A higher potash topdressing to redcurrants, gooseberries and tomatoes will improve flavour. Alternatively quick-acting nitrogenous fertilizers like Nitro-chalk can be used to speed spring cabbage and wall-flowers into spring growth.

Remember, if you keep cropping the soil and taking goodness out then organic matter and plant foods must be replaced. The immediately available plant foods are, of course, soluble and easily taken up by the plant roots. Equally in light sandy soils, which drain freely, these plant foods are quickly leached. Apply fertilizers little and often on these soils.

Quickest acting of all are foliar fertilizers – the plant food here being taken up by the leaves and any run-off subsequently reaching the roots. They can be applied through the rose of a watering can and through sprayers.

The response will be seen in a few

A compost heap is an important part of any garden; it is useful to have two heaps, so that the compost can be turned and a new heap started.

Triangular offset paving gives variation and a feeling of space.

days if the weather is warm enough for rapid growth. All leafy subjects including apple, beetroot, spinach, carrots, hostas, peas and strawberries respond to foliar feeds.

PLANNING AND DESIGN

Once you have listed everything to be contained in your garden, the jigsaw puzzle, fitting them all in, can start. It is a good idea to list the requirements in priority because something may have to be left out.

Many gardens today are so small that landscape design and garden planning in the old sense has to give way to garages, fuel storage, caravan parks, clothes airers, children's sandpits and play areas, to name a few.

Even so a little careful planning and some good design ideas can make a small plot look larger than it is. Unsightly buildings and living areas can be screened or hidden behind decorative borders.

I quite like the serried ranks of neat vegetables growing vigorously in a small plot quite close to the house. Others may prefer such areas to be screened and well away from the back door. Greenhouses which need regular attention are best sited near the house, especially if electricity or gas has to be connected.

Bringing buildings like sheds and oil tanks very close to the house often makes them easier to hide, rather than taking them down the garden where the vista from indoors widens. A small area for the compost heap and perhaps incinerator is best reserved well away from the house.

Scale plans are fine for gardeners practised in working from a measured drawing. The less experienced may find it easier to mark the various areas

When making or reconstructing a garden, first level the site and mark out the proposed features and areas for buildings.

Here × *Cupressocyparis leylandii* is being planted to screen the background.

Gardens constantly change as plants grow. Compare this picture of a bed in the author's garden, with the one below, taken six years later.

The small silver *Chamaecyparis pisifera* 'Boulevard' in the picture above is now 5 ft (1·5 m) high, and the pyracantha has screened the wall.

out with pegs and strings. Plotting them then on squared paper helps keep the record.

Don't forget the speed of growth of trees and shrubs. Marking the site and likely size in ten years can be quite a revelation. Equally a 3 m × 2·6 m shed or greenhouse may not look anywhere near so big once marked out by canes to the area and height of the building.

A paved area close to the house serves many purposes, from sitting out in the sun to giving a dry area to clean shoes before entering the house.

Raised flower beds can be constructed on a terrace, tubs set on patios and even raised areas built for a small water garden. Having the water garden above soil level reduces the chances of someone – especially young children – falling into a pool by mistake. Raised gardens of any kind, at 20 in. (50 cm)

high, with a broad surrounding ledge, are convenient places to sit.

All the marking out and thought about likely growth apply equally to established gardens where the layout requires change and new features are to be constructed. If possible lay paving slabs on a firm base but without cement. This allows further quite simple rearrangement later.

Try to keep the lawn in one large piece, this is not only easier to mow but gives the largest possible area for children to play and adults to sit out.

Where vegetable plots are surrounded by paths many crops can be gathered without getting shoes covered in mud. Also, in wet conditions much of the cultivation can be done from the paths, reducing the damage to soil tilth.

Siting of paths to give clean and easy access to clothes airers, sheds, compost heap and greenhouse is important. Setting slabs like stepping stones in a lawn is often a good way to achieve this in a small garden.

There are three common shapes which affect small modern garden layouts. Where a row of houses is built around a crescent-shaped road, the houses on the outer circumference have narrow boundaries close to the house which spread out as one looks down the garden from the house.

A good evergreen shrub border each side of and close to the house hides the boundary and gives a feeling of space.

Houses built on the inner circumference have triangular gardens and a projection of evergreen growth two thirds of the way down one side, and half way down the other, helps screen the reduction in size.

Long, narrow gardens and small square ones can be made to look more spacious by running a path and border away from the parallel as you look down the garden.

Colourings, too, can help with optical illusions. Pale colours, preferably light blue, give a distant feel while bright colours, especially scarlet and yellow, give emphasis and bring things closer.

Variations on a plan

Taking the most common rectangular garden shape, some of the permutations in design can easily be illustrated by taking the plan shown opposite. Working from the house we start with the paved area. The example has a 3 m × 4 m vegetable plot set in the paved area. This could equally well be an attractive greenhouse structure,

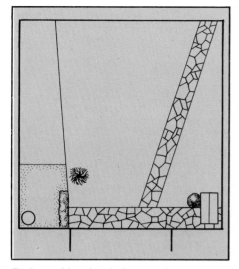

Paths and borders help to make a square garden look more spacious.

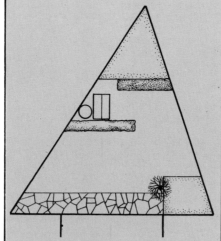

Cleverly placed hedges help to hide the converging lines of a triangle.

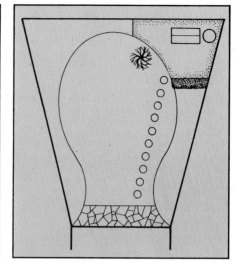

Planting shrubs close to the house help to hide closely fenced boundaries.

a sandpit or a raised water garden.

A small deciduous tree at the end of the terrace provides a little shade, is attractive in itself and can be used to hang bird feeders in the winter.

Two borders run out on either side, one on the left filled with dwarf conifers, Heathers, azaleas and rhododendrons underplanted with bulbs and given height with a Silver Birch. The other border has a manhole screened by evergreen camellias and is filled closer to the house with herbaceous plants and flowering annuals.

Two upright trees (1) and (2) mark the tips of the two borders and give a walk through to a possible vegetable plot (A), and fruit plot (B). These plots could be reversed if any taller fruit trees needed to be sited to the north of the plot to avoid casting shadows.

This design has been used to good effect in a plot bordered on east, north and west by very high walls. It could equally well be used in an open site with hedges planted around the boundary for shelter.

Just as long as each section gets a little direct sunshine each day most plants can be grown. Where the area is totally shaded then plants which thrive in shaded conditions must be chosen.

While books and catalogues indicate the conditions best for each plant, remember quite adequate growth is usually obtained with siting compromise. For example planting camellias away from east-facing walls is often recommended because rapid thawing in morning sun can turn the petals of open flowers brown. In practice the number of times this happens in a year is hardly significant and it is much better to plant east-facing if that is the

Move the various features in the plan to achieve the best overall layout. Trees 1 and 2 mark the path through to vegetable and fruit plots A and B.

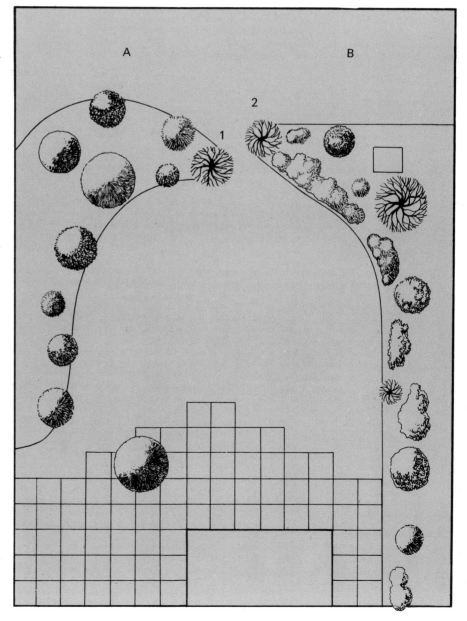

An evergreen close to the house screens the fence and triangular rose border gives a greater feeling of space in a short narrow garden.

only site available rather than have to manage without this plant.

Camellias prefer a sheltered site but in the high wall-surrounded garden mentioned, fierce wind turbulence between the walls stripped leaves off the camellias and yet they still thrive and flower. Efforts are being made to plant more bushy shrubs to reduce the wind damage and get better growth, proving that far from ideal sites can be mastered, with worthwhile results.

PROPAGATION
Plants from Seeds
Gardeners repeatedly refer to good tilth, crumbly fine soil and the need for sterile seed and potting composts because this is what you require for high germination of seed. All seeds need the right amount of moisture, ample oxygen and the right temperature to break dormancy and germinate.

There are some alpine, shrub and tree seeds which need a period of cold, even frosty conditions before they will germinate. This cool treatment is called stratification and often involves storing outside all winter in a layer of sand. Even after stratification these seeds still need warmth, air and moisture to grow.

Overwatered soil 'caps' and excludes air, waterlogged compost has insufficient air, dry soil prevents seeds absorbing moisture, swelling and cracking into growth, and low temperatures prevent growth. This may sound a formidable list but in practice it means sow in nicely moistened sterile compost indoors and in damp crumbly soil outdoors when the temperature is warm enough for growth.

If you sow too early, when the temperature is low, moistened seeds are very susceptible to fungus diseases.

Sowing outdoors
Winter frosts, the warming and cooling, wetting and drying all break down winter-dug soils to give lovely surface conditions for spring seed sowing. Where spring and summer cultivations have given hard lumpy soils try mixing a good layer of well moistened peat into the top 1–2 in. (3–5 cm).

When preparing all dug soils for seed sowing knock the lumps down with a fork or cultivator. Then tread over the surface to consolidate the soil somewhat before raking through to get a fine tilth.

Seeds can be sown broadcast and just raked into the surface – as you would for lawns or hardy annual flowers. More often we draw out a shallow drill with draw hoe, trowel tip or piece of wood. The larger the seeds the deeper the drill can be. In practical

Break cloddy soil with a fork. If surface is sticky, work in damp peat.

Large seeds, such as broad bean, can be sown with a trowel.

A piece of wood can be used to draw out the seed drills.

terms this means sufficient soil just to cover the seed and 1 in. (2·5 cm) is sufficient for most.

Where the soil is rather wet and you cannot reach to draw the drill and sow from the path, tread on a wide board to prevent soil compaction. Large seeds such as broad beans and Sunflowers can be sown individually with a trowel.

Most of us are tempted to sow seeds too thickly and while it is perhaps an insurance to sow plenty, the more seeds that germinate the more time we need to spend thinning out the seedlings to the required spacing.

Soil can either be shuffled back over the seeds, using the toes of both shoes, or pulled over with a rake. If using a rake be careful not to rake the seeds out when pulling the soil over.

If you don't know what the emerging seedlings will look like mix a little fast-germinating lettuce or radish with them. Once they germinate you will see where to hoe and exactly where the desired seedlings will follow. The indicator seeds are pulled out with the thinnings.

Thinning is best done in two stages, the first to half the final spacing; this reduces the possible losses from slugs, birds or other pests.

There are one or two other guidelines with seeds. Peas and beans are best sown in soil on the dry side – don't soak them in water before sowing as this depresses germination and subsequent root growth.

Accumulation of fertilizer in the surface reduces germination, especially where the whole season's fertilizer application is applied before sowing. Sowing seeds with low germination percentage, for example old seed, will

If seedlings become rather tall and drawn see they are planted well down in the compost when pricked out singly.

often give less vigorous growth. More vigorous seeds give more vigorous plants.

When storing seeds, every time the temperature is dropped 5°C the life-span is likely to be doubled, between 50°C and 0°C. Keep foil-packed seeds cool to maintain high germination. Seeds in paper packets need keeping dry because again each time moisture content is lowered by 1 per cent (within

the range from 14 per cent to 4 per cent) the germination life is doubled.

A cool, airtight tin is by far the best and most convenient storage place for most seeds.

Sowing indoors

Seed and potting composts must in no way be confused with well-rotted garden compost used to improve soil outside. Seed compost is designed to germinate seeds and can be used to root some cuttings. Potting composts are used to grow seedlings on into larger and mature plants.

The name compost probably comes from the original constituents for mixes when good turf was cut and stacked to rot down – that is, be composted – to provide loam, and leaves from beech and oak were given the same treatment to provide leaf-mould. These two materials formed the basis of many recipes used by skilled gardeners.

Today we increasingly come across the term 'growing medium' and this more aptly describes the very carefully formulated mixes for seed raising and container plant cultivation.

The British John Innes Institute did much basic research and brought about

Space seeds carefully down the row to reduce the need to thin out later.

Keep the soil between the seedlings hoed to control weeds.

Loosely fill the container before firming the compost evenly.

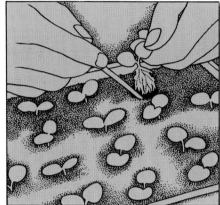

Cover all but the smallest seeds with a light sprinkling of compost.

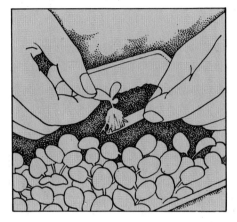

Always handle seedlings by their leaves, lifting with a stick.

Seedlings should be pricked off into boxes or pots, and spaced evenly.

a reduction in the number of recipes. They introduced a seed compost and a potting compost with a range of fertilizer strengths, but the basic ingredients are the same.

These were later followed by the University of California (U.C.) soilless (loamless) mixes based on peat and sand. Now we have many commercial brands of soilless mix, some so refined that one compost is adequate for seed and cuttings as well as plant growing.

It is the steam sterilized loam in the John Innes (JI) formula which separates it from the others. Having this sterile loam in the mix gives weight to the compost and widens the margins for error when it comes to watering and feeding.

Where you have access to good loam and the facility to sterilize to kill pests, diseases and weed seeds, there is no reason why you should not mix your own. The formula is as follows:–

John Innes Seed Compost
2 parts by volume loam (sterilized)
1 ,, ,, ,, peat
1 ,, ,, ,, sand
    To each 1·28 cu ft or 1 bushel (36

litres) of the mixture add 1½ oz (40 g) superphosphate and ¾ oz (20 g) ground limestone.

John Innes Potting Compost
7 parts by volume loam (sterilized)
3 ,, ,, ,, peat
2 ,, ,, ,, sand
    To each 1·28 cu ft or 1 bushel (36 litres), add ¾ oz (20 g) ground limestone and 4 oz (110 g) John Innes Base fertilizer to make JI potting compost No. 1; double the base fertilizer for No. 2, and use 12 oz (340 g) for No. 3.

The base fertilizer is made up of 2 parts hoof and horn meal, 2 parts superphosphate and 1 part sulphate of potash.

Mixing base fertilizers evenly right through the peat of soilless mixes, especially the small quantities of trace elements, is difficult. It is better to buy branded formulations and follow the maker's recommendation on subsequent liquid feeding.

You will find it easier to prick off seedlings from peat-and-sand composts because the sand produces a finer root more easily separated from the compost and its neighbours. You can

even add a little lime-free sand to all peat compost when seed raising, to make transplanting easier.

Moisture content of all composts is important, especially at seed sowing and seedling transplanting – the pricking-off and potting-on stages. The moisture content is right for all loam based mixes when a squeezed handful cracks open in one largish crack when you release the grip. Where the compost just crumbles when pressure is released it is too dry and if the lump retains the fingers and hand shape, without cracking, it is too wet.

Soilless composts are sufficiently damp if moisture just oozes from between the fingers when a handful is tightly squeezed. Shallow containers just 1 in. (2·5 cm) deep can be used for seed raising and these will use less compost, but remember that these shallow containers dry out quickly if not capillary watered.

Sow small quantities of seed in flower pots and seed pans – like flower pots but half the depth – larger quantities in seedboxes. Loosely fill the container to the brim with moist compost. Firm a little into corners and around the edge with fingers and then use a flat object; this will leave the firmed compost level and ½ in. (1–2 cm) or so from the top.

Space seeds over the surface; you can mix very small seeds with some fine dry sand to make the spread more even. Then sprinkle a little more compost over the seeds. Very fine seeds can be covered with fine sand.

Cover the sown seeds with glass to retain moisture and paper to reduce light. Alternatively place in polythene bags to achieve the same ends. A temperature of 55–65°F (13–18°C) is needed for quick germination of most

Seedlings damp off (see box on right) if sown too thickly in dirty boxes.

seeds. A few such as cucumbers are better at 65–70°F (18–20°C) and will be through in a day or two.

Watch the sown pots daily and as soon as you see the first signs of emerging shoots remove the covers, and water overhead with a fine rose to keep the compost damp. Move the pots as close to the glass as possible so that the seedlings get all available light. Left uncovered or even uncovered and away from the glass, seedlings will soon get long, pale coloured and unhealthy.

Once the first two leaves have unfolded and as soon as they are large enough to handle, prick them off singly into potting compost. Always handle seedlings by the leaves and never bruise the tender stem. Where the seedlings have become a little drawn it may help to lower the stem well into the hole when transplanting.

PLANTS FROM CUTTINGS
Softwood Cuttings

Very many plants can be increased by taking 2–3 in. (5–7·5 cm) long cuttings from soft young growing tips. More than half of the popular foliage house plants are propagated in this way. A lot of hardy shrubs and many flowering plants, from geraniums and fuchsias to heliotropes and double lobelia.

The method for all of them is the same. Trim the cutting just below a pair of leaves and remove the two bottom leaves. Use rooting hormone if you want to increase the number of roots and to get roots more quickly. Place the cutting in a damp, open compost. Moist sand or vermiculite will do, although the most common rooting compost is an equal mixture of peat and clean sharp sand.

Cuttings need light so the leaves can continue to manufacture plant food, but not so much sun that they wilt badly. Covering with a white polythene bag and placing in a sunny position is fine, except in high summer when the cuttings are better out of direct sunlight.

Remove the bag for a little while – half an hour or so – once a day or every other day, to dry the leaves and reduce the chance of wet rots affecting the leaves. Once the cuttings remain turgid with the bag off dispense with the bag. Misting over at midday from then on will help the cuttings to grow away.

Rooted cuttings are then removed and potted up singly.

Hardwood Cuttings

Once again cuttings are prepared from

To take a softwood cutting, select a shoot with six fully developed leaves.

Trim off cleanly just below the bottom two leaves, then cut off the two leaves.

Use a hormone rooting powder, and place round the outside of a pot.

Cover with a polythene bag and place in a light, warm position.

the current year's growth. Here we need the well ripened brown-barked wood, hence the term hardwood. These cuttings are taken in the autumn, late September through to November in Britain.

Plants propagated in this way include hedge plants such as Privet, flowering shrubs such as deutzia, forsythia, weigela, and fruit bushes (currants and gooseberries for instance), as well as trees like Poplar and Willow.

Vigorous straight growth 12 in. (30 cm) long, excluding the soft tip of growth in most cases, is pushed into soft sandy soil 6 in. (15 cm) deep. Alternatively make a slit with a spade, line the base with sand, put the cuttings in the slit and tread the soil back firmly. Twelve months later the rooted young plants should have rooted well and will then be ready for transplanting.

Because hardwood cuttings do not lose moisture as rapidly as softwood cuttings, there is little benefit in providing a close humid atmosphere.

Semi-hardwood Cuttings

Young growth with the stem just starting to harden and through a variety of stages to almost hard wood provides cutting material for many plants. Generally the more difficult subjects come under this heading. Plants propagated from half-ripe wood include cotoneaster, jasminum, pyracantha and evergreen berberis, ceanothus and Azaleas as well as many conifers.

It is best to tear off 4 in. (10 cm) long cuttings of conifers with a piece of the older wood at the base for good rooting.

Mist bench propagators and warm humid conditions are needed for the best results. Some of the hardier shrubs can be rooted in peat and sand under white polythene within a cold-frame.

July to September is the right time to take this type of cutting but the stage of wood maturity is important and varies with the different plants. Cuttings are likely to take from just over a month to eight months to root depending on the type of plant and rooting conditions.

Root Cuttings

Short lengths of root are the other means of producing new plants from cuttings. Seakale and horseradish, anchusa and phlox, raspberry and shrubby trees such as *Rhus typhina*, can all be propagated in this way.

Relatively thick pieces of root are selected to provide food reserves. Most cuttings are 3–4 in. (7·5–10 cm) long, taken in the dormant season and spaced in sandy soil outside to root.

TOOLS

Good gardens and satisfaction from gardening do not come from a great shed full of tools and equipment. Lay hands on a good spade and very many of the garden tasks can be completed adequately. There are literally thousands of clever gadgets and redesigned pieces of equipment, but few beat the well tried basic tools that have been developed over years of use.

One piece of advice I strongly recommend is to buy the best to suit your needs. A really good spade will last the ordinary gardener a lifetime. By good I mean a really comfortable handle and well-made cutting blade. If you are not too strong choose a smaller, lighter spade but still good quality.

Second choice must be a good pair of secateurs and once again the better quality will give the longest life and best value for money. Third in line for the average garden with a mixture of plants is lawnmower and shears. Remember with shears that stainless steel does not keep a good sharp cutting edge. You will get better value and a sharper cut for a longer period if you

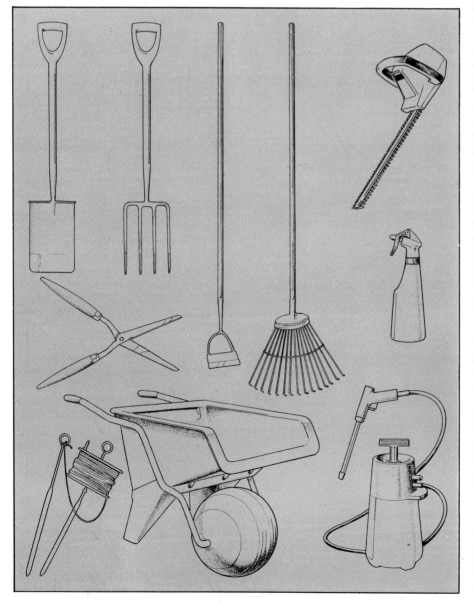

A good selection of hand tools which will allow most gardening jobs to be executed easily and quickly. Buy the better quality for a lifetime's use.

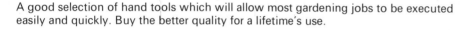

A good set of small hand tools and sharp secateurs are invaluable.

choose a steel with what is best described as a 'non-stick' finish. Metal treated in the same way as non-stick cooking pans stays sharp and, like stainless steel, does not rust when accidentally left wet and dirty.

All gardens with fertile soil will have their share of weeds and a regular surface hoe will kill off everything if used often enough and long enough. The Dutch or push hoes are best in my view. You work backwards with these and leave nice crumbly soil free of footprints. Where the draw hoe is used and one works forward, inevitably some of the weeds are firmed back in.

New gardens and established ones being redesigned often need soil moved to change levels. Cement and sand have to be moved for paths and walls. All too often gardeners go out in a hurry and buy the cheapest wheelbarrow to move these materials. The carrying box is made of thin galvanized metal which rots in no time as rain collects in the bottom.

A barrow with a pliable plastic box will give much longer service. A pneumatic wheel will do less damage on wet grass and be easier to push over damp soil.

When it comes to sprayers for pesticide application there are small cheap plastic hand models which do an adequate job. We often need just a little insecticide or fungicide in smaller gardens and the small models hold just the amount for this.

Where you have a fruit tree or from 12–18 roses which need spraying regularly, the half gallon (2·27 litre) pump-up plastic models will give good service for many years. Be sure to use up all the diluted chemicals and wash out and drain the sprayer after use. Just a little water left in the nozzle or pump mechanism can split the plastic if it freezes.

Spring-tine lawn rakes serve several purposes and can be used for lawn renovation, leaf gathering and the production of a fine tilth for seed sowing. Where the amount of money to be spent is limited choose the wire spring-tine rake rather than one with rigid tines.

Power tools can be used to speed and ease the workload, especially in larger gardens. Battery operated tools are safest and quiet to use. Where mains electricity is used for hedge trimming and mowing, work systematically across the area to avoid cutting cables.

WATERING

Plants have tremendous powers to suck up water from the ground; just think of the distance from root to branch tip of large trees. Water evaporating from the leaves starts the power force which draws up moisture.

Where a plant cannot absorb water quickly enough the foliage wilts to conserve moisture. Occasional wilting will do little harm, although every check of this kind reduces growth.

Good cultivation reduces the chance of wilting, with strong rooted, well-established plants better able to absorb moisture from the soil in hot weather. Waterlogged soil conditions suffocate plant roots and with a checked and less efficient root system plants are more susceptible to drought when weather conditions change.

Soils which remain flooded in the winter need the drainage improved. Pipe drains are the ideal way of achieving this, draining out from the pipes into boundary ditches. This is not practical however for many sub-urban areas where gardens are small and packed closely together.

The only answer here is to raise up the soil level of these areas where fruit

Layflat polythene tubing can be very useful for watering, and is one of the simplest and most efficient forms of irrigation.

bushes, vegetables and flowers are to be grown. Select plants which withstand the wet in the remaining garden areas.

Something like 1 in. (2·5 cm) of rain evaporates from the soil via plant leaves in 8–10 days of sunny warm weather. The more plants and the more leaves, the faster moisture will be lost.

Replacing the water loss is best done in good heavy doses applied occasionally. Just wetting the surface does more harm than good.

A watering can is the number one piece of equipment and long-spout designs are easiest to use. The longer the spout the lower the angle it is to the ground. Thus when tipped the water doesn't shoot out quite so forcefully and can be more gently applied to soil around plants.

Where deep water penetration is required a slowly dripping nozzle is most effective. Sprinklers which spray water right up into the air in a great

arch suffer a loss from evaporation before the water hits the soil.

Simple and cheap black 'lay-flat' polythene tube with holes punctured every 6–12 in. (15–30 cm) along its length will drip or produce light water jets close to the soil. The wider the hole spacing the longer the run of tubing you can use on the ordinary household hose.

The same principle can be used to help recently transplanted trees suffering in hot weather. Tie a large thick walled polythene bag to the tree stake. Fill the bag with water and prick a small hole in the base so that the water drips out against the trunk and runs down the root deep into the soil. This is a good system for watering small fruit trees in the garden.

Oscillating sprinklers, self-rotating sprinkler heads and a wide variety of nozzles can be used to irrigate lawns and areas of ornamental and cropping garden where there is an abundant water supply.

Repeated watering in this way can cap the surface soil. Hoeing over the surface just as it starts to dry will retain the crumbly surface tilth and also help reduce evaporation from the surface.

If you are not sure how damp the soil is, take a spade or trowel and dig down several inches. Often the surface will be dry when there is plenty of moisture below. Where the soil is dry and you water heavily, mulch the wet surface with garden compost, straw or lawn mowings to retain moisture.

Where it is not practical to lay proper land drains, wet soils can be worked quite satisfactorily by raising the level of the beds.

Trees and shrubs can be bought with bare roots, like those the author is holding, and conifers are often 'balled', but most are sold in containers.

CONTAINER PLANTS

Over the past ten years there has been a complete change in the way nurserymen grow very many plants. Up to the mid 1960's, in Europe all but a few species of shrubs, conifers, herbaceous plants, trees, fruit bushes, roses and climbers were grown in open fields. Transplanting was then restricted to the dormant late autumn to early spring period for deciduous plants, and spring and autumn for evergreens.

Now most plants are available grown in pots or are, to use the accepted term, 'container grown'. Quite apart from the commercial implications of this change, it allows the gardener to plant perennial subjects the year round, as long as the soil is unfrozen and not too wet. Container-grown plants are also transplanted with virtually no root damage and the chance of losses after planting are very much reduced, if not entirely eliminated.

Plants grown in the open field and lifted to dispatch to gardeners, either bare-root in the case of trees and shrubs or with a hessian-retained soil-ball in the case of conifers and evergreens, are still available and

sometimes cost less when delivered by public transport. Such plants still serve the gardener well if planted carefully, but the trend is very much to container growing.

It is important to check that container plants are well established and fully rooted into the pot. Growers often lift plants from the field and containerize them. If purchased before they are fully rooted into the pot they have as much root disturbance as the plants sold straight from the field and the container-grown advantages are lost.

There are several ways of checking container-grown plants. First, if you lift the plant carefully by the stem the compost and container will come too with no harm done. Freshly potted plants will come out of the compost. If when you start to lift you see the compost cracking on the surface and feel the plant starting to come from the pot, replace quickly and leave until it is fully rooted.

Container-grown plants will often have roots coming out of the base of the pot, showing the roots are right through the compost. Avoid plants

which have great quantities of root through the base. This usually means they have outgrown their pot and may well be root-bound (masses of root in the pot) and the growth starved and checked as a result.

Young plants growing strongly without experiencing a check to growth will always be the best buy. Larger and older plants appear to be better value for money, but if they have been short of food and water such that growth is checked, the younger stock will grow away more quickly and be the better buy.

One other sure sign of plants fully rooted in the container is mossy and small weed growth on the surface. Newly potted plants have fresh clean compost on the surface; as they stand in the open and the compost settles some form of green inevitably develops.

Very many different materials are used to make the container, such as soft and rigid plastic, some from biodegradable material, and metal. Where plants are in metal containers be very careful with the cut edges when transplanting because they are very sharp and hazardous to handle. I prefer to remove *all* containers when planting. Even the biodegradable ones will sap up nitrogen at the plant's expense if left in place. Even worse, in dry soil conditions and dry weather the container can dry right out and isolate the root-ball within the container.

Follow all the good soil preparation rules, whatever kind of propagation and growing method has been used. Once the soil has been dug over one or two spade's depth and plenty of peat and/or well-rotted compost mixed into it, take out a good-sized hole.

Remove the container before planting, which is easy with the plastic type.

Always water the container well before planting. It is a wise precaution to water and leave for several hours and water again to ensure the container is wet right through. A little liquid fertilizer in the last watering will give the plant a good start in life, especially where the container is full of roots.

Place the container-grown plant in the hole and check that the depth is right. This will leave the compost in the container 1 in. (2·5 cm) or so lower than the soil surface. It is ideal if the compost is just covered after the soil has settled.

Once the hole is right remove the container. I also like to unravel some roots very carefully if they have fully circled the base of the container. Spread these roots out around the bottom of the hole and fill in with good soil, firming with your feet as you work.

A final watering to settle the soil around the plant roots will be needed in dry soil and dry weather. Mulch with peat or compost to cover the surface soil and reduce the rate of drying. Where the soil is wet and sticky at planting time, mixing in peat will make the texture crumbly and easier to handle. It is wise not to firm wet soil too much or it will cake hard once it dries. Another firming may well be needed if planted in wet soil, once it has dried a little.

Tall-growing shrubs, conifers and trees will need some form of support until the root system is fully established in the soil. Larger specimens in big containers will have a heavy root ball to help anchor the plant against wind but the larger the stem and branches above ground, the greater the wind resistance.

Pushing a stout cane right through the compost and into the soil below gives good anchorage for many plants, including young trees. Where stout stakes are needed it is often best to insert them into the ground at a 45–60° angle to the stem and away from the root-ball to avoid excessive root damage.

Secure the uppermost part of tree stems to the stake for maximum support. Check the ties every 2–3 months during the growing season. Fast-growing conifers can have the soft bark girdled in weeks if tight plastic or wire ties are not loosened regularly.

If for any reason it is necessary to lift and transplant a container-grown plant after a season or two, you will find the root-ball in the container remains firm and makes transplanting easier.

If roots have encircled the base of the container, carefully tease some of them free without damaging the main ball of roots, which must remain intact.

To give the plant a good start, it is wise to work a liberal quantity of peat into the surface. Alternatively compost can be used.

Lawns

An area of neatly trimmed grass can make a garden complete, and it is difficult to imagine the average home garden without its patch of lawn. Grass is so versatile that we can use it for many purposes, from purely utilitarian grass paths and play areas, to beautifully kept lawns, which can be a perfect foil to formal ornamental gardens.

It is too easy to take the lawn or grassed area for granted and forget that plants are involved – plants which are subjected to constant cutting and wear. Give grass the same care bestowed on vegetables and flowers, and the effort will be repaid many times.

PREPARING THE SITE
Grass grows well in nearly all situations, although densely shaded areas and very steep banks are best avoided. In fact, where the slope is great it is more sensible to cover it with shrubs.

To sustain acceptable growth the year round, some 6 in. (15 cm) of reasonable topsoil is needed. This soil must be graded sufficiently to give a surface level enough to mow, although a slight slope overall is no bad thing.

Heavy clay soils and those which can lie wet should ideally be drained, although the small garden owner often has nowhere to drain the excess water. Should you have a ditch or water course at the lowest point of your garden, then a 3 in. (7·5 cm) diameter line of pipes set 18 in. (46 cm) deep across the area to be grassed would be an advantage. Cover the pipes with 12 in. (30 cm) of either clinker or gravel before filling with the last 6 in. (15 cm) of topsoil.

If the laying of drainage pipes is not possible, the next best thing is to add peat and coarse gritty sand to improve drainage. Raising the surface slightly overall will also help. At least 14 lb (6·3 kg) of sand to each square yard or metre and a 1-in. (2·5-cm) depth of peat will be needed for good results.

Light sandy soils present no drainage problems but they dry out very quickly in hot weather. It is equally important, therefore, to add plenty of organic material to these soils.

Debris left by builders is best removed from the site. It is sometimes possible to bury sub-soil at the same time as bringing buried topsoil up to the surface. Should the site only have very inferior topsoil, then either a 6 in. (15 cm) depth of topsoil will need to be brought in or a very heavy dressing of organic material worked into the soil over a season or more to improve it. Do not attempt to take short cuts when preparing a site recently left by builders. The effort will be rewarded.

Lime is not usually required, and in fact a slightly acid soil will encourage the desired finer grasses. It is a good practice to crop a new garden with early potatoes, to improve soil structure and help level the site.

It is much easier to cultivate, level and grass down the whole area, cutting out beds and borders later. Digging the young turf into such areas considerably improves the soil for other plants.

MAKING A LAWN
Where an area of cultivated garden is just left and the resulting weed growth regularly mown, an area of indigenous grasses will quickly become established. These can form an acceptable play area and a quite reasonable sward and are useful for reducing cultivated areas in large gardens. Commercial fruit growers call this 'tumble down' grassing.

Whether grassed 'tumble down', by seeding or by turf, the initial preparation is the same. After rough levelling and the removal of tree stumps and roots, the whole area needs to be dug to the depth of the blade of a spade. Thick perennial roots like dock, twitch or couch grass and thistle should obviously be removed at the same time. Organic material like peat should be mixed in the top 3 in. (7·5 cm) on really heavy and poor soils.

Once dug, the soil should be left to settle and to weather. Several weeks, if not months, and a good heavy rain will be needed to settle the soil properly. Ideally, you should dig in early autumn for spring grassing, or in spring for autumn grassing.

To level a site, prepare pegs with the top 2 in. (5 cm) marked off. Use a straightedge and spirit-level to align them, then level soil against the marks.

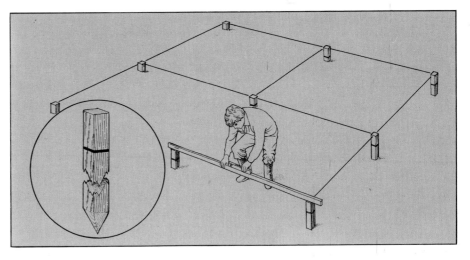

It is important to firm the soil before sowing or laying turf, and treading the soil helps to reduce the chance of subsidence later.

Levelling

A smooth lawn, free of bumps and hollows, begins with careful preparation. It is best to tackle the job in stages, using a multi-tined hand cultivator first and removing large stones at the same time. Rolling and treading is the next stage, though a dry surface is needed for this. While it takes time, treading – shuffling across the plot moving the body weight from one foot to the other – reduces the chance of subsequent subsidence, the cause of small hollows and humps.

Gentle slopes across the area and undulation can improve the appearance of some garden designs. But a flowing surface is needed to prevent mowers cutting into the soil. Flowing but even and perfectly flat surfaces are achieved by careful use of the rake, and this is the final stage of levelling.

Weeding and Feeding

It may take many weeks to complete all the preparatory stages, and, if the weather is mild, many weed seeds will germinate. This is no bad thing as they can then be cut off before becoming established.

Good garden soil will need little fertilizer, but areas around new houses where the soil has been badly damaged by builders' equipment, and impoverished sites, will need feeding. One of the proprietary *autumn* fertilizers should be used because they have a greater proportion of phosphate, which encourages root growth.

A branded fertilizer should be applied according to the manufacturer's recommendations, or you can apply a mixture of $\frac{1}{2}$ oz (15 g) sulphate of ammonia, 1 oz (25 g) superphosphate and $\frac{1}{2}$ oz (15 g) sulphate of potash to each square yard or metre. Any fertilizer should be raked in a week or so before sowing.

Seed or Turf?

Whether you create a lawn from seed or turf depends on what you want from your lawn, and the advantages and disadvantages of each method are set out in the table opposite.

Without question I prefer to use seed, though new methods of growing turf using loamless composts and good seed mixtures are promising. Such turf is likely to be more expensive than seed but on the other hand it will be quicker to establish as a lawn.

A Lawn from Seed

There are many different kinds of grass. Garden shops usually offer mixtures of several kinds, for varying sites, soils, and uses.

All the mixtures sold fall into one of three main groups: mixtures of only fine grasses, mixtures of coarser hard-wearing species, and mixtures for shady areas.

Fine-leaved mixtures make superb lawns but they require a high standard of cultivation to maintain and need fairly close mowing. A mixture of 80 per cent Chewing's Fescue *(Festuca rubra commutata)* and 20 per cent Browntop Bent *(Agrostis tenuis)* is a well-tried recipe for fine lawns, succeeding on either acid or alkaline soils and resisting dry conditions.

Coarser-leaved mixtures are quicker to establish, and they recover better after wear. They usually include hard-wearing grasses such as Perennial Ryegrass *(Lolium perenne)*. A common recipe which is competitively priced and suited to average garden conditions contains 40 per cent Chewing's Fescue, 30 per cent Perennial Ryegrass S23 strain, 20 per cent New Zealand Crested Dogstail *(Cynosurus cristatus)*, and 10 per cent Rough-stalked Meadow Grass *(Poa trivialis)*.

Shade mixtures are usually made up of 50 per cent Rough-stalked Meadow Grass, 30 per cent Smooth-stalked Meadow Grass *(Poa pratensis)*, and 20 per cent Creeping Red Fescue *(Festuca rubra rubra)*.

Variation to these standard recipes will be made by seedsmen according to supply and price. Choosing a mixture is basically a matter of looking for one with or without ryegrass, or one for shade.

When buying lawn seed remember that although the coarser seed mixtures are cheaper they often have to be sown more thickly than finer mixes. This is because there are more seeds to a given weight with finer grasses.

SEED OR TURF?

SEED

The case for
Cheaper to buy.
Easier to put down, less weight to handle.
Easy to purchase and hold until weather conditions are right.
Choice of grass mixtures to suit site and purpose.

The case against
Takes longer to get established.
Can suffer more from weed competition.
Birds can damage emerging grass seedlings.
Seedling grass can be infected by disease in cold, wet conditions.

TURF

The case for
Quick to establish and ready to use earlier.
Less soil preparation needed as long as site is level.
Longer period of time when turf can be laid successfully.

The case against
Difficult to obtain in good quality.
Heavy to handle and takes more time to lay.
Must be put down within a day or so of delivery.
More expensive.
Turves shrink and gaps open in dry weather.

Sowing: You need to sow when the soil is damp and warm enough for speedy germination and establishment. This ideally means spring or early autumn, September being best of all. Apart from the depths of winter, however, a lawn can be sown the year round.

The standard seed rate is $1\frac{1}{2}$ oz (45 g) per square yard or metre, although with the cheaper, coarser mixtures and with ideal growing conditions sowing rates can be a little less than this.

After raking the surface, divide the seed to be broadcast into two equal halves and apply one half, walking over the area in one direction. Then sow the remainder walking at right angles, to get an even spread. Avoid applying the seed through a fine sieve because this can separate out the different grasses from the mixture and give uneven growth across the lawn.

When the soil is moist and the surface dry, choose a calm time and keep the hand well above the soil to spread seed. Cast the seed gently upwards and it will float down to give an even spread. If you have not sown grass seed before, practise first with an equal volume of dry peat to get the knack.

Once sown, just very lightly rake into the surface; running the back of the rake over the soil is often all that is required. Do not roll or water immediately after sowing because this may cake the surface and damage the good crumbly conditions.

Do not worry either about some seed remaining on the surface, or about birds taking seed. The sowing rates are ample to allow for some minor losses. Sometimes the seed has been treated to make it unattractive to birds. Where birds damage the surface soil by taking sand-baths, just stretch a few strands of black cotton on sticks a few inches above the soil.

When very dry weather follows seeding, the grass will often lie dormant, growing away strongly once the weather changes. Poor growth in difficult autumn weather will often recover in the following spring, so in all cases be patient. And do not worry about the presence of some seedling weeds: these are inevitable.

Right: To achieve even coverage scatter seeds gently upwards into the air.

Below: Broadcasting too close to the soil will result in uneven coverage.

Stack turf carefully until you are able to lay it, which should be as soon as possible. Start at one corner of the plot and stagger the joins. Work from a plank to avoid damaging the newly laid turf.

A Lawn from Turf

The very finest sea-washed turf, usually referred to as Cumberland Turf, is excellent for smooth fast-running surfaces such as bowling greens. It is, however, difficult to maintain in most domestic gardens because coarse indigenous weed grasses can quickly appear. Transport charges also make these fine turves expensive.

Most gardeners have to use local turf which is usually no more than fairly weed-free meadow land, mown down to a manageable height. If at all possible try to inspect the source of supply before ordering to ensure the grasses are not too coarse and that it is weed-free.

A few specialist growers raise turf from seed mixtures, which are certainly worth the high price. It is also sometimes possible to select the mixture from seed grown in a sterile medium.

Laying Turf Once delivered the turf should be laid within a day or two. Should wet weather prevent laying then unroll and unfold each piece in a shady place and keep well watered until it can be put down properly.

September to early March, whenever the soil is frost-free and not too wet, is the best time to lay. If this job is carried out in late spring and summer, hot dry weather will cause shrinkage and cracks between the turves, unless regular heavy watering can be given.

Start putting the turf down from one corner or one side of the plot. Once the first row or two is down, place a board on the laid turf and work outwards over the unturfed area. At the edges overlap the turf to leave sufficient for edging back in a few months' time to give the final straight edges.

Stagger each row of turf to give a brick-laying pattern and lightly roll the whole area twice in opposite directions to finish off. Tight contact between turves and soil ensures rapid root establishment into the new soil and the complete knitting of roots between the edges of each turf.

Turf laid in autumn or early winter is unlikely to need cutting before the spring. Don't be afraid to mow grass as soon as it is 1½–2 in. (4–5 cm) long, but keep the mower blade high, just trimming off the tips. Any openings between turves can be filled with sandy soil. Where these are too wide for the sward to cover in a few weeks, some grass seed should be scattered over the soil, where it will soon germinate.

GRASSLESS LAWNS

Plants other than grass can be used to give a green, close-knit surface. The best is chamomile, the fragrant non-flowering *Anthemis nobilis* 'Treneague'. Small divisions of this are just pushed into the soil 4–6 in. (10–15 cm) apart.

Mosses in damp shade and thyme in light sandy soils are other possibilities to consider.

Under the dense shade of trees, if even the special shade mixtures of grass will not thrive, it is best to use ground cover plants such as Rose of Sharon (*Hypericum calycinum*), or Ivy.

The well-known rock garden plant *Sedum acre* with its ground-hugging habit and small but bright yellow flowers is another possibility.

This unusual lawn of sedum shows what imagination can do for a garden.

Everyone's idea of a good lawn is one with neat alternating stripes. These are achieved by mowing in the method described below, but a roller and cylinder type of mower is required for this effect.

CUTTING GRASS

The average lawn will be cut some 50 times a year and it is this treatment which will have more effect on the sward than any other. Very fine grasses will stand quite close mowing, say $\frac{1}{2}$ in. (13 mm), and regular close mowing is one way of reducing rough, coarse grasses.

Most lawns with a wider mixture of grasses are best cut with the mower blade 1 in. (2·5 cm) high and cut at least once, and in warm, damp weather twice, a week to give the best sward and appearance.

It is advisable to collect the grass mowings at the time of cutting. This is much tidier, it gives a firmer turf, reduces the build-up of dead organic matter on the surface, and reduces the spread of unwanted seed heads from grass and weeds.

Start mowing in spring with the blade set high, at 1$\frac{1}{2}$ in. (4 cm), reducing the height as speed of growth increases. It is advisable to raise the mower blade slightly in very hot weather. A longer grass leaf is better able to sustain good green colour in hot, dry conditions in high summer.

Drawing either a large brush or heavy sack over the lawn before mowing knocks off dew and speeds drying. It also helps to scatter worm casts and lifts and exposes straggly stems to the mower. It is best to cut grass when the surface is dry, and brushing early in the day certainly helps achieve this in spring and autumn.

Cut two widths of the mower at the top and bottom of the lawn before cutting the remainder in parallel lines. While it is easier and quicker to cut in the direction of the length of the lawn, occasionally cut in the right-angle direction to remove straggly stems.

To create a striped effect, first cut across both ends of the lawn, then mow in alternate directions in even widths.

Choice of Mower

The roller and cylinder mower is essential for the best finish on lawns. These can be manually pushed, powered by petrol engines, and by mains or battery electric motors. Battery mowers are comparatively quiet, easy to use and avoid the risk of cutting a live power cable, but you must remember they are heavier than other machines and it is necessary to keep the battery charged.

The parallel stripes typical of an English lawn are only achieved with a roller and cylinder mower. The more blades to the cylinder and the more cuts per yard, the finer will be the finish.

See that the cylinder and base blade are finely set to cut the grass clean and avoid leaving bruised and browning ends. The test for correct setting is the ability to cut thin paper the length of the base blade by rotating the cylinder by hand.

Where the cylinder is set just touching the base blade and yet is still easy to rotate, the cylinder is virtually self-sharpening. After 15 years of regular use my mower has required no sharpening or repair. The only requirements are a stone-free surface, the occasional drop of oil and the blades and rollers kept clean, especially after cutting damp grass.

Rotary blade mowers are best for longer grass, and for wet and rougher conditions, especially on banks and under trees. There is a choice between rotary hover mowers without wheels, which are light to use, especially on uneven ground, and the rotary type with wheels. Modern designs powered by electricity are very easy to use and keep quite large areas of grass under control. Once the garden exceeds $\frac{1}{4}$–$\frac{1}{2}$ acre (1,000–2,000 sq m), then a ride-on mower becomes a great work and time saver.

Size of machine required is related to the area to be cut. Hand pushed mowers of 12–14 in. (30–35 cm) are adequate for the average small garden. Increase the mower cut from 12 to 18 in. (30 to 45 cm) and you increase the area cut in a given time by two and a half times. A motor mower with a 30 in. (75 cm) wide cut will cover an acre (4047 sq m) in approximately an hour.

LOOKING AFTER THE LAWN

Repeated mowing and the regular treading as people use a lawn inevitably compacts the surface on all but the most sandy, free-draining soils. Decaying old leaves and roots also accumulate to cause a matted surface.

Regular maintenance is needed to counteract this wear and tear, and September or October is the best time for this. First, thoroughly rake the surface using a spring wire-tined rake or a similar tool. Next aerate with a special tool, such as a hollow-tined fork, or by piercing some 4–6 in. (10–15 cm) deep with an ordinary garden fork. The garden fork, a hollow-tined fork and really strong machine-powered aerators are best.

Some of the many types of mowers. Top row, from l. to r.: ride-on rotary mower, petrol rotary, electric rotary; bottom row, from l. to r.: hover mower, rotary with grass collection hopper, cylinder hand mower, wheeled hand mower.

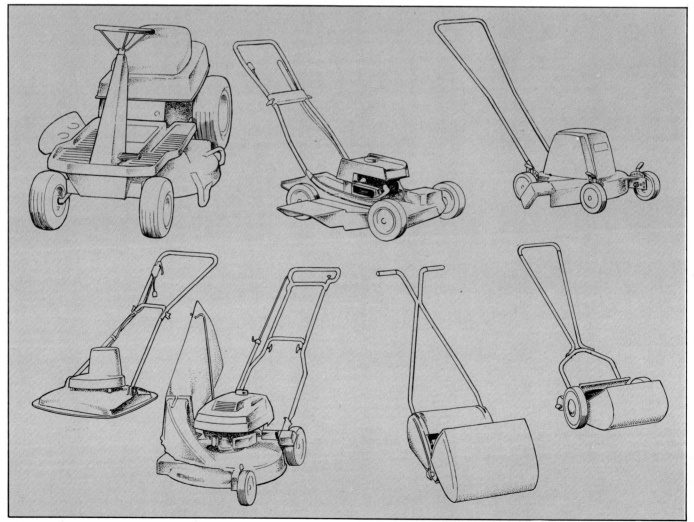

Aeration holes should then be filled by brushing or raking in a turf dressing at 2–7 lb per sq yd (1–3 kg per sq m). The dressing can be lawn peat and sand, screened soil and sand, or similar combinations of material which will encourage new root growth and improve drainage from the surface. Any sand used must be sharp, gritty and free from lime.

The best way to get suitable material for this turf dressing is to stack old turf in 6–9 in. (15–23 cm) layers, sandwiching with 3–5 in. (8–12 cm) layers of well rotted manure, garden waste and peat. Leave such a heap for 12 months before cutting down, sieving and mixing with sand.

It is important not to apply so deep that the grass is suffocated. Rubbing the mixture into the surface with the back of a rake works it into holes and hollows as well as uncovering the grass. If wet weather prevents autumn treatment, aeration can be undertaken in early spring.

Slight hollows in the lawn can be filled at the time of top dressing, although it may take several years to build up to the required level.

Dips and hollows are more quickly straightened by cutting the turf over the area in question, lifting it back and either removing soil or infilling before rolling back the turf. Where gaps are left between returned turves they should be filled with a soil mixture similar to that for aeration treatment and seeded.

Keeping a Trim Edge

Neatly trimmed edges to the lawn are almost as important as a well cut surface – they both give a finishing touch to a good garden. Once or twice a

Sweeping the lawn early in the morning with a wide broom knocks off the dew, and the grass dries more quickly for mowing. Worm casts are also spread.

year it is necessary to cut the grass and soil back to a line. A guide is needed for the half-moon edging tool and this can be either a string line between two posts or the straight edge of a piece of timber. Curved edges can be marked out with a supple hose (stiff hoses are more likely to fall to the desired shape if warm). Really sharp, even curves can be cut using a string as radius attached to the edging iron.

Make sure the cut edge slopes outwards at the base, as this strengthens the edge and reduces the chance of it breaking away. Once soil has been cut subsequent trimming is best done with long-handled shears. Here the secret is to hold the left hand still and work the right-hand handle to achieve the cut. The left hand moves the shear along after each cut as the right hand opens up the shear to take the fresh cut of overhanging grass.

Where a small area of edge breaks back it can be repaired by cutting out a rectangle of turf, reversing the turf so that the hole is inside and filling this with compost ready for seeding. Paths which have become too narrow by repeated edging can also be widened by cutting turf along each edge, moving the turf outwards, then infilling the centre and seeding. This retains a good outside edge of well-established turf.

It is unwise to have a grass path much narrower than say 2½–3 ft (75–90 cm), for convenience of cutting.

Watering

Generally speaking the average garden lawn is best left unwatered. Where a rich green lawn is required right through the summer then irrigation should start before the soil gets really

A half-moon edging tool is used with a batten to cut a straight edge.

A hosepipe can be used to create an evenly curved edge.

29

YEAR-ROUND LAWN CARE

Operation	Nov–Feb	Mar	Apr	May	June	July	Aug	Sept	Oct
Sow lawn seed* (new lawns or worn patches)			● ●	○ ○	○ ○	○ ○	○ ○	● ●	● ○
Lay turf* (new lawns or worn patches)	● ●	● ●	● ●	● ○	○ ○	○ ○	○ ○	● ●	● ●
Apply selective weedkillers			●	● ●	● ●	● ○	○ ○	○	
Apply lawn sand (to kill moss and weeds)		●	● ●						
Control fungus diseases including toadstools	● ● ○ ○	○ ○	○ ○	○ ○	○ ○	○ ○	○ ○	● ●	● ●
Apply high nitrogen fertilizers†			●	● ●	● ●	● ●	●		
Apply autumn fertilizers								● ●	● ●
Rake, aerate, topdress	○ ○ ○ ○	● ○	○					● ●	● ●
Rake up leaves	● ● ● ●								●
Mow	○ ○ ○ ○	○ ●	● ●	● ●	● ●	● ●	● ●	● ●	● ○
Shape lawn edges		●	● ●	○ ○	○ ○	○ ○		● ●	● ●
Level hollows, lumps and bumps		● ●	● ●	●				● ●	● ●
Water					○ ○	● ●	● ●	● ●	○ ○
Service mower	● ● ● ●	●							

Key   ● ● ● ideal time
○ ○ ○ you may get away with it

* mow with the blades set high as soon as grass grows
† use dilute liquid feeds in very hot weather

---

dry and be continued right through any dry period. Occasional watering will just encourage surface roots which soon shrivel back with the first really hot, dry day.

There are many sprinklers for lawns. Choose a size to suit the area.

Some 5 gallons (22 litres) of water will evaporate from a square yard in a week of hot weather, so even small lawns will need considerable quantities of water to retain all the moisture needed. Aeration in the autumn to encourage deeper rooting is far better than occasional watering.

Either oscillating lawn sprinklers or trickle hoses are needed to apply all the water needed slowly and gain good penetration. The higher the spray of water the greater will be the loss in evaporation before the much needed water actually reaches the grass.

Feeding

While raking in a lawn top dressing after aeration feeds the lawn, additional fertilizers will be needed to retain a rich green colour. The same general principles apply for grass as for other crops when selecting fertilizer. Nitrogen is needed for strong green leafy growth in spring and summer. Superphosphates encourage root growth and are best applied in autumn and early spring. Potash is not required in great quantity but a little at some stage in the year encourages good strong growth, and gives resistance to dry conditions, wear and disease.

Lime is not generally required, and alkaline conditions encourage unwanted clover. Occasionally, however, old lawns on thin acid soils will become excessively acid, particularly when organic matter has built up on the surface. A sure sign of this is greener grass along the lime-washed lines for sports areas. Where this does occur, and it is not often, then lime should be applied at 2 oz per sq yd (60 g per sq m).

The average lawn only needs one dressing of autumn lawn fertilizer and one general lawn fertilizer in the spring. Occasional early summer dressings high in nitrogen, best in

Above: Spike the turf with fork tines in the autumn.

Right: After tining, work in a lawn dressing with the back of a rake.

liquid form, maintain a good colour through the summer.

Most of us are well served by the proprietary brands of fertilizer, but should you wish to mix your own the following are dependable recipes.

Autumn dressing: 7 parts (by weight) bone-meal to 3 parts sulphate of potash, applied at 2 oz per sq yd (60 g per sq m).

Spring dressing: 2 parts (by weight) sulphate of ammonia, 1 part hoof and horn (or similar slow release nitrogenous fertilizer), 2 parts superphosphate, 1 part steamed bone-flour, and 1 part sulphate of potash. Apply at the same rate as the autumn dressing.

The early summer nitrogen supply can come from sulphate of ammonia applied at ½ oz per sq yd (15 g per sq m). It will be necessary to dissolve it in water or mix it with sand to get an even distribution.

Select a time when the soil is damp to apply general fertilizers, and should the weather remain very dry for a day or two after applying, it is wise to water it in well.

Care must be taken when applying lawn fertilizers because uneven distribution will cause uneven colouring, and perhaps scorch where an excess is put down. Hand application is still the most widely used method and if the fertilizer is bulked up and well mixed with *dry* sand, soil or peat, even distribution is easier to achieve.

Like grass seed application, it is best to split the quantity to be applied in half and apply one half walking in one direction and the remainder walking at right angles.

Special mechanical fertilizer spreaders can be purchased and sometimes borrowed from garden sundries retailers and these make spreading easier. Do a test run over newspaper and weigh the delivery to a given area to check the correct rate is being applied. Be sure the spreader covers the whole area with no gaps or overlaps to avoid discoloration in lines across the lawn.

Diluters to attach to the hose are also available for the easy application of liquid lawn fertilizers.

When deciding to feed the lawn, remember that much grass is being removed with repeated cutting, yet excessive nitrogen fertilizer will give tremendous soft leafy growth, which will increase the need to mow. Keep things in balance to provide a good colour without the need to mow excessively. Rich and heavy soils will need less fertilizer than poor, sandy soils to maintain balanced growth.

Weeds

The importance of starting as free of weeds as possible has already been stressed, but some will still appear.

Many germinating with newly sown grass seeds will be destroyed with repeated mowing. Strong growing, healthy grass will also smother out weeds, while raking and brushing before mowing exposes the trailing stems of weeds like Clover to the mower. Removal of large single weeds by hand using an old kitchen knife or something similar can prevent weed spread.

Apart from these mechanical methods of weed control there is an armoury of chemical weedkillers. The oldest is *lawn sand* whereby the caustic action of the mixture scorches broad leaved weeds and mosses but falls from the upright grass. Lawn sand is made from 3 parts (by weight) of sulphate of ammonia, 1 part sulphate of iron, and 20 parts dry sand. It is applied at 4–6 oz per sq yd (120–180 g per sq m) in spring, ideally when there is a touch of dew for the sand to stick to. Dead growth can be raked out after about three weeks, according to temperature (the warmer the weather the faster the effect of the lawn sand). Where there is the risk of hot, dry weather following

To ensure even application of weedkillers or fertilizers, mark the area off into yard or metre squares. Garden canes are satisfactory for this.

application, make two dressings, reducing the rate by half to avoid scorching the grass.

Hormone weedkillers are also freely available and the proprietary materials are usually a combination of two of the following: MCPA; 2,4D; mecoprop; fenoprop; and dichlorprop.

Applied correctly these materials will give adequate control of nearly all weeds but good cultural treatment is also needed to avoid regrowth and reinfestation by weeds. These hormone weedkillers are most effective when plants are growing strongly as they are then translocated rapidly.

If you plan to use a hormone weedkiller, these are the steps to take:

1. Apply the spring fertilizer at least two weeks before the weedkiller.

2. Cut the grass and leave for one or two days, to encourage new weed growth to absorb the hormone.

3. Choose a warm *still* day and water on the selective weedkiller. Remember, this spray will kill other garden plants if allowed to drift on to them.

4. Wait at least three days and ideally seven before mowing again;

see that the clippings from the next three cuts are composted separately for at least six months to prevent damage to other crops. They can also be used to mulch under mature trees as long as left undisturbed on the surface for at least six months. Wait six months for turf and twelve

months for seed-raised lawns before applying hormone weedkillers. Where bulbs are underplanted do not apply selective weedkillers until the foliage has completely died down.

Very persistent weeds may need more than one treatment but be sure to select a suitable branded weedkiller combination for your most difficult weed. Mecoprop in early summer for White Clover; MCPA for Buttercup and Plantain, for example. It is also possible to buy wax sticks impregnated with hormone, and aerosols for spot weed treatment.

Hand removal of single weeds and the very occasional use of selective weedkiller is all that is needed to keep a lawn free of weeds.

LAWN PROBLEMS

Bare patches are not only the result of pests and diseases. Humans and animals can also create problems. Areas which take a great deal of wear, for instance, can go bare, and the introduction of paving slabs to take this wear is one answer. There are also open, honeycomb-like bricks which can be set into the soil and seeded over. The bricks take the heavy wear and help to protect the grass, and they are ideal where cars occasionally go over the grassed area.

The main animal pests are moles and dogs! Moles seeking worms and insects burrow through newly seeded lawns and fertile soils, causing much damage. Deterrent smokes and traps can be used, and prickly leaves like holly in the tunnels will also act as a deterrent.

Dogs' urine, especially bitch urine, causes small brown patches. Dousing

Some common lawn pests. Top left, leatherjacket; top right, wireworm; bottom left, cutworm; bottom right, larva of a cockchafer.

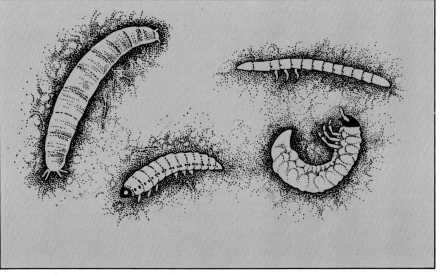

32

Weeds such as daisies are quickly and easily removed by hand.

Bare patches left where weeds have been removed can be reseeded.

Where fairy rings are a persistent problem the only sure cure is the removal and destruction of infected turf, digging the soil 9 in. (23 cm) deep and fumigating with a solution of formaldehyde.

Pests

Ants can be a problem, especially in light sandy soils where small ant-hills are thrown up. Several powders are available for killing ants.

Leatherjackets are blunt ended brown grubs about $1\frac{1}{2}$ in. (35 mm) long. They are, in fact, the larval stage of crane-fly or daddy-long-legs. The grubs can infest the turf and in extreme cases cause dead patches from March to May as they eat roots and base of the grass stems. One method of control is to thoroughly soak the turf with water, cover overnight with black polythene to bring the grubs to the surface, then to sweep them up or let the birds take over. Alternatively, water with HCH (BHC) in mid-September to kill the recently hatched larvae.

Earthworms are usually encouraged in gardens but on the lawn the worm casts of soil provide the perfect site for seedling weeds. When wet the casts also spoil cylinder mower blades.

To control the number of earthworms, maintain an acid soil by the use of a peat turf dressing, sulphate of ammonia fertilizer and sulphate of iron. In extreme cases a proprietary worm killer can be applied in the autumn.

the area with water, ideally just behind the dog, is the only treatment.

Although starlings in numbers pecking into the soil in spring after rain look horrifying, they are usually to be welcomed. They are after leatherjackets, and the pecking does little damage and can even help to aerate the surface. Kill the leatherjackets to prevent the birds probing.

Moss can be another nuisance. Poor drainage and wet surface conditions encourage the growth of moss, and aerating the soil and raking out the dead thatch improves conditions and reduces its effect. A spring application of lawn sand will burn off moss growth, or you can apply proprietary moss-killing chemicals in the spring to back up the autumn aerating treatment.

Diseases

White mould in the grass is caused by fusarium patch; red threads in the grass are caused by the corticium fungus. Both can be controlled by watering with a mercury-based lawn treatment (such as calomel) or benomyl in late summer and early autumn. Benomyl is best for home garden use.

Small brown patches which spread are likely to be caused by dollar spot (sclerotinia), and once again benomyl will give control.

Toadstools and fairy rings can disfigure a lawn, and need to be controlled. Start by spiking the turf and watering well, to penetrate the mycelium growth of these fungi, then apply a proprietary copper or mercurial chemical.

Six widespread and troublesome lawn weeds: top row, left to right: Plantain, Clover, Yarrow; bottom row, left to right: Buttercup, Dandelion, Daisy.

Hedges

First priority in any garden must be the introduction of hedges and screens. Not only is it important to mark out the boundary of your property, you will also need the shelter and protection it will provide.

A well-chosen hedge plant, carefully planted and tended will give years of good service. It will be much cheaper and usually longer lasting than wooden fencing.

Many hedging plants are attractive in themselves and make a very good backcloth to other planting schemes.

List the qualities you want before making the choice of plant. Protection from two- and four-footed invaders will be provided by thorns, especially the deciduous Quickthorn, which remains our best country hedge plant, and the evergreen Holly.

All plants will provide some protection from wind. Plants are better than solid fences for this, as it is preferable that the wind filters through rather than hits an impenetrable barrier and bounces over with even greater force. The higher the hedge the greater the extension of shelter; as a general guide one unit high gives seven units length of wind shelter beyond.

Even in open-plan front gardens informal groups of low-growing shrubs will give valuable shelter from wind.

Privacy can also be brought to the garden with hedge plants. Fast and tall growing kinds will soon prevent private gardens being overlooked. Unsightly objects can be screened completely. The summer foliage of deciduous plants and the year-round foliage of evergreens reduce noise and help to minimize the aggravation of traffic and other unwanted sounds.

Gardeners in the past used low hedges to surround vegetable plots, and the advantages of earlier and heavier crops obtained from such shelter should not be forgotten.

On very exposed sites it is a good

The Hornbeam, *Carpinus betulus*, makes a tall hedge and is a good alternative to Beech, being equally happy on chalk or clay soils.

plan to erect either metal or concrete posts and plastic or wire netting around the boundary. The hedge plants are then planted just inside this fence. They get shelter from the netting, are supported by it in the early stages of growth, and quickly grow to cover it completely.

A few plants like the small-leaved evergreen *Lonicera nitida* require the support of posts and wire to prevent them blowing over when more than 18 in. (45 cm) high.

CHOOSING THE RIGHT PLANTS

The first step is to decide whether you want an evergreen or deciduous hedge. Remember, too, that there are a few deciduous plants like Beech and Hornbeam that retain russet-brown leaves through the winter if clipped

regularly. Others drop their leaves to unmask richly coloured bark like the purple-leaved plums, or highly coloured berries in the case of plants like *Berberis wilsonae*.

Some evergreens, like pyracantha and cotoneaster produce masses of bright berries to contrast with the evergreen and semi-evergreen foliage.

Select those with dark foliage to throw up lighter coloured plants in front of them. For example, the yellow winter-flowering *Hamamelis mollis* and pale pink *Viburnum ×bodnantense* are more eye-catching against a background of evergreens. Light green and golden plants contrast well with copper Beech and *Prunus* 'Cistena'.

Generally speaking the evergreens make better hedges. They give year-round seclusion and offer more pro-

Hedges do not have to be high and impenetrable to serve a useful purpose. Lavender makes a low boundary hedge that's both colourful and fragrant.

tection. Deciduous flowering plants like forsythia and Flowering Currant make excellent informal screens even if they can be seen-through in winter.

Plants for Low Hedges

The plants in this group can normally be contained to form a low hedge no more than 3 ft (90 cm) high.

Common Box, *Buxus sempervirens* 'Suffruticosa', will make a very low evergreen hedge and there are a number of forms with golden and creamy white leaves which grow taller. *Berberis thunbergii* 'Atropurpurea Nana' has purple foliage and the leaves turn yellow before leaf-fall in autumn. Kept trimmed this makes a neat and self-protecting low hedge, as it has sharp thorns.

The evergreen *Euonymus fortunei* 'Emerald 'n Gold' and 'Silver Queen' make neat hedges if kept trimmed. Some of the evergreen veronicas or hebe, are also attractive low hedge plants, best lightly trimmed once a year after flowering and allowed a less formal shape.

Lavender makes one of the most popular low hedges. *Lavandula spica* 'Hidcote' has compact growth and makes the neatest low hedge to 30 in. (75 cm), while the ordinary *L. spica* will form a much larger and somewhat rougher hedge. Trim lavender back after flowering and choose a sunny, well drained site.

Lonicera nitida, with its tiny evergreen leaves, will quickly form a neat low hedge. But it needs regular trimming to keep its shape – almost monthly through the summer. Golden Privet, *Ligustrum ovalifolium* 'Aureum', does not grow as tall or as quickly as the green kind. It makes a neat low hedge and needs less frequent trimming. Both lonicera and ligustrum root easily from 8–12 in. (20–30 cm) hardwood cuttings in late autumn.

A favourite low-growing plant of mine is *Mahonia aquifolium*, best cut back after flowering in April or May and allowed to produce a natural semi-formal shape. It grows well in most soils once established, in sun or shade.

Two silver foliage plants, *Santolina chamaecyparissus* (the best for a neatly trimmed low hedge) and *Senecio laxifolius* can also be recommended. Trim them back in spring.

The best deciduous plant for low hedging is *Prunus* 'Cistena', commonly called 'Crimson Dwarf'. Blush-pink star-like flowers in April and May are followed by rich copper foliage. Trim this plant quite hard back after flowering to retain shape and size; this will also help to produce plenty of richly coloured young foliage.

Plants for Medium Hedges

The plants in this section will form a hedge up to 10 ft (3 m) high. However, there can be no hard and fast rule on speed of growth and ultimate height because both soil and the quality of the young plant will influence growth rate. This grouping is only a guide, and plants need to be clipped and pruned back to retain their size.

The evergreen *Berberis × stenophylla* has showering branches of bright yellow flowers in April or May and makes a completely impenetrable hedge. As it is not easy to root cuttings (which should be taken in summer and kept in a cold frame), it is best to buy container-grown specimens for successful transplanting.

Much easier to propagate is *Cotoneaster simonsii*, with seed-raised plants much cheaper to buy. Upright in habit, this species is semi-evergreen with large scarlet berries close to the stem, which are more clearly seen as the leaves fall.

Less formal hedges are produced with escallonia, which is good for seaside areas but not recommended where exposure to very cold winter winds is likely. Prune back after the

Wind filters through hedges and open fences but bounces over walls. Every metre height of hedge offers protection for seven metres.

pink or red flowers have finished in late summer and try to avoid cutting back too hard.

Another good seaside plant for informal screens is the hardy fuchsia, again best kept to warmer areas. *Fuchsia magellanica* cultivars are recommended. *F. m.* 'Riccartonii' is the strongest growing, with scarlet and violet flowers; *F. m.* 'Variegata' is smaller but has cream and pink edged leaves. Any cutting back is best done in spring when the chance of winter dieback has passed.

The strong-growing green Privet serves us very well in this size grouping. While the twice-yearly trimming may be considered by some to be unnecessary work, this plant does grow quickly in rough conditions. It is cheap to buy and easy to root from hardwood cuttings, taken in early autumn.

Plant a double row of Privet if you want a dense impenetrable hedge quickly. But despite its strong growth, Privet can easily be kept in bounds with an electric hedge trimmer.

Completely deciduous but with fragrant flowers is the philadelphus commonly known as Mock Orange. Other excellent hedges can be created with the yellow forsythia or the white-flowered *Spiraea × arguta*. Also justifiably popular is the red Flowering Currant; just prune out some branches with secateurs after flowering.

The purple-leaved Plum, *Prunus cerasifera* 'Pissardii', is an attractive alternative to the usually more expensive copper-leaved Beech. It does not, however, hold its leaves in winter and is not as popular as *Prunus laurocerasus*, the evergreen Common Laurel. Both, left unpruned, will reach 16 ft (5 m). On very chalky soils try to plant the darker and smaller evergreen Portugal Laurel, *Prunus lusitanica*.

Another recommended evergreen is the recently introduced *Thuja occidentalis* 'Smaragd', a very neat-growing conical conifer which forms a good compact hedge. Also good are *Griselinia littoralis* (good for seaside planting), and the Common Yew, *Taxus baccata*. The Yew will grow much taller than 10 ft (3 m) but can be kept to any size by trimming in August.

Plants for Tall Hedges

The plants in this section will exceed 10 ft (3 m) quite rapidly. The common Hornbeam, *Carpinus betulus*, is a good example of a plant that will soon reach 10 ft (3 m), then if left alone will grow into a small tree. Clipped once or twice

Hedges need never be dull – even in leaf. This picture illustrates how purple leaved *Prunus cerasifera* 'Pissardii' and *P. E. M. myrobalan* contrast to provide interest.

a year it is a good alternative to Beech, thriving on chalk or heavy clay soil.

Evergreen conifers of the Lawson type also form upright trees, but careful clipping of the young growth in August will contain their size. Seedlings of *Chamaecyparis lawsoniana* are cheapest and can give a variety of colourful foliage.

The native Quickthorn *Crataegus oxyacantha*, and Beech, *Fagus sylvatica*, are widely used for hedges. Thorn remains the best boundary hedge, keeping out cattle and trespassers of all kinds at a low cost. Planting a double row of seedlings up to 18 in. (45 cm) tall and cutting them back by half a few weeks after planting gives the best hedge.

Seedling Beech is very attractive in late April and May when different leaf colour unfurls. The rich green summer foliage is then followed by brilliant autumn shades to make this a most attractive hedge and screen. Be sure to clip in August if you want beech to retain its leaves over winter. Clipping the tips off prevents the production of a hormone which causes the leaves to fall in autumn. They then drop when new growth starts in spring.

Finally, two more evergreens. *Thuja plicata* 'Atrovirens' makes a splendid hedge, being especially useful because it responds well to quite hard cutting back when space is outgrown. The other one, *×Cupressocyparis leylandii*,

Beech hedging cut hard back soon shoots out new growth to cover the cuts.

Upright cultivars of *Chamaecyparis* make a good screen.

Green privet makes one of the best hedges. Trim to leave it wider at the base. Try not to leave it too long between cuts, and collect the trimmings on a sheet (see below).

The time to transplant bare root plants is October and November or February and March. Plants in this category usually include the cheaper kinds like Thorn, Privet, Beech and cotoneaster. While all plants lifted from the open ground need their roots kept damp it is especially important with Beech. Let their roots get dry and transplanting losses can be very high.

The closer you plant the quicker a dense hedge forms but the more it costs, as a general rule. Good specimens of the larger growing container-grown evergreens can be planted 3 ft (90 cm) or more apart. Leylands at this spacing will give a good screen in three years.

Evergreens can be transplanted in September and October or March and April if not too old and established. It is best to spray the foliage with an antidessicant before lifting, and to take up a good ball of soil with each plant to keep root disturbance to a minimum (see the advice for transplanting conifers on page 71).

All newly-planted stock will need watering in dry weather until well established. Evergreens benefit from syringing with water in drying winds and hot weather.

KEEPING A GOOD SHAPE

Once planted and established, growth will be improved with feeding. A well-balanced general fertilizer applied in spring and early autumn and hoed in around the plants will considerably speed growth.

Trimming is the only other regular cultural treatment required. The general rule here is to cut young deciduous plants back regularly to encourage branching from the base. Evergreens, especially Leylands, are

is perhaps the most popular screen plant of all. It will grow 3–5 ft (1–1.5 m) a year and can be clipped in August to retain size and improve its bushiness. An excellent alternative to the dark green Leyland is ×C. l. 'Castlewellan', this cultivar being bushier than the green type and is bright yellow in May and June when new growth forms.

Always plant either pot or container-grown Leylands; and you will find that smaller specimens 20 in. (50 cm) tall get away quickly.

Planting a Hedge
Careful preparation will give a good long life and the speedy establishment usually needed. On good to average soil, digging over the site one spade deep, and adding plenty of peat and similar organic matter, is usually sufficient. For the very best results, however, it is worth digging out a trench one spade deep and forking organic material into the base before returning the improved topsoil. If there is grassy turf on the site, dig this into the sub-soil.

It is a good idea to stretch out a plastic or cloth sheet at the base of the hedge to catch clippings. Simply lift up four corners to carry trimmings away.

Hedging plants with large leaves can look unsightly if trimmed with shears.

best cut back by 6–12 in. (15–30 cm) before the ultimate required height is reached. The tip growth then develops to cover the cuts and takes the hedge or screen up to the final height.

Where long, straight edges have to be cut, erect posts and string to guide the shears.

Large-leaved evergreens are best cut with secateurs, pruning out branch tips. Shears and hedge trimmers are more suited to the smaller-leaved plants and conifers where shaping the outer edges is all that is required.

Some plants will respond to very hard cutting back, and renovation of old overgrown hedges is easy with these. Beech, Privet, thuja and Yew are good examples. Hedges 3 ft (1 m) or more thick, cut back one side at a time, can be reduced by half and soon produce new growth. Evergreens like *Chamaecyparis*, ×*Cupressocyparis* will not respond to this hard cutting.

Growth is naturally stronger at the top so clip to give a wider base and narrower top. This will not only produce more dense growth but reduce the chance of snow damage.

Where topiary work is planned it is a good idea to make a wooden jig which can easily be placed in position, and cut to this.

YOUR GUIDE TO HEDGES AND LIVING SCREENS

Plant	Common name	Spacing	Height in 4–5 years	Ultimate height	When to trim
Berberis Xstenophylla (E.F.)	—	1½–3 ft*	5–6 ft	6½ ft	After flowering
Berberis thunbergii 'Atropurpurea Nana' (F)	—	12–20 in.	1 ft	1½ ft	After flowering
Buxus sempervirens (E)	Common Box	1½–3 ft	2 ft	4 ft	July/August
B.s. 'Suffruticosa' (E)	Box Edging	6 in.	6 in.	12 in.	July/August
Carpinus betulus	Hornbeam	1½–3 ft	5–6½ ft	20 ft+	July/August
Chamaecyparis lawsoniana (E)	Lawson's Cypress	3 ft	5 ft	20 ft+	July/August
C.l. cultivars (E)	—	3 ft	5 ft	20 ft+	July/August
Cotoneaster lacteus (E, B)	—	1½–3 ft	5 ft	10 ft	Early spring
Cotoneaster simonsii (B)	—	1½ ft	5 ft	6½ ft	July
Crataegus monogyna	Quickthorn	1 ft	5 ft	23 ft	Twice in summer
Crataegus oxycantha 'Paul's Scarlet' (F)	—	1½ ft	5 ft	23 ft	July/August
XCupressocyparis leyandii	Leyland's Cypress	1½–2 ft	8 ft	30 ft	April and August
Euonymus fortunei radicans (E)	—	1 ft	1 ft	1½ ft	May
Euonymus japonica 'Ovata Aurea' (E)	—	2 ft	2 ft	4 ft	June
Fagus sylvatica	Beech	1–1½ ft	5–6½ ft	20 ft	August
Fagus sylvatica 'Riversii'	Copper Beech	1½ ft	5–6½ ft	20 ft	August
Fuchsia magellanica (F)	Hardy Fuchsia	1½ ft	2 ft	4 ft	March/April
Hebe brachysiphon (E)	Shrubby Veronica	1½ ft	1½ ft	1½ ft	May
Hippophae rhamnoides (B)	See Buckthorn	2 ft	5 ft	10 ft	July/August
Ilex aquifolium cultivars (E, B)	Holly	2–3 ft	3 ft	13 ft	August
Lavandula spica (E, F)	Lavender	1½ ft	3 ft	3 ft	After flowering
Lavandula spica 'Hidcote' (E, F)	Lavender	1 ft	1½ ft	2 ft	After flowering
Ligustrum ovalifolium (E)	Privet	1½ ft	5 ft	10 ft+	May to August
L.o. 'Aureum' (E)	Golden Privet	1½ ft	2½ ft	5 ft	May to August
Lonicera nitida (E)	—	1½ ft	4 ft	6 ft	May to August
Mahonia aquifolium (E, B)	—	1½–3 ft	2½ ft	3 ft	Informal – May
Prunus cerasifera 'Pissardii'	Blaze	1½ ft	5 ft	10 ft	July
Prunus 'Cistena' (F)	Crimson Dwarf	1½ ft	2½ ft	4 ft	May
Prunus laurocerasus (E)	Cherry Laurel	2½ ft	6½ ft	10 ft	July/August
Pyracantha (E, B)	Firethorn	3 ft	6½ ft	13 ft	June and August
Ribes (F)	Flowering Currant	1½ ft	5 ft	6½ ft	May
Santolina chamaecyparissus (E)	—	1½ ft	3 ft	3 ft	March
Senecio laxifolius (E)	—	1½–2½ ft	3 ft	3 ft	March
Taxus baccata (E)	Yew	2½ ft	3 ft	10 ft	August
Thuja occidentalis 'Smaragd' (E)	—	3 ft	3 ft	13 ft	August
Thuja plicata 'Atrovirens' (E)	Western Red Cedar	3 ft	6 ft	26 ft+	August

Key E = Evergreen   F = Flowering   B = Berries

*1 ft = 0·3 m

Trees

The steady and continuing growth of trees is quietly reassuring in this energy-demanding era. If all mineral fuels are burnt we still have trees slowly building up wood year after year, regardless of our folly.

Trees do much more for us, quite apart from the many products made from wood pulp. They, more than any plant, purify the air taking in carbon dioxide and breathing out oxygen.

Great canopies of leaf give shade in summer, and masses of twiggy branches soften wind and help to reduce noise. And when the leaves fall they enrich the soil.

At last their many qualities are being appreciated. Each one of us has a responsibility to see that more trees are planted, but with decreasing garden size we need to be careful in selection.

I see no harm in using trees rather like indoor decoration material, replacing by other more appropriate kinds as their growth and the family's requirements change; rapid growing and relatively short-lived Poplar and Willow, for example, can be used to give near-instant effect in a small new garden and then be cut down as soon as they grow beyond the space available.

Slower-growing trees planted at the same time can then be left to develop once the quick-growing space fillers are removed.

While you may be unable to grow what I call forest and field trees in the garden, try at least to instigate the occasional planting in your locality, be it in school playing field, churchyard or roadside. Real giants like the white candle flowering Horse Chestnut *(Aesculus)* and the beautiful deeply grooved bark of Sweet Chestnut *(Castanea)*, green and copper Beeches *(Fagus)*, the tough, hardy black-budded Ash *(Fraxinus)*, town-pollution-withstanding London Plane *(Platanus)*, huge Oaks *(Quercus)*, and Elms *(Ulmus)* are such a welcome feature of our land.

Robinia pseudoacacia 'Frisia' will make a colourful addition to any garden; container-grown plants transplant best.

Many people are unnecessarily worried about trees close to buildings. Very many country and town houses have stood for centuries unmoved with large trees within touching distance. Large buildings on strong foundations will not be affected. Dwelling houses built on heavy clay can, however, be cracked in periods of extreme drought where tree roots suck out moisture.

Rapid-growing trees like Willow will draw many gallons of water each day from clay soils. This causes shrinkage and soil cracks which can affect the house. Roots of these trees also seek moisture from every source when the soil is dry. Where drainage pipes have the slightest crack roots will penetrate and in extreme cases block the pipe with root.

Plant trees from one to one-and-a-half times their ultimate height away from houses to be absolutely safe. Small trees will, of course, have a much lower water requirement and closer planting is acceptable.

There is always a rush to get trees planted in a new garden to give added height and some privacy. While I am all in favour of getting trees in and away, take a little time over the choice. Never rush the selection, for the choice of species and variety can be vitally important in a small garden.

Less care is needed over the quick-growing kinds treated as expendable, but once in the remainder are likely to be there a long time. My advice is always cultivate the soil and grass first, then hedges, screens and specimen trees can be planted.

Where trees are to be planted on the boundary and in cultivated soil, as opposed to lawn, then once the choice is made there is no need for more delay.

CHOOSING A TREE

We have tree shapes, sizes, speeds of growth and leaf colours for nearly every situation with the Maples, or acers as they are known botanically. Most are easy to grow in all soils and situations.

Where space is available for a specimen that will form a large shrub or small tree, choose a Japanese Maple or a Snakebark Maple. The Japanese *Acer japonicum* and *A. palmatum* types are more often grown as shrubs, often with several stems. All have beautiful autumn leaf colour and several have rich red summer leaves.

The rich yellow leaves of *A. j.*

Autumn leaf colour is an attraction on the cut-leaved Japanese Maple.

'Aureum' will scorch in strong sunlight and the young growth burn in spring frost, so find a partially shaded site for this plant. All the Japanese Maples are better given protection from wind and will thrive in partial shade. Add plenty of peat to the soil to get strong growth and the richness of young foliage. They associate well with azaleas, Lilies and the natural stone of rock banks and gardens.

Coloured bark is the feature of the small tree *Acer davidii*, with green and white snake-skin-like colouring. For birch-like papery peeling brown bark seek out *Acer griseum*.

Very common and widely planted in gardens are *Acer negundo* 'Elegans', which has leaves margined yellow, and *A. n.* 'Variegatum', with white-edged leaves; this is commonly called Box Elder. They can also be grown in tubs and as tall shrubs but need any shoots of all-green foliage cut out promptly. The illustrations below show how these plants can be treated as either shrub or tree, depending on the situation.

Large trees are well covered by the Norway Maples, *Acer platanoides* – the ordinary species grows quickly and has good autumn leaf colour. There are rich summer coloured kinds including *A. p.* 'Crimson King', with copper-purple leaves, and *A. p.* 'Drummondii', with green leaves edged cream.

Often confused with the Norway Maple is Sycamore, *Acer pseudoplatanus*, a very easily grown large tree which seeds freely; in fact seedlings can

Acer negundo can be treated as a shrub. Prune back in spring to retain size and give strong new growth.

Another example of *Acer negundo,* this time grown as a tree. There are forms with cream and white variegation.

be a problem in the garden. There are a number of very attractive garden forms without the seeding problem. My favourite is *A. p.* 'Brilliantissimum', with rich pink new spring growth and creamy-orange young leaves on a small mop-head tree.

Larger growing are the green, yellow and pink splashed *A. p.* 'Leopoldii' and yellow-leaved *A. p.* 'Worlei'.

The Chestnuts demand space, especially the large ordinary Horse Chestnut, *Aesculus hippocastanum* with its sticky buds which can be cut in early spring to open in water, eye-catching white flower spikes, and prickly conker cases. Red-flowered *A.* ×*carnea* 'Briotii' is of medium size and does not produce conkers. Large-growing Sweet Chestnut is a different plant, *Castanea sativa*, and hot summers are needed for the best edible chestnut crops. Grow this either as a specimen for its attractive deeply ridged bark or cut back every few years to provide a quick-growing shelter belt.

Tree of Heaven, *Ailanthus altissima*, also responds to hard pruning as a young plant. The strong new shoots carry huge attractive leaves. Left unpruned it becomes a large specimen withstanding city dirt and pollution.

Wet soils suit the Alders. *Alnus cordata* is larger than the medium-height *A. glutinosa*; both are useful for shelter belt planting. Better suited to gardens is *Amelanchier*. This small tree or large shrub has white flowers and rich copper young leaves in April, beautiful in association with spring-flowering bulbs. Rich autumn leaf colour and purple fruits, attractive to blackbirds, follow the spring spectacle.

One of the few evergreen trees other than conifers is *Arbutus unedo*, the Strawberry Tree; it is slow to establish and eventually makes a small tree. White flowers are produced in autumn at the same time as seeds from the previous year's flowers ripen on small strawberry-like fruits. Always plant pot-grown specimens as root disturbance causes a severe check.

Most graceful of all, the Birches with silver bark and rich yellow autumn leaves are superb for the garden.

Smallest is *Betula pendula* 'Youngii', a lovely weeping tree, seldom reaching more than 10 ft (3 m) unless the growing tip is kept tied upright until the wood hardens. The spreading, weeping habit produces a flat-topped tree.

All young Birches have brown bark and only as they age over four to six

The young yellow leaves of *Gleditsia tricanthos* 'Sunburst' are one of the attractive features of this tree. It makes a small to medium tree.

years does the silver-white colour develop. *Betula papyrifera* has really striking white bark and grows a little larger than the common Birch, *Betula pendula*. Container-grown trees are easier to transplant successfully than bare-root plants.

While Hornbeam, *Carpinus betulus*, is very hardy and easy to grow, usually seen in copses, woodland and hedges, there is one form which deserves greater use. The cigar-shaped *C. b.* 'Fastigiata' really puts a 'spire-on-the-bungalow' in a reasonably sized garden. The upright habit is neat and compact, and the leaves nicely colour yellow in the autumn.

Much more spreading but of similar medium size, *Catalpa bignonioides*, the Indian Bean Tree is more suited to large gardens, parks and street planting. Large trusses of white flowers with yellow and purple throat are followed by long bean-like seed pods in hot summers.

Neat rounded, light-green leaves are the attraction of *Cercis siliquastrum*, commonly called the Judas Tree because legend indicates this was the tree on which Judas Iscariot hanged himself. Masses of purple-pink flowers are produced in May on tall shrub or small tree shapes. A good hardy subject, but best transplanted from containers as it does resent root disturbance.

Very tough and easy to grow in all soils and conditions are the flowering Thorns, with carmine-pink flowered *Crataegus oxyacantha* 'Paul's Scarlet' most popular of all. When planting bare-root trees be sure to keep the roots damp at all times and be patient, it may take several months into the spring before new growth develops on newly transplanted trees.

While children should be encouraged to grow Oaks and Horse Chestnuts from seed and watch them develop over the years, impatient adults will get quicker returns from *Eucalyptus gunnii* grown from seed.

This tree grows at a tremendous speed. The young growth produces rounded silver-grey leaves and then older branches produce sickle-shaped grey-green leaves. If cut back when one to two years old, the single-stemmed seedlings will be forced to shoot up several branches. All are useful for flower arranging and the cut branches can be stood in glycerine (one part) and water (two parts) to produce excellent preserved material for indoor arrangement.

Only one Beech, *Fagus sylvatica* 'Purpurea Pendula', is small enough for most gardens today. This cultivar is ideal with its very weeping branches, reaching down to the soil, covered with rich purple leaves.

The common Beech and its weeping variety *Fagus sylvatica* 'Pendula' are truly graceful giants with beautiful early leaf colour, rich summer green and rich autumn gold that falls to unmask the light grey bark. Even greater impact on the skyline is made by the purple-leaved *F. s. purpurea*. Give these plants space to develop and their full beauty, as branches sweep to the ground, will be seen in future years; a perfect choice for the surrounds of sports and playing fields.

Mention must be made of the Ash, *Fraxinus excelsior*, to encourage planting where disease has killed stately Elms. Fast growing, tough and easy to grow, the Ash has black buds in winter and attractive rich green leaves in

Autumn colour on small acers seen through the spread of *Platanus orientalis*.

A good example of how plants can be combined to enhance each other. *Clematis montana* types will happily scramble through a tree such as laburnum.

summer. In more formal planting use the yellow-barked *F. e.* 'Jaspidea' with its rich yellow autumn foliage, and *F. oxycarpa* 'Raywood' with more sharply defined leaves, and rich purple autumn colour on more compact trees.

Best suited to the drier south-east of England, *Gleditsia triacanthos* 'Sunburst' makes an attractive small to medium sized garden tree. Certainly do not plant it in waterlogged soils. The fern-like leaves are light yellow when young and they turn light green with age. Avoid the strong-growing Honey Locust, *Gleditsia triacanthos*, in gardens because it grows quite rapidly to a large tree and is armed with long vicious thorns. It is, however, a good choice for public ground where young boys need to be deterred from climbing!

Another tree for our heirs is *Juglans regia*, the common Walnut, which will provide edible nuts in warm summers. The wood can fetch a high price.

The common name of Golden Rain Tree is easier to cope with than *Koelreuteria paniculata*. It gets its common name from the large clusters of dainty yellow flowers produced in August in hot sunny weather. The attractive deeply divided leaves turn rich yellow before falling in the autumn. Small to medium sized, it is suited to the larger garden.

Don't confuse Golden Rain with the common name Golden Chain tree which some people use to describe laburnum, one of the most popular flowering trees. Best for garden use is *Laburnum* 'Vossii' because it has great long trusses of scented yellow flowers

Giant *Populus nigra* 'Italica' need plenty of space. They make very good windbreaks but cut the tops out while you can reach in restricted spaces.

Magnolia grandiflora, a really magnificent evergreen. The large shiny light green leaves have a brown furry underside, and huge cup-shaped richly lemon scented cream flowers appear late summer or early autumn on the tips of the branches. This tree can also be planted free-standing in most parts of the country.

Jostling with *Prunus* for pride of place in providing garden trees are the *Malus*, or Ornamental Crabs. Small to medium-sized trees provide flowers, attractive fruits and, in the case of upright-growing *Malus tschonoski*, the Bonfire Tree, brilliant autumn foliage.

All the fruits are edible but pretty tart and it is as well to use only the largest fruiting kinds for jelly and wine. Best for flowering in my opinion is the neat small tree *Malus floribunda*; crimson buds open to pale pink and cover the rounded head with flowers.

Good for flowers and large colourful fruits is *Malus* 'John Downie', the fruits tend to drop quite early, however, and can make a mess on paths. Better is the more upright *M.* 'Golden Hornet', which has pale pink flowers and masses of rounded rich yellow fruits which hang on well into the winter. Both 'Jown Downie' and 'Golden Hornet', are of medium size and good for pollinating eating apple varieties.

There are two kinds of Siberian Crab, *Malus* ✕*robusta* – red fruited and yellow fruited; both are attractive in flower and fruit. One of the best for flower is the compact and upright-growing small tree *M.* 'Van Eseltine', while *M.* 'Profusion' and *M.* 'Royalty' have rich copper leaves, flowers and tiny fruits. The foliage of 'Royalty' is especially spectacular.

There is a delightful weeping form,

The most suitable Poplar for garden use, *P. candicans* 'Aurora'.

and sets few seeds. Laburnum seeds are poisonous and best not introduced where undisciplined children play.

A comparatively short-lived tree, similar to Birch and many of the *Prunus*, it is easy to grow in all soils including light sandy and chalky types.

Damp, but not waterlogged, and acid soils are required for *Liquidambar styraciflua*, the Sweet Gum. It is beautiful in autumn when the five-lobed palm-shaped leaves turn yellow, orange, red and almost purple. Given the right soil conditions it will grow to a large tree.

Newcomers to gardening sometimes confuse *Liriodendron tulipifera*, the Tulip Tree, with the magnolia, which follows it in so many catalogues. Liriodendron makes a large specimen with unusual shaped leaves. The

greenish-yellow flowers are produced at the tips of branches on well-established trees.

There is nothing to compare with the visual impact of a multi-branched, small tree-sized specimen of *Magnolia* ✕*soulangiana* in full flower in April ahead of the leaves. Once established – ideally transplanting container-grown specimens to avoid damaging their succulent roots – they are hardy and withstand a variety of soils, even quite heavy clay. See that plenty of peat and organic matter is mixed into the planting site for the best growth. Cold winds and spring frost can damage the April flowers so choose a protected site if possible. The flowers apart, this tree is quite hardy.

It will be advisable to provide the shelter of a wall in cold areas for

The Flagpole cherry, *Prunus* 'Amanogawa', makes a neat column of colour.

M. 'Red Jade', with pale pink flowers, bright green leaves and small red fruits.

Taking us back to the giants is the London Plane, *Platanus ×hispanica*. It is easy to grow, responsive to very hard pruning to retain size, and very resistant to adverse city conditions.

Many Poplars are equally large and are some of the fastest growing trees we have. They grow easily and quickly even from cut lengths of branch put in the soil in winter. Poplars are good plants for wet soils but best kept away from houses, drains and buildings.

The white underside leaf of *Populus alba* is very attractive and the yellow autumn leaf colour is bright. A recent form, *P. a.* 'Racket' has upright growth as well as leaves glossy green above and grey beneath.

The only candidate for garden use is *P. candicans* 'Aurora', growing to medium size. Under poor soil conditions the young leaves are cream,

Pyrus salicifolia 'Pendula' with lead branch weeping over.

green and pink. It is best cut hard back every year or every second year to produce plenty of young growth and coloured foliage. If over-fed the leaves will stay green.

Ornamental almonds, cherries, peaches and plums all have a place in gardens. Earliest to flower are the almonds, *Prunus dulcis* (syn *P. amygdalus*) which will produce edible nuts, and the peach, the best of which is the rich double pink *P. persica* 'Klara Meyer'. Sadly both are susceptible to the disease peach leaf curl.

Troubled only by the odd caterpillar and easy to grow, the Purple Leaved Plum, *P. cerasifera* 'Pissardii' has masses of tiny white flowers in March or April followed by dark purple leaves.

This leaves the cherries, the most free-flowering of all trees. Nothing can compare with the flowering abundance of double pink *Prunus* 'Kanzan', its branches stretching upwards like an umbrella blown inside out, on a medium-sized tree.

Weeping cherry *P.* 'Kiku-shidare Sakura' has flowers of similar colour but this small tree with branches to the ground is ideal for small gardens. In marked contrast is the Flagpole Cherry, *P.* 'Amanogawa'; growing very upright and with pale pink flowers it is also suited to small gardens.

There are many cultivars of medium-sized flowering cherry trees, but for shape of head, and large white flowers contrasting with young copper leaves, I like *P.* 'Tai-Haku'. For rich shiny mahogany bark choose *P. serrula*, the Birch Bark Cherry, and for winter flowers select small to medium-

A good example of carefully sited flowering *Prunus* planted among prostrate and upright growing conifers and deciduous and flowering shrubs.

Prunus 'Shirofugen' is one of several flowering cherries suitable for a small garden.

sized *P. subhirtella* 'Autumnalis'.

Grey-leaved Weeping Pear, *Pyrus salicifolia* 'Pendula', is another perfect small garden tree. Left with the lead shoot untrained upwards it makes little more than a shrub. Masses of white flowers in April are followed by rich silver willow-like leaves. This tree seems to take everything, all soils, coastal conditions and town pollution.

I can but plead for *Quercus robur*, the English Oak; if you can find the place and the space this tree is a must. Where space is restricted the upright *Q. r.* 'Fastigiata' is the alternative.

The *Robinia* is closely related to *Gleditsia* and it is easy to confuse the two. Best for the garden, a quite outstanding small tree is *Robinia pseudoacacia* 'Frisia'. Bright yellow leaves like Maidenhair Fern grace the branches from spring to autumn.

All the *Robinia* are hardy, quite quick growing and once established are easy in most soils, though preferring lighter, sandy soils and sunny conditions. Container-grown trees are easiest to transplant successfully. The branches tend to be brittle so avoid very windy situations. *R. pseudoacacia*, the Common Acacia, grows very rapidly and tends to sucker; also its branches are quite fiercely thorned.

Many gardeners are attracted by the yellow bark and shoots of the Weeping Willow, *Salix ×chrysocoma*. It grows much too large for most gardens, however, unless used as a temporary filler, cutting it down after a few years. The best choice of Weeping Willow for small gardens is *S. purpurea* 'Pendula'; very small, it is slow growing and not easy to cultivate.

Willows (*Salix*) are very striking and beautiful trees, but many species do need space, so careful selection is necessary. This is S. × *chrysocoma*.

Flower arrangers will like the twisted branches of *S. matsudana* 'Tortuosa', seen at its best in winter against a blue sky. While not quite so large as the Weeping Willow it will still require space unless cut back regularly.

Two popular groups of garden trees are listed under *Sorbus*, the Mountain Ash, *Sorbus aucuparia*, and the White-beam, *Sorbus aria*. There are quite a number of different cultivars to choose from but all are easy to grow, even in chalk. They are not terribly long lived in comparison, say, with Beech, and are of small to medium size.

Although there are a variety of berry colours the red *Sorbus aucuparia* remains very popular with both gardeners and blackbirds. I would like to see *Sorbus aria* 'Lutescens' planted more widely, its creamy white leaves are especially attractive in spring before turning to the more typical grey-green of *S. aria* in summer and yellow in autumn.

Most of the *Sorbus* are neat and upright in habit, especially in their early years. Branches may bend over and spread out a little when carrying heavy bunches of fruit but the compact shape suits smaller gardens.

Finally the Limes, *Tilia*, and the Elms, *Ulmus*, again need space – but we owe it to our heirs to plant more of these important landscape trees.

PLANTING

Once you have selected the kind of tree you want, be sure to purchase the right shape. Many ornamental trees are grown in just the same way that nurserymen grow bush, half-standard and standard fruit trees (see fruit training section, page 123). Where trees are in grass and need to be mown underneath, and where you plan to sit

When planting a tree or shrub, make sure there is room to spread the roots.

Use the existing soil mark on the stem as a guide to planting depth.

Always position the stake on the windward side before filling the hole.

Carefully return the soil to the hole, shaking it between the roots.

It is essential that the earth is firmed well, using the feet to tread the soil.

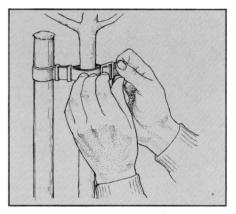

To complete the job, trees should be tied, using a specially designed tie.

under the tree, then full standards with a trunk of 6 ft (2 m) should be purchased.

Full standards will need a good strong stake at least 7½ ft (2·5 m) for support until well established. One- and two-year-old trees are often sold, and the term used here is 'feathered'. This refers to the small side branches coming out from the main stem, the trunk of the tree.

Once well established the feathers can be pruned off to give the clear trunk of a full or half standard 3–5 ft (1–1·5 m). Side branches are left the first year or two to help speed the thickening of the main stem.

Soil preparation really cannot be done too thoroughly, once planted the tree may well be there for a hundred years and there will be no second chance to add well-rotted compost, peat and similar material to improve water retention and drainage, to improve soil and speed root growth.

When planting bare-root trees in autumn to early spring, do not let the roots become dry, and prune off any roots which are twisted or broken. While bare-root deciduous trees can be planted at any time the soil is not frozen during their dormant season, the earlier they are planted the more time there is for root development before the demands of new spring growth.

Container-grown trees can be planted the year round without check. Where trees are well established in the pot and roots are completely circling the base of the container, it is well worth gently unwinding them and spreading them out to improve anchorage, and get them off to a good start.

PRUNING

When cutting large limbs from trees always cut into the underside of the branch first, then finish cutting from the top. This prevents the weight of the branch breaking the last piece of wood and tearing it back.

Once cut off, carefully pare around the edge of the cut bark to leave a clean finish which quickly heals over.

Make a cut on the underside of large branches before sawing from the top.

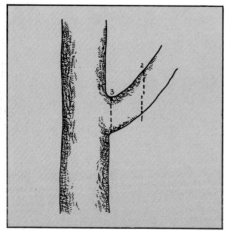

Carefully pare around the edge of the cut to leave a clean wound.

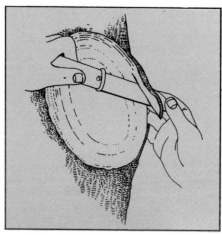

48

GARDEN TREE SELECTOR CHART

Name	Common name	Soils	Likely ultimate height	Shape	Garden value
Acer davidii	Snake-bark Maple	A	40 ft*	1	Coloured bark
Acer platanoides	Norway Maple	N	80 ft	1	Easy to grow, autumn leaf colour
A.p. 'Crimson King'		N	65 ft	1	Crimson-purple leaves
A.p. 'Drummondii'		N	60 ft	1	Creamy-white edged leaves
Acer pseudoplatanus 'Brilliantissimum'		N	20 ft	1	Pink and cream spring foliage
Amelanchier lamarckii	Snowy Mespilus	N/M/C	23 ft	2	White spring flower, autumn leaf colour
Betula pendula	Silver Birch	N	60 ft	1	White bark, autumn leaf colour
B.p. 'Youngii'	Young's Weeping Birch	N	20 ft	3	Small weeping tree
Carpinus betulus 'Fastigiata'	Fastigiate Hornbeam	N/C	50 ft	4	Spire-like shape
Cercis siliquastrum	Judas Tree	N/C/D	25 ft	2	Pink spring flowers
Cotoneaster 'Hybridus Pendulus'		N	10 ft	3	Masses of red berries
Crataegus oxycantha 'Paul's Scarlet'	Red May	N	25 ft	1	Double red spring flowers
Eucalyptus gunnii	Gum Tree	N	65 ft	1	Silver-blue leaves
Fagus sylvatica	Beech	C	100 ft	1	Autumn and spring leaf
Gleditsia triacanthos 'Sunburst'	Golden Honey Locust	D	33 ft	1	Thornless cultivar with rich yellow leaves
Laburnum 'Vossii'	Golden Chain	D/C	25 ft	1	Yellow spring flowers
Liquidambar styraciflua	Sweet Gum	M	65 ft	1	Autumn leaf colour
Magnolia Xsoulangiana		N	25 ft	2	Large spring flowers
M. grandiflora	Evergreen Magnolia	N	33 ft	2	Large glossy leaves, huge scented flowers
Malus 'Golden Hornet'	Flowering Crab	N	30 ft	1	Flowers and fruits
M. 'Red Jade'	Weeping Crab	N	25 ft	3	White flowers and red fruits
M. tschonoskii	Bonfire Tree	N	35 ft	1	Upright growth and autumn leaf colour
Populus candicans 'Aurora'	Variegated Poplar	N/M	45 ft	1	Colour of young leaves
Prunus 'Amanogawa'	Flagpole Cherry	N	25 ft	4	Pale pink spring flowers
P. cerasifera 'Pissardii'	Purple-leaved Plum	N	33 ft	1	Dark copper leaves
P. 'Kanzan'		N	40 ft	1	Double, pink spring flowers
P. 'Kiku-shidare Sakura'	Weeping Cherry	N	13 ft	3	Double, pink spring flowers
P. serrula		N	33 ft	1	Shining coppery bark
Pyrus salicifolia 'Pendula'	Weeping Willow-leaved Pear	N	15 ft	3	Silver leaves
Robinia pseudoacacia 'Frisia'		N/D	25 ft	1	Golden-yellow foliage
Salix caprea 'Pendula'	Kilmarnock Willow	N/M	13 ft	3	Umbrella-shaped weeping tree
S. Xchrysocoma	Weeping Willow	N/M	65 ft	3	Golden-yellow shoots and weeping habit
Sorbus aria 'Lutescens'	Whitebeam	N/C	60 ft*	1	Silver-white young leaves
S. aucuparia	Mountain Ash	N	33 ft	1	White flowers and red berries

Key N = suitable for neutral and most garden soils   A = suitable for slightly acid soils   C = suitable for slightly alkaline (chalky) soils
M = suitable for moist soils   D = suitable for dryish soils

*25 ft = 7·6 m

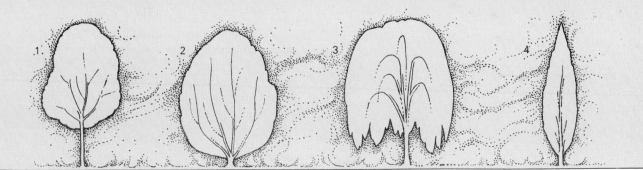

Shrubs

Shrubs are all too often neglected in smaller gardens because for many people a shrubbery conjures up a gloomy and dusty border densely planted and perhaps 7–10 ft (2–3 m) high. Shrubberies like that only exist because planting has been done carelessly, without due attention to selecting the right kinds of shrub for the right place and space. Frequently such errors in planning are made much worse by neglect of even the small amount of pruning and feeding that shrubs require.

Consider the true qualities and value of shrubs in the garden and their adaptable nature, then the invaluable contribution they make to a balanced garden soon becomes apparent.

Shrub borders in large gardens give colour and interest the whole year, with the minimum of effort. Even a small shrub border can include a wide range of species that reflect the diversity of shrubs. There are shrubs in flower every month of the year. Taking the winter months of December and January alone, the fragrant chimonanthus and hamamelis can be in flower at the back of the border, with the sweet-smelling evergreen mahonia mid-border and Heathers covering the foreground. Add to all that the winter berries and the coloured barks of shrubs such as the Dogwoods, and it will become apparent that there is nothing dull about shrubs even in winter. If this can be achieved in the bleak months, how much more there is to look forward to for the rest of the year, when the weather is kinder.

Planning a Shrub Border

Plan a border like an artist using colour, selecting each plant to build the complete but ever-changing picture. Do not overlook the importance of height – trees on a clear stem can provide this, while taller and upright-growing shrubs can be used in the

Shrubs play a vitally important part in any garden design. This is part of a shrub border in the author's garden.

centre and back of the border. Prostrate, ground-hugging types should be used to cover the ground underneath larger specimens. Such ground-cover plants are attractive in their own right, but also make gardening easy by smothering weeds and reducing maintenance.

Do not overlook the usefulness of evergreens. Besides green foliage being attractive in its own right it is also a useful winter foil for winter-flowering shrubs such as hamamelis. The chapter on conifers offers many possibilities in this direction but there are other choice evergreens such as *Garrya elliptica* and the hebes, some with attractive variegation. Evergreens are useful for furnishing the garden in winter, for filtering winds and deflecting noise.

Quantity and brightness are obvious qualities required from ornamental fruits and berries, but equally important is the length of time they remain on

the plant – and how attractive they are to birds. The fruiting crab 'John Downie', for example, will ripen and fall long before 'Golden Hornet', which will hold its abundant yellow fruit well past Christmas. The yellow and orange-berried pyracanthas seem to be less attractive to birds than the red kinds, and where birds are a problem this is worth considering when making a selection. One shrub that usually retains its large fruits right through the winter is chaenomeles, the Japanese Quince.

When young shrubs are seen in a nursery or garden centre it is sometimes difficult to visualize their final size and form, yet this is vital if a balanced border is to be created.

Speed of growth and ultimate height will of course depend on district, soil and situation, and heights quoted are the averages likely to be reached under normal conditions. Impoverished soil

A few well-chosen shrubs can transform a garden. Here forsythia contrast well against Silver Birch and bring a spring garden to life.

Balled plants, which have been lifted with a soil-ball, held firmly in place with sacking-like material, allows transplanting with very little root disturbance.

Container-grown plants are subject to the least disturbance of all, and unlike the others can be planted at any time of the year. Such plants grow away with no check because roots are undisturbed when transplanting.

When purchasing a container-grown plant try lifting it by the stem – an established plant will hold the full weight of the pot and compost; a recently potted specimen will not and should be avoided.

Where possible it is best to visit a garden centre or nursery to choose well-shaped, vigorously growing specimens. But this is not always possible, and some shrubs may have to be ordered from a reputable nursery. Cheap offers and low-priced plants are usually inferior and are likely to prove a false economy.

Vigorous young plants will tend to grow away quickly and become established more readily than larger specimens that suffer a more severe check when moved, especially where bare-root plants are concerned. Because the younger plants tend to grow away more strongly, they often overtake larger plants of the same kind. As younger plants are usually cheaper to buy, do not be influenced by size alone.

PREPARATION AND PLANTING
Although plants will cling tenaciously to life despite unsatisfactory conditions, they will establish themselves far more readily if they are given the benefit of well prepared soil – which is not much to ask considering the many years most shrubs decorate a garden.

Alkaline soil turns the leaves of many shrubs yellow, even this pyracantha.

and also cold, dry positions will restrict growth, while warm, rich soils and high rainfall can increase the ultimate size. Plants grown in shade may become drawn.

The other problem encountered in establishing a new border is the *rate* of growth, for some will grow rapidly, while others take many years to reach a mature height.

The appearance of a new shrub border can be improved by planting groups of perhaps three or five plants of a single kind, thinning over the years until just one good specimen remains. The extra plants will give an appearance of maturity more quickly, and three plants, to be thinned to one finally, could cover the ground in a season and save a couple of seasons of hoeing the ground every fortnight to control weeds.

Besides their accepted role in borders, shrubs can make an attractive feature in their own right, just like specimen trees. They also provide protection, privacy, and a pleasant vista. The range of shrubs available is wide, but the key to success is to select carefully in the first place, matching the plant to soil and situation.

Most shrubs are tolerant of quite widely differing soils, and it is usually only where extremely alkaline (chalk) or acid (peat and thin sands) soils occur that special care must be taken when selecting species. The chart on page 63 indicates which shrubs will grow well on difficult soils, and if this is read in conjunction with the notes on specific plants it should be possible to select the best for your situation.

BUYING SHRUBS
How well your plants grow away after planting will depend to a large extent on the state of the root system. The roots may be bare when you buy the plant, wrapped in a soil-ball, or be growing in a container.

Bare-root plants have been lifted from the field and transported without soil, although the exposed roots should have been wrapped to keep them moist. This keeps carriage costs down, but avoid these plants unless you are sure the roots have not been allowed to dry out.

The minimum depth to which the site should be dug is 1 ft (30 cm) but forking over the lower soil is advisable. Both heavy and light soils will benefit from the incorporation of peat and well-rotted compost. Remember that although it is simple to add fertilizers later, it is not so easy to improve soil structure once the shrubs are planted.

While annual weeds are easily dealt with later, deep-rooted perennials are more difficult, so every effort should be made to clear these from the ground during soil preparation.

The newly prepared ground should be left to settle before planting.

Planting

Always dig a hole large enough to accommodate the roots without cramping. If there is nowhere convenient to place the earth during planting apart from the lawn, use a sheet of plastic to protect the grass and provide a clean finish to the job.

Be sure to protect bare roots from cold drying winds while preparing the holes, covering them with a damp sack or cloth if necessary. Bare roots should be spread out well in the bottom of the hole, but try not to disturb the soil-ball if there is one. When the shrub is in position, fill round the roots with damp peat and good friable soil. Bare-rooted shrubs need to be eased up and down a little during this process to make sure there are no large air pockets left in the soil.

The sacking-like hessian round balled plants can be left in place as it quickly decays in the soil. Any plastic root wrap which will not rot must be removed.

Firm the soil as infilling progresses by treading firmly. The surface footprints should be forked out once complete however, as if left the structure of the soil will be affected and become wet and muddy, then dry into a hard cake. For the same reason, try to avoid planting in wet conditions.

Planting should also be delayed if the ground is frozen. In wet or icy conditions it is best to wait until the weather improves. Container-grown plants will not come to any harm provided they are not allowed to dry out. Bare-rooted plants should be left in the wrapping in a frost-free place and kept damp. If plants arrive before the ground has been prepared, they can be 'laid in' temporarily by placing the roots in a spare piece of ground and covering with moist soil, gently firmed. Container-grown plants are the

Broom can be pruned after flowering by cutting back the previous summer's growth by about two-thirds.

easiest to handle as the hole only needs to be fractionally larger than the container, and the plant placed in the hole before removing the container. The gap can then be filled in with fine soil and firmed.

Deciduous shrubs can be planted from mid-October till the end of March. Evergreens are best planted in September and October or March and April. Container-grown plants can, of course, be planted at almost any time provided the ground is not frozen.

Staking

Specimen plants and large shrubs need staking until they become established. If a stake is necessary, try to position the stake in the hole ahead of the plant. To determine the position, try the stake and plant in the hole together first, with the stake to the windward side to reduce the chances of chafing. Then the shrub can be removed while the stake is driven in firmly, and the planting finished normally.

Make sure the stake is tall enough to support the heaviest part of the plant. It is important that ties hold the plant firmly without chafing the bark, and must also allow for adjustment as the trunk or branch increases in girth.

PRUNING

The majority of shrubs need very little regular pruning, and in many cases it is quite sufficient to remove dead flower heads and trim to retain good shape.

Although there are very many different kinds of shrubs, pruning can be simplified into four groups – spring, summer and winter-flowering deciduous, and evergreens.

Those which flower in spring and early summer such as Flowering Currants, forsythia and Lilac, should be pruned immediately after flowering, cutting back old shoots that have flowered to fresh young growths on the main branches. Weak growths and crowded shoots should be thinned out at the same time.

Shrubs which flower in late summer or early autumn on the current year's growth, such as *Buddleia davidii* cultivars, the fuchsias, potentillas and caryopteris are best pruned hard in early spring.

Winter-flowering shrubs should have diseased and weak branches cut out in spring, otherwise just prune to keep the plants within a restricted space.

Evergreens are best pruned in April, when they will quickly produce new growth to hide any unsightly cuts. Normally only weak, straggly or diseased shoots need to be cut out. A few plants however, such as Box, Lavender, rhododendrons and Cotton Lavender, respond to hard pruning; if they are bare at the base and have grown too large they can be cut back in spring.

Before attempting any pruning, be sure to have a good sharp pair of secateurs – for the sake of the plant and your own comfort. It will be easier to remove a large branch if downward pressure is applied on the branch, and away from the blade.

SOME GOOD GARDEN SHRUBS

Acer (Maple) These deciduous trees are grown for their attractive foliage and bark. The Japanese type will tolerate some lime, but they grow best in slightly acid, peaty soil. As those with finely-cut, coloured leaves are easily damaged by late spring frost and strong winds, plant them in a sheltered position and out of direct early morning sunshine.

The cut-leaved forms are well suited to growing on banks, as specimen subjects in lawns, or in association with stone. Japanese Maples and lilies make a good planting combination.

Acer negundo 'Variegatum', which has broad white margins to the leaves, makes a nice pot-grown tree, and is effective planted with purple-leaved prunus. Among the Japanese Maples, *A. palmatum* 'Atropurpureum' is a popular purple-leaved shrub, but for a dwarfer, slower-growing plant try *A. p.* 'Dissectum Atropurpureum'.

Amelanchier (Snowy Mespilus) This large shrub or small tree should be more widely planted. The young pink to copper foliage contrasts with clusters of massed white flowers in spring. It also associates well with spring bulbs. The leaves have rich autumn colour before falling.

Prune back hard after flowering to retain a compact size.

Aucuba japonica A good town plant as the evergreen foliage will withstand shade and grime. Best planted in a position with some shelter from very

The Barberries are justifiably popular shrubs, with a variety of forms and leaf colour. This is a deciduous species, *Berberis thunbergii* 'Rose Glow'.

cold wind. The variegated forms retain their colour longest if grown in full sun. If male and female specimens are planted, red berries are produced.

Prune in May or June to restrict size and retain shape.

This versatile plant can also be grown in tubs or urns, and even makes a nice houseplant.

Aucuba japonica is a good, attractive shrub for town gardens.

Azaleas There are two main groups – evergreens and deciduous. The evergreen and semi-evergreen include Japanese Azaleas, and these are quite hardy, though late spring or early autumn frosts can damage flower buds. For this reason, and because some flowers fade badly in strong sunlight, plant in a position sheltered from early morning sun. A partially shaded site under trees is good.

Slow-growing plants, they may take ten years to reach 3 ft (1 m). Deciduous azaleas tend to grow taller, and the flowers are larger.

All types can be grown in tubs, but keep them well watered with lime-free water.

If azalea gall shows itself as white and pale green swellings, remove the galls and spray with benomyl.

Berberis (Barberry) This is another shrub with evergreen and deciduous forms – all with sharp spines which can make them useful as a deterrent hedge.

The evergreens are grown mainly for attractive deep green foliage, but some are grown for their flowers. *B. darwinii* and *B. ×stenophylla* are both widely planted, the latter for hedges.

Deciduous types are grown for their attractive autumn foliage and bright berries. This group is dominated by *B. thunbergii*.

To avoid planting losses, purchase container-grown plants. Prune only to remove weak old growth and to retain shape – the deciduous kinds in spring, the evergreens after flowering.

Buddleia (Butterfly Bush) A wonderful plant if you want to encourage butterflies to visit your garden. The most widely planted types are the July to September flowering *B. davidii* cultivars, but *B. globosa* the Orange Ball Tree is a complete contrast with its orange balls of flowers in June.

Prune *B. davidii* hard in March, but *B. globosa* only needs to be trimmed to shape after flowering.

Calluna (Heather) Although some ericas (Heaths) will tolerate limy soils, the callunas will not. Apart from this, the major difference between callunas and ericas is in the leaves – those of callunas being softer and thicker.

The cultivars grown for their silver, golden or red leaves generally have insignificant flowers, but others have good flowers over a period from June to November, according to variety.

Full sun is needed for plenty of flower and a good colour to the foliage. Trim the flower heads back lightly in March every few years.

Camellia The exotic waxy flowers of the camellia make it the hardy shrub equivalent of the orchid. The glossy, evergreen foliage is a bonus.

The plants are hardy, but because the flowers are produced in winter or

Camellias are spectacular spring-flowering shrubs that are very rewarding to grow. The variety illustrated is *C. japonica* 'Elegans'.

early spring some protection is needed from early morning sun after frost. In northerly areas the plants need a sunny site to ripen the wood and encourage flower bud formation. Avoid lime and chalk, and incorporate plenty of peat when planting.

If growing in tubs or pots, water regularly with lime-free water to avoid flower bud drop.

Ceanothus This includes one of the best blue-flowered shrubs, though a warm site in full sun is required. The evergreen kinds also need the protection of a south or west facing wall.

Cold wintery weather may damage the soft young shoots, and these are best pruned back to green wood in April. Evergreen types need little other pruning apart from trimming to retain shape after they have flowered. Deciduous kinds should have flowering shoots cut hard back to within 3 in. (8 cm) of the previous year's wood in March.

Chaenomeles (Japanese Quince) This outstanding garden plant used to

be known as cydonia. It is completely hardy and thrives in all soils. The attractive spring flowers are followed by golden-yellow fruit in the autumn. The red cultivars are the most spectacular for a north wall.

Chimonanthus (Winter Sweet) A delightful, fragrant shrub that flowers from December to February. It thrives on a chalky soil, and a well-drained sheltered site is ideal. It responds well to the protection of a south or west facing wall. The plants take several years before they start flowering so do not be impatient, the result is worth the wait.

Choisya (Mexican Orange Blossom) The heavily fragrant flowers in May make this an ideal patio plant or for planting beneath a window. It prefers full sun, and some shelter. A well-drained soil is best. Pruning only consists of removing frost-damaged shoots in March.

Cornus (Dogwood) Coloured foliage and bark are the reasons for growing

Chaenomeles is a hardy spring-flowering shrub, once known as cydonia.

Cotinus in the foreground of a mixed border. This used to be known as *Rhus cotinus*, and its fluffy flower heads give rise to the name Smoke Tree.

Dogwoods. Those grown for the winter bark succeed in partial shade and are happy in most soils. Some Dogwoods have nicely variegated foliage like *Cornus alba* 'Elegantissima' one of the most popular of all shrubs. A few, such as *Cornus mas* and *C. florida*, are grown for their flowers.

Those kinds with coloured bark should be cut back very hard every-other March to encourage new growth.

Corylus (Hazel) *Corylus avellana* 'Contorta', the Corkscrew Hazel, can be quite a conversation piece, with its twisted and contorted branches.

Totally different but still attractive is the Purple-leaf Filbert *C. maxima* 'Purpurea'.

Prune in March after the catkins, cutting back even into three- and four-year-old wood.

Cotinus (Smoke Tree) This used to be called *Rhus cotinus*. It is grown for its fluffy flower heads that give rise to its common name. There is a purple-leaved form, 'Royal Purple'. Cotinus is an excellent plant for a mixed border,

contrasting with golden foliage.

Pruning is normally unnecessary, though any unwanted growth can be cut out in March.

Cotoneaster These are among our most important hardy shrubs. There are both evergreen and deciduous kinds, and a wide range of form and habit. Colourful autumn foliage and brilliant berries are their main attraction, but their ease of culture also explains why they are so widely planted.

Among the evergreen cotoneasters there are many that are good for carpeting a bank, such as *C. conspicuus* 'Decorus' and *C. dammeri*, the latter growing only a few centimetres high but each plant spreading over a 4 sq m area. One of the best weeping trees for a small garden is *C.* 'Hybridus Pendulus'. Grown as a standard it is really eye-catching when festooned with brilliant red berries.

Among the deciduous cotoneasters, *C. horizontalis* is one of the best, and is invaluable for north and east walls. It is also excellent on banks. The common

name Fish Bone Cotoneaster describes it well. This species has good autumn colour.

There are some species best described as semi-evergreen, and this group contains the popular hedging plant *C. simonsii*.

If any trimming is necessary, do it in spring.

Cytisus (Broom) The Brooms, with their tumbling sprays of spring flowers cascading like a waterfall, are excellent garden plants. They will be happy in most garden soils, provided the extremes of acid and alkaline soils are avoided. Full sun and good drainage are important.

Brooms do not take kindly to transplanting, so buy container-grown plants. Prune after flowering by cutting back the previous summer's growth by up to two-thirds. Hardened wood does not respond to pruning, so leggy specimens are best replaced with new plants.

Daphne *Daphne mezereum* is one of the most popular February-flowering plants. It has a delicious fragrance.

A well-drained soil is required, and chalk is tolerated. Full sun or partial shade are both acceptable, but the soil must not be allowed to dry out. If planting near a wall, be sure to add plenty of organic matter to retain moisture.

The scarlet berries which follow the flowers are poisonous.

Deutzia These summer-flowering shrubs are often planted too closely in a mixed border, where their beauty is not

Cytisus × praecox is one of the most graceful Brooms, ideal for small gardens.

A ground covering of *Erica carnea* 'Vivellii' and *E. c.* 'Springwood Pink'.

A pleasing group of *Erica cinerea* 'White Dale', *E. c.* 'Pink Ice' and *E. carnea* 'Foxhollow'.

seen at its best. When planting be sure to allow sufficient space for development. An open sunny site will give the most balanced growth, but pink-flowered forms will hold their colour better in the light shade of overhanging trees.

Occasional removal of old wood from the base will keep the plants vigorous and attractive.

Elaeagnus Useful evergreen plants. *E. pungens* 'Maculata' is attractively variegated with yellow, and is popular with flower arrangers. *E.* ×*ebbingei* has

Ground-covering *Euonymus fortunei* 'Emerald 'n' Green'.

fragrant white flowers in the autumn and can be grown in coastal areas.

Any all-green shoots that appear on variegated forms should be cut out as soon as they are noticed.

Erica These useful ground-cover plants have become justifiably popular. Young plants spaced 15 in. (38 cm) apart will cover the ground in two seasons.

An acid soil is preferred, and if the soil is chalky the choice should rest with *E. carnea*, *E. mediterranea* or *E.* ×*darleyensis*.

Mulch annually with moistened peat or composted bark to speed growth. Dead flower heads can be removed with shears in spring, but do not cut the plants back too hard.

Escallonia Any well-drained soil is suitable for these shrubs, and they will survive even in those that are very light and dry.

In cold northern areas away from the coast the protection of a wall may be necessary.

If used as a screen or hedge they should be spaced so that hard pruning is unnecessary. Trimming back should be done after flowering.

Euonymus (Spindle) The evergreen forms of euonymus are becoming popular because of their attractive foliage and compact growth.

Euonymous japonicus 'Ovatus Aureus' has bright yellow variegation. Several forms of *E. fortunei radicans* are excellent ground cover plants. The variegated kinds need full sun to produce the best colouring.

Forsythia One of the most brilliant of spring-flowering shrubs, it is also one of the easiest to grow. Any reasonable soil will give good results.

Besides the popular *F.* ×*intermedia* cultivars, 'Lynwood' and 'Spectabilis', there is a species with a rambling, weeping habit – *F. suspensa*. This is effective trained against a wall, on steep banks, or sprawling over fences or walls.

Do not prune too hard – only remove old flowering shoots immediately after flowering.

Branches cut after Christmas and placed in water indoors can be forced into flower.

Fuchsia Although even hardy species tend to be cut back by frost, they produce new shoots from the base in spring. Protection from severe frost can be given by covering the base of the plant with 8–12 in. (20–30 cm) of dry peat in the autumn. Open sunny sites or shade are both satisfactory.

On established plants, shoots can be pruned to ground level in spring in areas where frost causes die-back. Otherwise just remove dead wood.

Garrya elliptica The glossy evergreen foliage of this shrub will withstand the onslaught of city smoke and dirt. The real prize comes with the long tassels of catkins in January and February, which makes it attractive as a free-standing bush or planted against a wall.

Ideally a south-facing wall is the best place for planting as cold winds burn back the leaves. It will survive on a north wall in mild, sheltered districts.

To avoid transplanting losses, buy pot or container-grown plants.

Genista Closely related to Broom, the genistas *G. hispanica* and *G. lydia* are excellent plants for covering dry banks. A hot, sunny site suits them best, and poor soil produces the most flowers.

Hamamelis (Witch Hazel) One of the most popular garden shrubs, bringing as much interest and colour to the garden in mid-winter as the forsythia does in spring. Small branches can be cut to bring their fragrance into the house.

A soil heavily enriched with peat or leafmould is required.

Hebe These plants, which used to be listed under veronica, have shiny evergreen leaves, some of them being variegated. The flowers, which may persist for many months, are also attractive in their own right.

Hebes are excellent coastal plants, and also stand up to the dust and grime of city life. Long, severe spells of cold can damage some cultivars.

Hibiscus These spectacular shrubs, with their large almost hollyhock-like flowers, make good solitary plants as well as mixed border subjects.

Protection will be required throughout the winter in cold northern areas, but do not be impatient in spring, for this is one of the last plants to start into growth.

Hydrangea Many hydrangeas find their way into gardens after serving their time as a pot plant indoors. These are the *Hydrangea macrophylla* cultivars, but there are other interesting species such as *H. paniculata* 'Grandiflora', which produces cone-shaped white flower heads. This is also hardier. As the *H. macrophylla* cultivars are not completely hardy they may need some protection in winter from severe frost in the form of straw or sacking. As the dead flower heads offer

The Witch Hazel, *Hamamelis mollis*, is a fragrant winter-flowering shrub that enjoys a moist, acid soil.

some protection, do not remove them until March.

Hydrangeas are useful for planting in troughs and tubs, but watering must never be neglected. Use rainwater whenever possible.

Some pink varieties turn blue in acid

Large, single, yellow flowers typical of deciduous and evergreen hypericum.

soil, but if it is not very acid a special blueing powder can be applied to ensure a good flower colour. White varieties will not change colour.

Hypericum (Rose of Sharon) A wonderful ground-cover plant, *Hypericum calycinum* is evergreen and has large, yellow buttercup-like flowers in profusion. It will give a good show in full sun or semi-shade, and grow freely in all but waterlogged soil. Semi-evergreen *H.* 'Hidcote' is a free-flowering taller shrub.

Ilex (Holly) There are many beautiful variegated forms.

As male and female flowers are carried on separate plants, be sure to plant both kinds if you want a good crop of berries. Where only one plant can be used, select 'J. C. van Tol', or 'Pyramidalis', which are self-fertile.

Container-grown plants avoid difficulties sometimes experienced with transplanting.

Jasminum nudiflorum (Winter Jasmine) The yellow-flowered *J. nudi-*

One of the most popular magnolias is *M.* × *soulangiana*, which has large tulip-like flowers in April.

florum makes a good wall shrub for winter flowers, but avoid an east-facing site.

Prune side shoots after flowering.

The white-flowered *J. officinalis* is summer-flowering (see climbers).

Kalmia This needs special soil conditions, but it is worth providing them. It needs a moist, acidic soil free from lime or chalk. A peaty soil in semi-shade is ideal.

Once established it will require no further attention except removing dead flowers.

Kerria japonica An undemanding free-flowering plant that suckers from the base to form a many-stemmed shrub. There is a variegated form which needs the protection of a wall in cold districts.

Prune back flowered shoots in early June.

Lavandula (Lavender) Space should be found in every garden for this shrub. One of the best dwarf forms is *L. spicata* 'Hidcote'.

Magnolia Most gardeners are familiar with the splendid April-flowering species. The most widely planted species is *M.* ×*soulangiana*, which has large tulip-like flowers, but another gem is *M. stellata*, which grows only slowly to reach 9 ft (3 m), and is laden with white star-like blooms in March and April. Other species flower later in the year.

Magnolias are best in a reasonably rich, deep and lime-free soil, but they will grow in clay and stand the atmosphere of towns quite well.

Container-grown plants are the easiest to establish. Protect newly planted specimens from cold winds.

Mahonia These excellent evergreen plants have sprays of yellow flowers early in the year. *M.* 'Charity' has exquisitely scented flowers from December to February, with a fragrance rather like Lily-of-the-Valley.

Although not fussy about soil, several species take a season or two to settle down, but require little attention once established. *M. aquifolium* can be encouraged to maintain low and lush green growth by cutting back hard in April after flowering.

Osmanthus This shrub will grow on most soils, in sun or partial shade. It is best to avoid exposure to cold northern and easterly winds.

Paeonia (Paeony) The Tree Paeonies are quite as showy as roses, but unfortunately they are not as hardy. The tender young shoots produced in the spring are sometimes damaged by late frosts, and it is worth covering them with sacking on cold nights and leaving until the frost has thawed in the morning.

Tree Paeonies are best planted in groups to the front of mixed borders, or as specimens in sheltered gardens if they can be given a position protected from early morning sun.

Philadelphus (Mock Orange) This plant derives its common name from the fragrance of the flowers, which is like orange blossom. It is an almost perfect garden plant, with a good habit and undemanding nature. It will thrive in the poorest conditions, including chalk. Little pruning is required apart from thinning out old wood after flowering.

Pieris These plants are grown for the bright scarlet young shoots in spring. For greatest impact grow *P. formosa forrestii* and *P. f. f.* 'Wakehurst'. These will require a sheltered site protected from the swift thawing of early morning sun, but *P.* 'Forest Flame' is hardier.

A lime-free soil is required, and they

Potentilla fruticosa 'Red Ace' is brightest red in cool weather.

Pyracantha 'Orange Glow' is one of the best Firethorns, with its long-lasting orange-red berries carried on strong upright plants.

Rhododendrons come in great variety; choose dwarf kinds for small gardens.

will appreciate a bed of acid peat. Pieris are useful for planting with heathers and rhododendrons, which have similar requirements.

Potentilla For sheer flower power it is difficult to better the shrubby potentillas, which produce their single rose-like flowers from June to the first frost. All are easy to grow, but they do best on a light well-drained soil, and although shade is tolerated they will be more prolific in full sun.

Besides being useful in mixed shrubberies, and low hedges, they make a good ground cover, and some cultivars are suitable for sunny banks and the back of rockeries.

Pyracantha (Firethorn) The pyracanthas have so many uses that no garden would be complete without at least one of them. Sheets of white flowers in spring are followed by bright red or orange berries carried well into the winter. One of the best to grow is *P*. 'Orange Glow', a strong upright plant smothered with orange-red fruit for many months.

All garden soils, including chalk, are suitable, and they thrive in both sun and partial shade. Their thorns make the plants useful for creating an impenetrable hedge, but they look most attractive against a wall. Any pruning for shape should be done in May or June.

Buy pot or container-grown plants to avoid transplanting losses.

All willows, *Salix*, thrive in damp soil, even the low-growing shrubs.

Rhododendron Although rhododendrons are often seen to best effect in large stately gardens, there are species and hybrids well suited to gardens of more average size. Some grow only 6 in. (15 cm) high and are suitable for the heather garden or rockery.

All rhododendrons require an acid soil – lime turns the leaves yellow. An application of flowers of sulphur 4–6 oz per sq yd (100–150 g per sq m) will reduce alkalinity.

Where conditions are not right naturally, it is worth creating a special peat bed, and watering with Sequestrene to overcome the yellowing of the leaves.

Never allow rhododendrons to become dry at the roots; leaf edges rolling under and tips browning indicates a dry soil.

Remove dead flower heads as this encourages the formation of next year's flower buds.

Rhus (Sumach) These easily grown plants have splendid autumn colour, and are useful in city areas where they withstand the atmospheric pollution better than many plants. If cut back in February, vigorous new shoots will be produced. This plant tends to produce suckers round the base, and these can be a nuisance in a small garden.

Ribes (Flowering Currant) One of the most common garden shrubs, the Flowering Currant will grow well in ordinary garden soil in full sun or partial shade, though the flowers will be more colourful and profuse in a sunny situation.

Prune out old wood after flowering to keep the plants growing vigorously and to provide plenty of one-year-old wood to produce the flowers.

Spirea bumalda 'Gold Flame' carries richly coloured shoots in spring.

Salix (Willow) Although many people think of the Willow as a large tree, there are shrubby species. Some, such as the prostrate Woolly Willow, *Salix lanata*, barely reach 3 ft (1 m) in height.

Any ordinary garden soil is suitable, including those that are occasionally waterlogged. Light, dry soils will need large quantities of peat or leafmould adding when the site is being prepared.

Little, if any, pruning is required for the dwarf types, although stronger-growing kinds, selected for their coloured bark, will need cutting back hard in spring.

Senecio greyi Widely planted and popular with flower arrangers, the silver-white leaves of this low spreading shrub are very attractive.

This is a plant happy in most soils and situations, although like most other silver-leaved plants it prefers full sun.

If *S. greyi* becomes too large it can be cut back quite severely in spring and will soon produce new growth.

Skimmia Skimmia is a neat evergreen shrub that grows little more than 3 ft (1 m) high. It has clusters of tiny scented white flowers in March and April. Male plants have more flowers, but the female plants have abundant brilliant red berries the size of large peas, which remain on the bush right through winter. To be sure of having plenty of berries, plant one bush of each sex together, or one male to three females. *Skimmia reevesiana* carries male and female on the same plant.

Avoid alkaline soils. Pruning is rarely necessary.

Spartium (Spanish Broom) This plant looks like the common yellow

White felt-like leaves throughout the year and yellow flowers in summer are produced by *Senecio laxifolius* and the very similar *S. greyii*.

Broom, but is more vigorous and the branches are circular in cross-section. It will tolerate a wide variety of soils, but does less well on chalk. Good drainage and full sun help it to thrive.

This is a subject that resents transplanting, so buy pot or container-grown plants.

Plants which have become leggy or too tall can be cut back in spring provided only young wood is pruned.

Spirea The spring-flowering spireas have white flowers, but the summer-flowering kinds usually have pink or red flowers. The various types can add colour and interest over a long period. All are easy to grow and are not fussy about soil.

Spring-flowering types need a light pruning after flowering to restrict size, but the summer-flowering kinds need harder pruning in spring to produce large flower spikes.

Symphoricarpos (Snowberry) This is a suckering shrub which has tiny

blush-white flowers during the summer followed by shiny white berries that remain on the plant for many months. There are also some cultivars with coloured berries. Snowberries are quick to become established and will furnish the wilder parts of the garden and fill waterside banks very rapidly.

Syringa (Lilac) Few shrubs are better than Lilac for fragrance, for garden decoration or for cutting. There are many very good named forms, though the flowering season tends to be short.

Lilacs thrive on almost all soils, including chalk. However, they quickly impoverish poor soils. Full sun is required for a good show of flowers.

One of the best methods of pruning is to cut the branches in flower for indoor decoration. Even so it will occasionally be essential to prune hard, cutting out thin unproductive wood, and this is best done immediately after flowering.

Any suckers coming from the base of the plant should be cut out.

Viburnum opulus, the Guelder Rose, has bright red berries in autumn.

Tamarix This shrub has a graceful habit of growth that makes it a good choice for mixed borders or as a lawn specimen.

Though delicate in appearance, it is quite tough, and will do well on most soils, though a well-drained and sunny position is preferred.

Up to two-thirds of the current season's growth should be cut out – after flowering for the early-flowering species, in winter or early spring for *T. pentandra*.

Viburnum There are many different kinds of viburnum, with a range of qualities. It would almost be possible to furnish a garden with viburnum alone, and it is worth considering a special border of just viburnums – once established there would be interest all the year, and it would require the minimum of attention.

There are evergreen and deciduous kinds, some deliciously fragrant, others with bright autumn foliage, and yet others with richly coloured fruits. Most have white or whitish flowers. Main flowering seasons are winter, spring and early summer.

All types flourish in a wide variety of soils, though those that are moisture-retentive suit them best. Some species, such as *V. rhytidophyllum*, really thrive in chalk.

Weigela The easy and free-flowering nature of this shrub make it very popular. It can be used in borders, on banks, or to grow against a fence.

These plants prefer a well-cultivated soil, but will grow in either full sun or partial shade.

Quite hard pruning immediately after flowering will encourage production of plenty of flowers.

SHRUBS FOR SPECIAL SITES

North Walls	Shaded Sites	Ground Cover
Camellia	Aucuba	Cotoneaster
Chaenomeles	Buxus	Cytisus
Garrya	Camellia	Erica
Kerria	Euonymus	Euonymus
Mahonia	Hedera	Genista
Pyracantha	Hypericum	Hedera
	Ilex	Hypericum
Climbers	Ligustrum	Lonicera
Hedera	Lonicera	Potentilla
Hydrangea	Mahonia	Vinca
Jasminum	Phillyrea	
Parthenocissus	Rhododendron	
	Skimmia	
	Vinca	

SHRUBS WITH ATTRACTIVE BERRIES OR FRUITS

Name	Deciduous	Both	Evergreen	Acid soil	Alkaline soil	Clay soil	Sandy soil
Callicarpa	×						
Clerodendrum	×						
Colutea	×				●	●	●
Cotoneaster		×		●	●	●	●
Hippophae	×						
Ilex		×					
Mahonia aquifolium		×					
Pernettya		×	●				
Pyracantha		×				●	
Skimmia		×	●				
Symphoricarpos	×				●	●	
Viburnum		×			●		

SHRUBS WITH ATTRACTIVE FOLIAGE OR STEMS

Name	Deciduous	Both	Evergreen	Acid soil	Alkaline soil	Clay soil	Sandy soil
Acer	×			●			
Aralia	×					●	
Aucuba			×		●	●	
Buxus			×		●		
Cornus	×					●	
Corylus	×					●	
Cotinus	×					●	
Elaeagnus			×				●
Euonymus		×			●		
Fatsia			×				
Garrya			×				
Hebe			×		●		
Laurus			×		●		
Ligustrum			×		●		●
Lonicera		×					
Osmanthus			×			●	
Pieris			×	●			
Rhus	×				●		
Salix	×						
Senecio			×		●	●	

SHRUBS GROWN FOR THEIR FLOWERS

Name	Deciduous	Deciduous/Evergreen	Evergreen	Colour	Fragrance	Acid soil	Alkaline soil	Clay soil	Sandy soil	Jan	Feb	March	April	May	June	July	Aug	Sept	Oct	Nov	Dec
Amelanchier	×			W								●	●	●							
Azalea		×		W, Y, O, R, P, M	×	●							●	●	●						
Berberis		×		Y, O									●	●	●						
Buddleia	×			M, R, B, W, O	×		●									●	●	●	●		
Camellia			×	W, R, P	●							●	●	●	●						
Carpenteria			×	W											●	●					
Caryopteris	×			B														●	●	●	
Ceanothus			×	B		×	●								●	●					
Ceanothus	×			P, B		×	●										●	●	●	●	
Chaenomeles	×			W, O, R, P				●					●	●	●						
Chimonanthus	×			Y	×					●	●										
Choisya		×		W	×										●	●					
Clerodendrum	×			W	×													●	●		
Cytisus	×			W, Y, R, M					●						●	●					
Daphne	×			M	×						●	●									
Deutzia	×			W, P			●	●							●	●					
Erica/Calluna		×		W, R, P, M		●	●	●		●	●	●	●	●		●	●	●	●	●	●
Escallonia		×		R, P				●							●	●	●				
Forsythia	×			Y			●	●				●	●	●							
Fuchsia	×			W, R, M											●	●	●	●			
Genista	×			Y										●	●						
Hamamelis	×			Y	×					●	●	●	●								●
Hibiscus	×			W, P, M, B													●	●			
Hydrangea	×			W, R, P, B		●										●	●	●			
Hypericum		×		Y			●	●							●	●	●	●	●		
Indigofera	×			P					●							●	●	●	●		
Jasminum nud.	×			Y						●	●	●	●							●	●
Jasminum off.	×			W											●	●	●				
Kalmia		×		P		●									●	●					
Kerria	×			Y		●			●				●	●							
Kolkwitzia	×			P										●	●	●					
Lavandula		×		P	×				●							●	●				
Magnolia	×			W, P	×	●		●					●	●	●	●					
Magnolia		×		W	×											●	●				
Mahonia jap.		×		Y	×					●	●										●
Olearia		×		W		●										●	●				
Philadelphus	×			W	×		●	●								●	●				
Potentilla	×			W, Y, O											●	●	●	●	●		
Prunus	×			W, P								●	●	●	●						
Rhododendron		×		W, Y, R, P, M		●							●	●	●						
Ribes	×			Y, R, P				●					●	●							
Rosa	×			W, Y, R, P	×										●	●	●				
Skimmia		×		W	×	●							●	●							
Spartium	×			Y											●	●					
Spiraea	×			W, P				●					●	●	●	●	●	●			
Syringa	×			W, Y, R, P, M, B	×		●						●	●	●						
Tamarix	×			P		●			●					●	●		●	●	●		
Viburnum		×		W	×		●	●		●	●	●	●	●	●					●	●
Weigela	×			R, P, M			●	●							●	●					

Key   W White   P Pink   O Orange   A solid dot under a soil type indicates the plant will grow well under these special conditions.
     Y Yellow   M Mauve
     R Red   B Blue

Climbing Shrubs

No list of shrubs would be complete without climbers, and there is room in practically every garden for at least a few of these useful plants.

Wherever there is a wall or fence, there's a possible site, and the great merit of climbers is that they usually clothe and enhance what would otherwise be bare areas, and for very little in the way of root space.

Many otherwise boring wooden fences can also be transformed into a living vista by careful selection of suitable climbers. Even old tree stumps that are too difficult to remove can be put to good use.

Some climbers need a little help with support until they get a grip themselves, but others such as the Virginia Creeper are totally self-clinging.

Clematis

Clematis are justifiably among the most popular climbing plants, and they deserve to be in every garden. They take up little soil space yet they can transform an otherwise dull wall or fence into a blaze of colour.

There are many superb large-flowered cultivars in shades of blue, white, pink and red, in single and double forms.

A collection of half a dozen will bring admiration from May till September, and from the numerous varieties available my personal selection would be:

'Duchess of Edinburgh', a large fragrant double white. Flowers in May and June.

'Ernest Markham', a glowing carmine-red that flowers from July to October.

'Jackmanii Superba', violet-purple and flowering from July to September.

'Lasurstern', a large deep lavender-blue. In flower from June to October.

'Nelly Moser', a pale mauve-pink with carmine bar. Flowers May to September.

'Vyvyan Pennell' is one of the best, with deep blue fully double flowers from May to July.

Pruning can sometimes be a little complicated with large-flowered clematis. Those which flower mid to late summer should be pruned hard in early spring, the others only need a light pruning immediately after flowering. If they become too straggly these too may need pruning back hard after flowering to rejuvenate them.

Of the six cultivars listed above

Climbers take up little root space, yet can produce a wealth of interest and colour. This is a charming combination of clematis and ivy.

'Ernest Markham' and 'Jackmanii Superba' need hard pruning in February, the rest should be lightly pruned after flowering.

Equally spectacular in a different way are some of the small-flowered clematis species. These are usually much easier to establish, grow more rapidly and are easier to manage.

Many of the cultivars of *C. montana* are magnificent plants, with their abundant fragrant flowers in May, followed by decorative seed heads.

The true species *C. montana*, which has masses of white flowers, is a very rampant grower.

Two rose-pink varieties are *C. m. rubens*, which has purple-bronze young shoots, and the larger-flowered *C. m.* 'Tetrarose'.

True species with attractive silvery seed heads are the yellow-flowered *C. tangutica*, which starts blooming in July, and *C. orientalis*, which flowers from August onwards. *C. orientalis* is commonly known as the Orange Peel Clematis because the thick orange sepals curl back to resemble the freshly cut peel of an orange.

The last two species should be pruned hard in early spring, but *C. montana* is best trimmed to size after flowering.

Clematis need a rich moist soil containing chalk. Although they like to have their heads in the sun, the roots appreciate a deep cool run, and it is useful to provide shade in the form of other shrubs or herbaceous plants.

All clematis will benefit from a mulch of manure each spring, and this will encourage vigorous growth.

Hedera (Ivy)

One of the most attractive ways to cover a wall, fence or pillar is to plant the creamy-white variegated Canary Island Ivy, *Hedera canariensis* 'Variegata', or the hardier *H. colchica* 'Dentata Variegata'. The latter has a richer more golden colour, but is not as fresh-looking as the Canary Island Ivy.

The smaller-leaved ivies, including the Common Ivy, *H. helix*, should not be overlooked, for in the right situation they can be very effective. There are also variegated forms of *H. helix*, including 'Glacier', which has silvery-grey, white-edged leaves, and 'Gold Heart', which is quite showy with its bold yellow centre to the leaves.

Although ivies will grow in the most impoverished soil and thrive in almost impossible situations, including dense shade, the variegated forms will have stronger colours if given a sunny site.

Ivies may need some support until the aerial roots have a chance to gain a hold. Wall plants can be pruned back in early spring.

Hydrangea

Hydrangeas do not always come immediately to mind when thinking of climbing plants, but one of the hydrangeas, *H. petiolaris* is a hardy self-supporting climber. Its large white flowers are similar to the Lacecap forms of hydrangea, and these cover the plant in June and July.

The glossy green leaves are also attractive when seen against walls or old tree trunks. It is a good plant for sunless north walls, though it may need some support until the aerial roots manage to take a grip.

The same plant can be grown as a free-standing shrub, but against a wall and given ample moisture it will grow very tall.

Jasminum (Jasmine)

The common white Jasmine, *Jasminum officinale* is a strong grower, and given the support of a trellis or old trunk, it will grow to 30 ft (9 m) high. The clusters of fragrant white flowers are carried from mid-summer to September, though vigorous leaf growth sometimes tends to hide them. For this reason avoid hard pruning.

Jasmine is excellent for furnishing bare walls and for screening.

Lonicera (Honeysuckle)

The Honeysuckles are also highly popular flowering climbers, and one

Hydrangea petiolaris is a very useful and attractive wall shrub.

reason for this is their sweet fragrance.

Although many climbing Honeysuckles are planted against houses, they tend to look better scrambling over arches, sheds and trellises.

These climbers like conditions similar to those for clematis, though they do not need the full sunshine that clematis require to flower well.

The wild plant of our hedgerows is *Lonicera periclymenum*, and this has

Clematis jackmanii is one of the most widely planted large-flowered varieties, flowering from July to September.

Clematis 'Nelly Moser' is a striking variety and will flower from May to September.

One of the popular Honeysuckles, *Lonicera periclymenum* 'Belgica'.

pale yellow flowers in July and August, followed by transluscent scarlet berries. Two cultivars commonly listed by nurserymen are *L. p.* 'Serotina' and *L. p.* 'Belgica'.

The flowering season is extended with the semi-evergreen *L. ×brownii* 'Fuchsoides', which flowers from June to September, and with *L. heckrotii* which flowers for a similar period.

The Japanese Honeysuckle, *L. japonica* 'Aureoreticulata' is grown primarily for its mottled foliage, which is popular with flower arrangers.

Regular pruning is not necessary, but mulching with peat or leafmould is definitely beneficial.

Parthenocissus (Virginia Creeper)

A wall covered with Virginia Creeper as autumn tints suffuse the plant is a very spectacular sight. They are self-clinging and need no help in their efforts to cover walls, fences or tree stumps.

The only problems come with the names, which have become very confused over the years. The true Virginia Creeper is *Parthenocissus quinquefolia*, and this has deeply cut five-lobed leaves. But the species best known and most widely planted, especially against old suburban houses, is *P. tricuspidata*, the Boston Ivy, occasionally listed as *Vitis inconstans*. *P. t.* 'Veitchii' has smaller leaves and the young growth is tinged purple.

Parthenocissus showing the different shape of adult and juvenile leaves.

The most colourful species is *P. henryana*, which has dark bronze-green leaves. If grown in the shade these show white and pink variegation.

Satisfactory results can be obtained in most garden soils that have been enriched with organic matter before planting, but the best growth will come from a rich loam with plenty of moisture.

Pruning is no more than removing unwanted shoots in summer.

Passiflora (Passion Flower)

A more refined climber is the Passion Flower, *Passiflora caerulea*, though it is best reserved for more sheltered gardens and preferably given a warm south or westerly facing site.

Given a warm and well-drained site, the Passion Flower will grow rapidly to 20–30 ft (6–9 m) high, supporting itself with tendrils, and giving a magnificent show of its exotic flowers from June to September.

Cold winters will damage the upper growth, but if this is pruned away in the spring, when the plant is cut back to limit size, new growth will sprout after all but the hardest winters.

Polygonum baldschuanicum (Russian Vine)

Another rampant grower is the Mile-a-Minute or Russian Vine, *Polygonum baldschuanicum* – an established plant can grow 16 ft (5 m) in a year. It may not have the most beautiful flowers, which are small and creamy-white, but it is a perfect subject for rapidly covering eye-sores such as oil tanks, sheds and garages.

Any site and soil will be adequate, including chalk, but it is worth paying a little attention to soil if you want it to become established rapidly.

Polygonum baldschuanicum, popularly known as Mile-a-Minute Vine, is a rampant grower, useful for covering sheds and garages.

There is little to match a well-grown wisteria in May, when the long trusses of fragrant mauve flowers cascade in profusion.

Pruning is more a case of hacking back if the plant is allowed to get out of control.

Wisteria

The real aristocrat of wall climbers must surely be the wisteria, which is an absolute joy in May when the great trusses of fragrant mauve flowers, 8 in. (20 cm) or more long, hang from the leafless branches.

The two most popular species are *Wisteria floribunda* and *W. sinensis*, the stems of the first twining clockwise and those of the second twining anti-clockwise. Both have a white-flowered form.

Perhaps most spectacular of all is *W. f.* 'Macrobotrys', which has the longest racemes of flowers.

Wisteria will grow in anything from heavy clay to quite light soils. Seed-raised *W. sinensis* may take many years to flower, but grafted plants of named cultivars are more free-flowering.

As these plants do not take kindly to root disturbance, container-grown plants are to be recommended. But do not despair if newly transplanted specimens are slow to break into growth, an occasional spray with water will help things along.

A sheltered site is preferable, ideally a south or west facing wall, to avoid damage to the flowers from late frosts.

Pruning can be done in two bites. All lateral side growths from the main branches can be cut back to within 1–1½ in. (2–4 cm) of the flowering spurs in February, then on very vigorous plants the current season's lateral growths can be shortened in August.

Conifers

There is a very wide and interesting range of conifers for use in the garden, whatever its size or shape. And although most people believe that all conifers are evergreen and do not shed their leaves each autumn, there are a few that do cast their leaves as the winter months approach. For instance, the Common Larch, with its beautiful light green shoots in spring when·the leaves are unfolding, is a magnificent sight. Also, there is the Maidenhair Tree, *Ginko biloba*, with its distinguished and uniquely shaped leaves which are brilliant yellow in the autumn.

Such is the diversity of their size, form and colour that entire gardens can be formed by using just conifers. There are excellent types for every purpose, from the Scot's Pine grouped in a copse to provide shelter, Leylands and Western Red Cedar for evergreen hedges, stately Cedars for specimen planting, different cultivars of Lawson's Cypress for year-round colour in large borders, prostrate junipers for ground cover and to replace lawns, to the miniatures for troughs, tubs and rock gardens.

Vigorous young plants set carefully in reasonable soil conditions really do give attractive gardens with the very minimum of work. It is, perhaps, the labour-saving value of these plants, coupled with the different leaf colour of the cultivars, which accounts for their increasing popularity.

While every conifer has its place in the garden and a number have several places and uses, the speed of growth and ultimate size are of great importance. Generally, garden catalogues list conifers under two headings – *conifers* and *dwarf and slow- or low-growing conifers*.

There is no problem with the ordinary stronger-growing conifers. Space can be given for them to develop over the years, especially where single

Chamaecyparis lawsoniana 'Ellwoods Gold' is one of the larger dwarf conifers, attaining up to 20 feet in height.

Juniperus scopulorum 'Blue Heaven' is an attractive juniper for any garden, with its year round blue foliage.

plants are grown as specimens. It is the dwarf and slow-growing kinds which cause the difficulties, especially as some are not as slow-growing as others! Even worse, some of the dwarfs are so dwarf that it takes too long to see their beauty in maturity.

Nurserymen often sell the different kinds of Lawson's cultivars and other tall growers in very small sizes. These are often one- and two-year-old cuttings at 5–6 in. (12–15 cm) high in $3\frac{1}{2}$-in. (9-cm) pots, and they look very attractive and appear ideal for rock gardens and troughs. Once established, however, they put on 15–18 in. (40–45 cm) of growth a year and quickly outgrow the space available to them.

There is no harm in using these attractive young plants of large conifers in restricted places, just so long as space is allowed for their future increase in size. Alternatively, they could be transplanted to a larger space in a few years.

When using young plants of stronger-growing kinds as fillers for gardens, we get a better appearance immediately after planting, and they also give protection to the very tiny true dwarfs which develop slowly and will eventually fill the allotted area.

DWARF AND SLOW-GROWING CONIFERS

It may generally be assumed that conifers classified as dwarf and slow-growing will reach no more than 10 ft (3 m) in ten years. Nurserymen have difficulty in classifying plants such as *Chamaecyparis lawsoniana* 'Ellwoodii' and 'Ellwood's Gold', which are very attractive for one to four years, when they are 6–24 in. (15–60 cm) high and set in tubs or the rock gardens. However, they eventually reach 14–20 ft (4–6 m) and, like most conifers, broaden at the base, taking them well outside the dwarf category.

Ideally, we would like plants which grow quickly to the size we want and

Conifers are versatile plants, and as well as making good specimen plants they are equally at home in a mixed border.

absorb some moisture, they prevent it reaching the roots. Dry roots will mean poor and slow growth. A thorough soaking in mid-summer, especially in hot and dry weather in drier parts of the country, will give strong new growth which improves the appearance and enriches the colour of the plants.

Mixing plenty of damp peat into the soil before planting is the easiest way to get a moisture-retentive soil. A mulch of either composted bark or similar material spread over the surface in spring will help retain the accumulated winter moisture.

Matching Plants to Soil

The following list of plants is a general guide to soil requirements. Abies, the firs, will not thrive in dry, shallow, chalky soils. *Picea omorika*, Serbian Spruce, will be better in these areas. Chamaecyparis, the False Cypress, is best in neutral to acid soils, while Juniperus, the Junipers, and Taxus, the Yews, thrive in all soils.

Larix, the Larches, and thuja are not happy in wet, poorly drained soils; Taxodium, Swamp Cypress, is better here. *Pinus sylvestris*, Scot's Pine, is not so successful in wet acid and dry chalky soils, while *Pinus nigra*, the Austrian Pine, will be better in alkaline areas. Given sufficient moisture, most of the dwarf and slow-growing kinds are successful in poor, thin soils – a factor which can be used to retain size.

Selecting the Site

An open and sunny site is needed to get the best colour on cream- and yellow-

then just stop growing. The fascination of gardening, however, is the continual development and changing scene through the years. One of the most attractive features of plants is the rich colour of new growth, and vigorously growing young conifers invariably look better than tired, old and starved specimens.

Make sure all conifers, especially the evergreen types, do not grow into one another or trespass on the territory of other plants. The foliage will go brown and die completely if shaded from light, and once a browned patch has been formed it is very difficult and often impossible to encourage new growth to replace it.

GOOD SOIL PREPARATION

All conifers will thrive in well-cultivated garden soils. Where the soil is especially difficult, choosing the right kind of plant can help, as will thorough preparation, such as adding lime to acid soils and adding plenty of peat, leafmould and well-rotted compost to heavy and sandy soils. On alkaline soils you can add peat and flowers of sulphur at 4–6 oz per sq yd (100–175 g per sq m).

Thorough preparation of the site before planting is essential. Once planted, conifers are likely to remain undisturbed for many years. In the case of cedars it may be several centuries. While the extremes of acidity and alkalinity may cause problems, the main aim must be to provide a rooting area which is free draining, especially in the winter, yet remains moist in the summer.

Evergreen foliage forms a canopy over the soil and, while the leaves

Individual specimen conifers add stature and impact to a garden scene.

leaved conifers. Several of the yellows tend to scorch in cold winds and in very hot and strong sunlight. The best conditions are found in a protected, sheltered garden.

It is often said the blue- and silver-foliaged conifers are best in partial shade. Although they will grow under these conditions, the best colour is produced in the open on fertile soils.

The accommodating × *Cupresso-cyparis leylandii* will grow vigorously and give shelter in all soils and sites, including exposed coastal areas. One of its less hardy parents, *Cupressus macrocarpa*, the Monterey Cypress, also grows well in coastal areas, as will *Pinus nigra*.

Chamaecyparis lawsoniana, Lawson's Cypress, and its many cultivars is not happy in very exposed sites and tends to brown if exposed to cold and drying northerly and easterly winds.

The prostrate and semi-prostrate junipers grow well in most sites, even north-facing slopes. They are ideal to retain the soil on steep banks.

TRANSPLANTING CONIFERS

Quite large specimens of many conifers can be transplanted from the open ground and it is not uncommon to see 15–20 ft (4–6 m) high *Cedrus atlantica* 'Glauca' being transplanted successfully. The best time to move conifers is either March and April or September and October. At this time the sun is not too hot and new root growth is quickly made to establish the plant before the onset of summer or winter respectively.

To ensure that the conifer transplants well, cut the soil to a spade's depth in a circle about 2–3 ft (60–90 cm) from the plant's trunk. This should be done about 6–12 months before actually moving it. We need to move as large a soil-ball with the roots as possible. Cutting around the plant with a spade 6–12 months ahead of lifting cuts the main side roots and encourages the production of fibrous roots.

The new site must be well prepared by digging the soil thoroughly to one or two spade's depths and mixing in peat or well-rotted compost. Dig out a large hole before digging around the conifer to be moved.

When the conifer is more than 2 ft (60 cm) high it will probably take two or more people to lift and transplant it. Ensure that the soil is well moistened and dig a trench around the plant 9–24 in (23–60 cm) out from the trunk. The larger the conifer, the greater the

Cedars make magnificent specimen plants where space allows. *C. atlantica* 'Glauca' (right) can be transplanted as a quite large specimen.

size of root-ball there is to be moved.

Having dug around the plant, cut underneath with a spade, as deep as is practical, remembering the soil-ball will be heavy. Roll up half of a large piece of sacking or polythene and, once you have cut halfway under the plant, push the rolled sheet under the root-ball. Cut through the other side, pushing towards the sheet. Eventually, roll the sheet around the root-ball.

Where the move is no great distance, it is easy to lift the four corners of the sheet and to carry the plant. Where distance and weight prevent carrying in this way, tie the sheet tightly around the soil-ball. This is best done by tying opposite corners, like the ends of a head scarf, against the trunk at soil level. As an added precaution, one or two pieces of strong string can be tied around the root-ball.

Once moved into the prepared hole the sheet is rolled back and removed. Well-moistened and crumbly soil is then firmed around the roots.

Conifers are often sold with a root-ball wrapped in hessian. Provided the wrap is not a plastic material, plant with it on, and firm the soil well.

Chamaecyparis lawsoniana 'Minima Aurea' makes a golden dwarf pyramid.

Spray the foliage with an anti-desiccant to reduce the loss of moisture from the leaves while new roots are made. Syringing over the foliage several times a day in hot, windy and dry weather also helps conifers survive the move.

Another method of protecting the plants from wind damage is to drive three or four stakes into the soil around the plant and fix hessian to them. Polythene can also be used, but ensure that the top is open and the polythene well out from the tree, to prevent excessive heat and drying in hot sun. When using polythene it is better to erect the polythene around the windward side of the plant only.

Large conifers will also need secure staking to hold them until new roots are formed.

Sometimes, when moving conifers, the soil-ball breaks away. This occurs especially with heavy soils and where the soil is dry. Should this happen, I find it advisable to remove the soil and pack very well moistened peat around the roots in its place. New roots are soon made into the damp peat and then out into the soil. If the air pockets and lumps of loose, dry soil are left in place, the roots dry out and the plant will go brown.

Where soil does break away extra care is needed in spraying with water and protecting from drying winds. I have successfully moved 3–4 ft (1–1·3 m) Lawson cultivars in dry conditions in midsummer, but the roots were packed around with wet peat and the foliage sprayed over several times a day for a week or two. If this can be done you should have no trouble at the correct transplanting times, except with Cupressus species, which do not take kindly to root damage.

While there may be some risk of damaging roots when lifting and transplanting from the open ground, all these problems are removed when container grown plants are purchased from the nursery or garden centre. Container plants can, of course, be planted at any time of year as long as the soil is not frozen or waterlogged. See that the compost in the container is just covered to get the correct depth.

What to buy

Conifers purchased with their roots balled in polythene and hessian must look fresh and in no way dull, a sure

This illustration proves that conifers are not only for large gardens. Dwarf conifer collections can be made to look very attractive in small front gardens.

sign that they have been allowed to dry out. The root-ball needs to be tightly held around the roots. Good nurserymen will see that the balled plants are regularly sprayed over with water, the root-ball buried in damp peat or similar materials to keep plants fresh and upright. It is advisable to remove all root wraps when planting, although the hessian wraps which rot in a few months in the soil can be left in place when planting.

Container-grown conifers should be able to be lifted by the stem without coming out of the soil. Recently potted specimens which start to come up out of the compost as you lift by the stem should be avoided.

Look for shapely specimens, nicely covered with foliage down to soil or compost level and without patches of brown on the outer surface. It is quite natural to find some inner browning in dense foliage types like *Chamaecyparis pisifera* 'Boulevard'.

Lighter, brighter coloured tips to the foliage are a good sign of strong, vigorous new growth.

After-planting Care
Once established conifers require little further attention. Specimens in grass and lawns need a circular bed, 2–3 ft (60–90 cm) out from the stem, of cultivated soil. Grass will compete for water in dry weather and where the grass is allowed to grow the lower branches of the conifer will go brown with the lack of light.

Conifers growing into one another and into other plants will also go brown at the point where they merge and careful thinning of plants or trimming back is needed to avoid this.

While fertilizer is not essential the application of a *little* general fertilizer in spring will give stronger new growth and richer colours.

USING CONIFERS FOR EFFECT
Stately Cedars in rolling acres of lawn give a relaxing atmosphere and the soaring tips of giant Californian Redwoods, *Sequoia sempervirens*, 300 ft (100 m) up in the air can be quite breathtaking.

While not everyone has room for these stately trees, there are different types with size and shape to suit every garden situation. Even the Californian Redwood could be planted in the local school playing field to provide generations of children with fun punching the spongy-reddish brown bark. Who knows, your planting may outlive the

Heathers associate well with dwarf conifers, as this picture of *Juniperus scopulorum* 'Sky Rocket' shows. Most dwarfs are equally suitable.

Picea glauca 'Albertiana Conica' makes an attractively shaped tree.

2200 years of the oldest recorded specimen.

If you want the romance of this great tree in your own small garden, then *Sequoia sempervirens* 'Adpressa' is the answer. Very slow growing, it has rich creamy white branch tips in summer. Once it gets its roots down and starts to produce strong lead branches, it must be pruned back to retain the dwarf habit and prevent it attempting to emulate its much more vigorous near relative.

Specimen Conifers
Gardens 30–40 ft (10–12 m) wide and 60 ft (20 m) or so long provide scope for one or several' specimen conifers, especially when set in lawns and among low-growing plants. The different coloured Lawson cultivars, the Juniper 'Blue Heaven' and Serbian Spruce are

A border of mixed conifers can provide year-round colour and interest.

Dwarf conifers can add much interest to a small garden.

good examples for this kind of use.

Take the space down even further and the very neat column-like growth of Juniper 'Skyrocket' or fastigiate Yews then come into their own. They can even be planted in a double line to give a colonnade leading to a formal rose garden. Semi-prostrate plants like the golden Pfitzer Juniper can also be used as specimens, either jutting out from walls and fences like buttresses or spreading out from paved areas.

Mixed Conifer Borders

Planting a collection of evergreen conifers in one bed or border is by far the most satisfactory way to use these plants. Each one can be positioned to contrast with and to show off its neighbour. More upright kinds at the back can be graded in height to the prostrate types in the foreground.

Once again space limitations are no problem, provided you select stronger growing kinds for large areas and the dwarf and slow growing types for small beds. These can be rearranged to fit in your favourites or similar types more freely available and suited to your area. Ensure that the different colours contrast to get the brightest year-round effect, and that the different foliage shapes contrast with one another.

Rock Garden Conifers

Very slow growing conifers can be positioned among rocks to give a miniature mountainside appearance. Lack of space really is no problem with the smallest species growing satisfactorily in sink and trough gardens.

Conifers can be grown alone and mixed with other alpine plants, according to taste. *Juniperus communis* 'Compressa' is a favourite, with an upright cigar shape, and the neat rounded shape of green *Chamaecyparis pisifera* 'Nana' and steel-blue *Picea mariana* 'Nana' are other popular choices.

Some of the stronger prostrate kinds like *Juniperus procumbens* 'Nana' look attractive over rocks but will need cutting back to retain their spread.

Specimens for Tubs

Two shapely evergreens each side of a door or path are popular with gardeners, and conifers can fit the bill. Attention first and foremost must be

Chamaecyparis lawsoniana 'Blue Nantais' is a lovely steel blue colour year round and especially early autumn. Seen here in association with potentilla and heathers.

given to compost and watering. A good, rich loam-based compost is ideal and a deep pot or tub is essential. I like to see the tub as deep as one-third, and certainly one-quarter, the height of tall upright conifers.

Once potted the tub conifer will require regular watering, especially in hot weather. The most popular plant for tubs is *Chamaecyparis lawsoniana* 'Ellwoodii' and a 3–4 ft (1–1·2 m) specimen will take up to 2 gallons (10 litres) of water a day in very hot weather. Other Lawson cultivars, *Chamaecyparis pisifera* types (especially 'Boulevard'), and *Thuja orientalis* 'Aurea Nana' are attractive in tubs.

Where the tub has good drainage holes in the base, over-watering is unlikely but giving sufficient water to tubs filled with root in very hot weather is not easy. Remember, dense evergreen foliage sheds water and even in showery weather it will be necessary to water the tub. Drying winds in autumn, winter and spring can be especially deceptive and if the conifer is allowed to become really dry and the foliage starts to brown it is very difficult to get the attractive new growth desired.

Half lifting the tub off the ground is the quick way to check moisture of compost. When wet the tub will be heavy, and as it dries it gets noticeably lighter. Once the tub feels light, water till moisture runs from the base, check then to see just how heavy the tub has become. Water again when the tub has lost weight.

Thuja orientalis 'Aurea Nana' is an attractive dwarf of neat shape.

Chamaecyparis lawsoniana 'Allumii' used for screening.

SCREENS AND WINDBREAKS

While close-clipped conifers for formal hedging are described in the chapter on hedges, mention must be made here of the usefulness of conifers for forming a natural screen, especially the taller and faster-growing kinds. Shelter from wind is desirable in most gardens, and on exposed and coastal sites it is vital.

A natural-looking belt of shelter can quickly be achieved in the larger garden with × *Cupressocyparis leylan-*

dii, Chamaecyparis lawsoniana, Picea omorika and *Thuja plicata*. Mix a few Larch and Pine in to give added variety, and where there is ample space plant a clump of Birch in the foreground – the white bark will show particularly well against dark evergreens in winter.

Ground and Manhole Covers

Prostrate Junipers offer the best opportunity of all for work-free gardening. Closely planted they give complete ground cover and weed smothering. Even better, on banks they not only provide an attractive appearance but the strong root growth helps to retain soil and prevent rainwashed erosion.

The different coloured forms of Juniper are best for this. Fortunately they grow well on virtually all soil types, including shallow chalky soils, partially shaded sites and in exposed positions.

The dark green leaf types like *Juniperus communis* 'Repanda', *J. procumbens* 'Nana' and *J.* ×*media* 'Pfitzeriana' are best on really tough soils and sites. Choose different habits and plant these in groups to get the most

As an alternative to grass, consider *Juniperus squamata* 'Blue Carpet'.

One of the merits of conifers is their variety of form as well as colour. *Juniperus × media* 'Mint Julep' holds its branches at an attractive angle.

It is often sufficient to trim conifers to shape with shears.

attractive combination. Place the taller growing Pfitzers with their branches jutting out at 45 degrees from the ground towards the top or back of the bank. Grade down to lower types like *J. × media* 'Mint Julep' and *J. virginiana* 'Grey Owl' in the middle, and very low types in the foreground.

Growth quite as attractive as short grass but without the need to mow can be achieved with *J. squamata* 'Blue Carpet' and *J. horizontalis* 'Hughes'. Extra colour can be added in the foreground with such types as *J. communis* 'Depressa Aurea', bright yellow in early summer turning red-bronze in winter, and the bright silver-blue *J. squamata* 'Blue Star'.

The perfect replacement for a well clipped grass is the quite flat growing *J. horizontalis* 'Glauca', commonly and quite aptly called the 'Carpet Juniper'. It smothers the ground no more than 4 in. (10 cm) high and will spread 5 ft (1·5 m) in 8–10 years.

Where good-sized, 10–12 in (25–30 cm) diameter, pot-grown plants are used a spacing of three plants per square yard (square metre) will give ground cover in two years. Very attractive combinations can also be achieved by using the taller types as specimens surrounded either by very prostrate Junipers or alternative ground cover plants like *Euonymus fortunei* 'Variegatus'.

TRIMMING AND PRUNING

Formal hedges of cupresses, thuja and yew will need regular clipping, and July is a good time for this. The first spring flush of growth has been made and the secondary late summer growth will cover the cuts and give a well-furnished appearance in winter.

Wherever possible use secateurs to prune out the unwanted branch tips neatly. While Leylands, thuja and Yew will grow again, even when cut hard back, most other evergreen conifers are

Juniperus communis depressa 'Aurea', yellow in spring, red in winter.

best cut no further back than the young green branches. Cut hard back into the brown hardened wood of Lawson types and you will have a permanent empty hole back to the trunk.

Most young conifers can have their shape improved by a light trimming in April or May. The skill here is to shave off no more than the tips with a sharp knife, then the side branches will soon produce two or more shoots behind every cut to give a more bushy and well branched plant. If you give this treatment to flat-sided Lawson cultivars the plants will soon develop into neat cone shapes.

Do not cut the top main growth of any upright conifers, save those which develop more than one central leader, in which case it is best to reduce to one if the straight conical shape is to be maintained.

Some prostrate conifers like *Picea pungens* 'Prostrata' will suddenly produce a strong upward-growing branch. Where this happens the upward branch must be cut out completely to prevent the plant losing its horizontal growth habit. Big cuts on *Picea* are best covered with a bitumen paint to reduce resin loss, and subsequent damage.

PROPAGATION

Many of the forest and larger conifers are raised from seed. It is not difficult and seeds of types like Larch, Lawson and Pine can be sown in the open garden in March and in two years seedlings a few inches high will be ready to transplant. These seedlings are slow-growing in their early years, however, and it is usually preferable to buy young plants.

The many cultivars with special colour or shape will not come true from seed and these have to be reproduced either from cuttings or, for those which do not root readily such as Cedar, Pine and Spruce, by grafting.

Young shoots 3–4 in. (7–10 cm) long, torn from the branch with a heel – a piece of the older bark at the base of the shoot – in August or September will root in sandy soil in a cold-frame. Once again the growth is slow and it will often take a year to get a small rooted plant.

A number of Lawson types and similar kinds will root more quickly given some bottom heat in propagating frames in a greenhouse. Dipping the base of cuttings in a rooting hormone chemical will help to speed rooting.

Quite different branch and plant shape is produced by different cuttings taken from the same plant. What is known as juvenile growth on a number of conifers is quite different from the mature growth. Take strong lead shoots from the top of *Thuja occidentalis* 'Rheingold', for example and it will quickly grow into a tallish conical shape. Take cuttings from the base of a more juvenile form and the growth will be more feathered and the shape nearer a mound than pointed. Eventually these juvenile cuttings will grow out into the mature form.

The garden plant *Cryptomeria japonica* 'Elegans' is a permanent juvenile form of *C. japonica* and the soft, much more 'frothy' growth is unrecognizable against the mature adult foliage.

Completely new cultivars of conifers can be secured by rooting cuttings which have 'sported', that is suddenly changed in appearance. The white-spotted Leyland is a good example.

Congested and fasciated growth also occurs on some types, especially the 'Witches Broom' out-growth on Pines

Picea pungens 'Prostrata' is a low-growing form of Colorado Spruce.

A beautiful golden conifer that deepens in shade by autumn, *Thuja occidentalis* 'Rheingold'. It grows slowly to about 6 ft.

and Spruce. Cuttings rooted from these can give completely new cultivars.

PESTS AND OTHER PROBLEMS

Pests Aphids and adelgids (sap sucking insects related to aphis and producing tufts of white waxy wool around them) can be a problem, especially on Pine and Spruce. Spray with malathion in late spring or early summer to control the pest.

Red spider mite can also affect *Picea* and attack is most likely in hot dry weather. Regular syringing with water reduces the chance of attack.

Diseases Honey fungus can affect many conifers and *Thuja plicata* appears to be particularly susceptible to this disease. Remove and destroy infected plants and sterilize the soil with formaldehyde.

Phytophthera on chamaecyparis can be a problem and it spreads in warm,

damp conditions. The first symptoms are dull appearance, with a loss of colour on certain branches, followed by browning. Infected plants are best destroyed and the site used for plants other than conifers, rhododendrons and heathers for a few years.

Browning of evergreens There are several causes of browning, not least of which is the attention of dogs in suburban areas. Apart from fencing, the use of deterrent sprays and planting back from pavements, there is little that can be done about this.

Cold, drying winds will burn back evergreens in the winter, and newly planted *Chamaecyparis* cultivars can be especially susceptible. Protecting young plants and the planting of a surround of tougher plants are the means of avoiding this.

Sudden browning of shoots on *Juniperus sabina* 'Tamariscifolia' is caused by wilt and is best pruned out.

CONIFERS: DWARF, SLOW GROWING AND PROSTRATE KINDS

Name	Common Name	Height 10 years	Ultimate Likely Height in Gardens	Ultimate Likely Spread	Soil Preference
Abies balsamea 'Hudsonia'	Balsam Fir	8 in. (20 cm)	30 in. (75 cm)	30 in. (75 cm)	Moist, pH 6–7
Cedrus libani 'Sargentii'	—	2 ft (60 cm)	3 ft (90 cm)	10–13 ft (3–4 m)	Most
Chamaecyparis lawsoniana 'Minima Aurea'	—	10 in. (25 cm)	4 ft (1·2 m)	30 in. (75 cm)	Free draining, pH 6·5–7
C.l. 'Minima Glauca'	—	12 in. (30 cm)	3 ft (30 cm)	3 ft (30 cm)	,,
C.l. 'Pygmaea Argentea'	—	10 in. (25 cm)	3 ft (30 cm)	30 in. (75 cm)	,,
C.l. 'Tamariscifolia'	—	3 ft (90 cm)	13 ft (4 m)	13 ft (4 m)	,,
Chamaecyparis obtusa 'Nana Gracilis'	—	20 in. (50 cm)	13 ft (4 m)	6·5 ft (2 m)	,,
C.o. 'Nana Lutea'	—	10 in. (25 cm)	30 in. (75 cm)	2 ft (60 cm)	,,
C.o. 'Pygmaea'	—	8 in. (20 cm)	3 ft (30 cm)	3 ft (30 cm)	,,
Chamaecyparis pisifera 'Boulevard'	—	3 ft (90 cm)	10 ft (3 m)	6½ ft (2 m)	Moist, pH 5·5–6·5
C.p. 'Filifera Aurea'	—	30 in. (75 cm)	10 ft (3 m)	10 ft (3 m)	Moist, pH 5·5–6·5
C.p. 'Nana'	—	6 in. (15 cm)	2 ft (60 cm)	3 ft (30 cm)	Moist, pH 5·5–6·5
C.p. 'Plumosa Aurea'	—	3 ft (90 cm)	16 ft (5 m)	10 ft (3 m)	Moist (not clay), pH 5·5–6·5
Juniperus chinensis 'Pyramidalis'	—	6½ ft (2 m)	13 ft (4 m)	8 ft (2·5 m)	Most, pH 6·8
Juniperus communis 'Compressa'	—	1 ft (30 cm)	3 ft (30 cm)	8 in. (20 cm)	Most, pH 6–8
J.c. 'Hibernica'	Irish Juniper	6½ ft (2 m)	16 ft (5 m)	12 in. (30 cm)	Most, pH 6–8
J.c. 'Depressa Aurea'	—	10 in. (25 cm)	20 in. (50 cm)	10–13 ft (3–4 m)	Most, pH 6–8
J.c. 'Repanda'	—	5 in. (12·5 cm)	6 in. (15 cm)	10–13 ft (3–4 m)	Most, pH 6–8
Juniperus horizontalis 'Glauca'	Creeping Juniper	4 in. (10 cm)	5 in. (12·5 cm)	13–16 ft (4–5 m)	Most, pH 6–8
Juniperus sabina 'Tamariscifolia'	—	10 in (25 cm)	20 in. (50 cm)	10 ft (3 m)	Most, pH 6–8
Juniperus squamata 'Blue Star'	—	12 in. (30 cm)	3 ft (90 cm)	3 ft (90 cm)	Most, pH 6–8
J.s. 'Meyeri'	—	4 ft (1·2 m)	8 ft (2·5 m)	3 ft (90 cm)	Most, pH 6–8
Juniperus virginiana 'Grey Owl'	—	12 in. (30 cm)	3 ft (90 cm)	13 ft (4 m)	Most, pH 6–8
Picea glauca 'Albertiana Conica'	—	28 in. (70 cm)	6½ ft (2 m)	3 ft (90 cm)	Most, pH 5·5–7
Picea mariana 'Nana'	—	4 in. (10 cm)	12 in. (30 cm)	20 in. (50 cm)	Most, pH 5·5–7
Pinus mugo 'Gnom'	—	2 ft (60 cm)	5 ft (1·5 m)	5 ft (1·5 m)	Most, pH 6–8
Pinus strobus 'Nana'	—	20 in. (50 cm)	6½ ft (2 m)	10 ft (3 m)	Most, pH 6–7·5
Pinus sylvestris 'Watereri'	—	5 ft (1·5 m)	16 ft (5 m)	13 ft (4 m)	Most, pH 5·5–7
Thuja occidentalis 'Lutea Nana'	—	3 ft (90 cm)	10 ft (3 m)	3 ft (90 cm)	Most, pH 5·5–8
T.o. 'Rheingold'	—	3 ft (90 cm)	10 ft (3 m)	6½ ft (2 m)	Most, pH 5·5–8
T.o. 'Smaragd'	—	6½ ft (2 m)	16 ft (5 m)	5 ft (1·5 m)	Most, pH 5·5–8
Thuja orientalis 'Aurea Nana'	—	2 ft (60 cm)	6½ ft (2 m)	3 ft (90 cm)	Most, pH 5·5–8
T.o. 'Conspicua'	—	6½ ft (2 m)	13 ft (4 m)	3 ft (90 cm)	Most, pH 5·5–8
Thuja plicata 'Stoneham Gold'	—	20 in (50 cm)	6½ ft (2 m)	3 ft (90 cm)	Most, pH 5·5–8

Leaf Colour	Purpose	Special Features
Dark glossy green	Rock garden	Forms a neat rounded hummock of growth
Blue green	Rock garden	Most attractive trained down a low retaining wall
Golden yellow	Rockery, heather garden	Flat shoots packed tightly together in neat rounded growth
Rich green	Rockery, heather garden	Neat, semi-globular shape
Green, silver-white	Rockery, sink and heather garden	Very bright foliage colour
Rich green	Shrub and heather garden	Semi-prostrate, excellent foil to coloured leaf forms
Bright green	Specimen, heather garden	Neat rounded branchlets, C.o. 'Nana' is slower growing and more rounded
Golden yellow	Rockery, sink and heather garden	One of the best dwarf golden conifers
Green	Rockery and sink garden	Reddish branches contrast with green foliage
Steel blue	Tubs, rockery and heather garden	One of the most popular dwarf conifers
Golden yellow	Heather garden, mixed conifer border	Finely cut foliage similar to Japanese acers
Dark green	Sink and rock garden	Compact, with tightly packed shoots
Golden green	Tubs, heather garden and mixed border	Feathery foliage which darkens in winter
Steel blue	Heather garden, mixed border	Beautiful colour, needs space to remain well-furnished with new growth
Light grey-green	Pots, rockery and sink garden	The finest cigar-shaped dwarf conifer
Light green	Specimen, heather garden	A superb columnar shape
Bright yellow, turning bronze	Ground cover, heather garden	Brilliant colour in full sun in spring
Dull green	Ground cover	One of the best and toughest ground covers
Steel blue	Ground cover	Quite as flat as grass
Grey green	Ground and bank cover	The traditional manhole-covering juniper
Silver blue	Specimen, heather and rock garden	One of the brightest foliage junipers
Steel blue	Specimen, heather garden	Best as a young plant, trim in spring to retain attractive young shoots
Grey blue	Ground cover, heather garden	Very easy, low shrubby ground covering
Bright green	Tubs, rockery and heather garden	Perfect cone shape, very attractive spring shoots
Blue grey	Rockery and sink garden	Neat bun shape of attractive foliage
Dark green	Rock garden	A small cultivar of the mountain pine
Light blue-green	Rock garden	A very attractive cultivar of Weymouth pine
Blue green	Heather garden, specimen	New growth forms attractive brown candles
Yellow green	Heather garden, mixed border	Colour deepens with the approach of winter
Old gold	Heather garden, tubs	Dense globose ground-covering shape, reddish in winter
Bright green	Low hedge	Very neat pyramid shape
Yellow to bronze	Tubs, specimen, heather garden	Dense growth in globe shape; one of the best
Rich yellow	Tubs, specimen, heather garden	T.o. 'Elegantissima' is similar but slower growing
Green/gold	Rockery, heather garden	Bicolour is especially attractive in winter

YOUR GUIDE TO CONIFERS: TALL KINDS

Name	Common Name	Height in 10 Years	Likely Ultimate Height	Soil Preference
Abies grandis	Giant Fir	10 ft (3 m)	260–300 ft (80–100 m)	Moist, pH 6–7
Araucaria araucana	Monkey Puzzle	5 ft (1·5 m)	80 ft (25 m)	Moist, loamy
Cedrus atlantica	Atlas Cedar	10 ft (3 m)	80 ft (25 m)	Moist soils – even to
Cedrus deodara	The Deodar	13 ft (4 m)	65 ft (20 m)	heavy clay provided it is not waterlogged
Cedrus libani	Cedar of Lebanon	10 ft (3 m)	60 ft (18 m)	,,
Chamaecyparis lawsoniana	Lawson Cypress	10 ft (3 m)	100 ft (30 m)	Free draining, pH 6·5–7
C.l. 'Allumii'	—	6½ ft (2 m)	50 ft (15 m)	,,
C.l. 'Columnaris'	—	6½ ft (2 m)	30 ft (9 m)	,,
C.l. 'Ellwoodii'	—	5 ft (1·5 m)	20 ft (6 m)	,,
C.l. 'Fletcheri'	—	6½ ft (2 m)	23 ft (7 m)	,,
C.l. 'Green Pillar'	—	6½ ft (2 m)	33 ft (10 m)	,,
C.l. 'Lanei' and C.l. 'Lutea'	—	6½ ft (2 m)	33 ft (10 m)	,,
C.l. 'Pembury Blue'	—	8 ft (2·5 m)	40 ft (12 m)	,,
C.l. 'Pottenii'	—	6½ ft (2 m)	33 ft (10 m)	,,
C.l. 'Stardust' and 'Stewartii'	—	8 ft (2·5 m)	40 ft (12 m)	,,
Chamaecyparis nootkatensis	Nootka Cypress	10 ft (3 m)	100 ft (30 m)	Most soils
Cryptomeria japonica 'Elegans'	—	5 ft (1·5 m)	20 ft (6 m)	Moist
X Cupressocyparis leylandii	Leylands	33 ft (10 m)	100 ft (30 m)	Most soils, pH 5·5–8
Cupressus macrocarpa	Monterey Cypress	16 ft (5 m)	65 ft (20 m)	Most soils
m. 'Goldcrest'	—	10 ft (3 m)	33 ft (10 m)	Most soils
Gingko biloba	Maidenhair Tree	10 ft (3 m)	60 ft (18 m)	Most soils
Juniperus X media 'Pfitzeriana'	Pfitzer Juniper	Spread to 13 ft (4 m)	6½–10 ft (2–3 m)	All soils, pH 5·5–8
Juniperus scopulorum 'Blue Heaven'	—	6½ ft (2 m)	20 ft (6 m)	Most soils
J.s. 'Skyrocket'	—	6½ ft (2 m)	23 ft (7 m)	Most soils
Larix decidua	Common Larch	16 ft (5 m)	100 ft (30 m)	Not too wet or dry, pH 5·5–7
Picea omorika	Serbian Spruce	10 ft (3 m)	70 ft (22 m)	Most soils, pH 5·5–8
Pinus nigra	Austrian Pine	13 ft (4 m)	100 ft (30 m)	Most soils, pH 5·5–8
Pinus sylvestris	Scots Pine	13 ft (4 m)	80 ft (25 m)	Most soils, pH 5·5–7
Taxus baccata	Common Yew	6½ ft (2 m)	20 ft (6 m)	Moist, pH 5·5–8
T.b. 'Fastigiata'	Irish Yew	6½ ft (2 m)	16 ft (5 m)	Most, pH 5·5–8
Thuja plicata 'Zebrina'	—	13 ft (4 m)	65 ft (20 m)	Most, pH 5·5–8

Leaf Colour	Purpose	Special Features
Glossy green	Specimen, achieves great size	Leaves fragrant when crushed
Dark green	Specimen	Resists wind, unusual overlapping leaves
Grey green	Specimen	C.a. 'Glauca' is beautiful silver blue
Silver to green	Specimen	
Dark green	Specimen	Heavy snow may break branches
Green	Hedge, screens	Better not clipped hard
Bluish green	Specimen, hedge	Columnar habit
Rich blue-green	Specimen, mixed borders	Very neat columnar habit
Blue green to light green	Specimen, tub and large rock garden	'Ellwood's Gold' has yellow tips
Grey green	Specimen, tub	A larger 'Ellwood'
Rich bright green	Specimen, hedge	Similar and better than 'Erecta Viridis' and 'Green Hedger'
Golden yellow	Specimen, tub and mixed borders	'Lutea' is more upright but not quite so golden
Silver blue	Specimen, mixed border	Conical shape, weeping at tips
Light green	Specimen, mixed border	Elliptical, crowded feather growth
Golden green	Specimen, tub, mixed border	The fastest growing golden Lawsons
Dull green	Specimen	Hardy, the golden C.n. 'Lutea' and weeping C.n. 'Pendula' are very attractive
Green, red bronze in winter	Specimen, mixed border	Attractive spring and winter colour
Rich green	Hedges, screens	The best fast growing screen
Bright green	Screening	Young plants are frost sensitive, compact habit, good by the sea
Rich yellow	Specimen	
Light green	Specimen and avenues	Deciduous, golden autumn leaves
Rich green	Ground cover	A very adaptable and useful plant. J.m. 'P. Aurea' and J.m. 'P. Old Gold' are good golden forms
Silver blue	Specimen, mixed border	Outstanding colour
Grey green	Specimen, tubs	Slender columnar growth, also called J. virginiana 'Skyrocket'
Light green	Copse	Beautiful light green spring leaves and deciduous golden autumn foliage.
Dark green above, silver beneath	Specimen	More decorative alternative to Christmas tree
Dark green	Wind breaks and shelter belts	One of the easiest and best pines
Blue green	Forestry	Reddish branches attractive on established trees
Dark green	Hedges and topiary	Easy to grow even in shade, hardy
Dark green	Specimen and tubs	Very neat columnar growth, T.b. 'Fastigiata Aurea' is a golden form
Green and creamy-yellow	Specimen	A good, conical shaped, variegated conifer

Garden Flowers

Some gardeners, and especially exhibitors at flower shows, are fascinated by one group of plants, and travelling the countryside I see gardens filled with just dahlias or summer bedding plants or roses. Most of us, however, prefer a happy mixture of flowering subjects and to my mind mixing the different groups gives the best effect and helps achieve year-round colour in the garden.

Bare patches in herbaceous beds and borders can be temporarily filled with either seed-raised annuals or summer-flowering plants grown from corms and tubers. Spring-flowering bulbs associate well with seed-raised biennial flowers and help to decorate rock gardens.

Most of the groups provide flowers for cutting and space must be found in the vegetable plot if a good supply of cut material is needed for indoors without plundering the ornamental garden.

Flower growing can be very inexpensive with many kinds quite easily raised from seed. As one's knowledge of gardening and eye for quality becomes more refined then selected named varieties, vegetatively propagated, become more significant.

When starting from seed don't begrudge a little extra money for the better quality packet. It will be money well spent. Generally speaking it is good advice to go for the better quality stock whether seed, bulb or plant, always allowing for the year's latest novelty introduction. If you want the interest and excitement of growing the latest introduction then by all means pay the premium. If you are looking for the best possible value for money then let your neighbours make the first-year trial and then pick out obvious winners when prices ease back.

I see nothing wrong with buying smaller and cheaper *vigorous* young plants; they will soon grow, given the

Many different kinds of plants can be used to bring colour to the garden.

right treatment. Older cut-price stock at the end of a planting season is usually not such a good buy, especially as we go into the hotter, dryer summer weather. The secret of success in all gardening, leave alone flower growing, is to get the job done in good time. If you happen to have forgotten or overlooked one sowing or planting job then it is better to wait . . . the next

season will come round all too quickly! If you happen to be the forgetful type, buying foil-packed seeds would be a wise precaution to take. Seeds packed in this way will hold their germination for a year.

Colour and fragrance

I have no fears about mixing flower colours, very few natural colours clash in the way man-made dyes will. A very pleasing effect can be achieved however by planting a harmonious group of colours in one garden or one section of the garden.

Silvers and pinks through to purple are a classic example. Silver and pink alone looks very fresh, as does green, deep blue and white. Rich copper foliage contrasting with scarlets and yellows to gold makes a bright, eye-catching combination.

Fragrance does need remembering and a few clumps of strongly-scented plants will bring a new breath of life to the garden air. Good examples are Hyacinths and Wallflowers in spring, Sweet Peas and Lilies in summer, Nicotiana and Stocks in the autumn.

SEED-SOWING TIME	Sept Oct	Nov Jan	Feb	Mar	Apl	May	June	July	Aug
Hardy Annuals to flower in 6–8 months	●●	▲	▲▲	▲●	●●	●●	●		
Half-Hardy Annuals to flower in 3–6 months		▲	▲▲	▲▲	▲▲	▲			
Biennials to flower next year					●	●●	●	●●	●
Perennials to flower next year and in successive years		▲	▲▲	▲●	●●	●●	●●	●	
Fuchsias			▲	▲▲	▲				
Dahlias					▲	▲▲	▲		
Lily–hardy	●●								
PLANTING OUT TIME									
Half-Hardy Annuals						●	●●	●	
Biennials	●●	●						●●	●●
Perennials	●●	●		●●	●●	●●	●		
Fuchsias and Dahlias						●	●●	●	

▲▲ indoors   ●● outdoors

Metre-square patches of hardy annuals grown from a March sowing.

HARDY ANNUALS

No group of flowers can challenge the hardy annuals for speed of growth from sowing to flowering, ease of cultivation and value for money. One packet of seed will, for a few pence, more than fill a square metre of garden. There are plants of varying height, from the neat low edging provided by linaria (Toadflax or Bunny Rabbits) which comes in mixed colours, the yellow and white tipped *Limnanthes douglasii* (Poached Egg Flower) and *Nemophila insignis* (Baby Blue Eyes), to the 5–6½ ft (1·5–2 m) Larkspur and lavatera, the pink Mallow.

The smaller-growing kinds are usually very quick to flower and are popular for children's gardens. Where the period from sowing to flowering is short it is worth making two or three sowings at three-week intervals in the same soil to provide a succession of growth and flower. Kinds like Virginian Stock will grow, flower, self-seed and grow again in the one season to give double, and occasionally treble, value for money.

Several kinds provide a strong fragrance, with the low edging plant Mignonette and taller Night Scented Stock good examples. Neither have brightly coloured flowers and it is worth mixing the Stocks, which looks dull and dirty in the daytime, with a bright flower like viscaria to provide both colour and fragrance.

Many hardy annuals are excellent subjects to cut and arrange in water. Obvious examples include: Annual Poppy, *Chrysanthemum tricolor*, calendula, Cornflower, Clary, *Gypsophila elegans*, Larkspur, nigella and Sweet Pea. The more flowers you cut, the

Nasturtiums are always bright and colourful, but 'Alaska' has the added attraction of brightly variegated leaves.

more new growth and additional flowers will be produced.

All the kinds listed can be sown outside in open ground in September (protected with cloches in colder areas), to produce earlier flowering next summer. In most cases the autumn sowing will produce bigger plants and better flowers than normal spring-sown plants.

When selecting a number of hardy annuals for a flower border, as well as heights, fragrance and cutting, remember the flowering season. A number flower quite late in the summer and into early autumn and these help to maintain colour. Useful in this respect are calliopsis, *Hibiscus trionum*, Love-Lies-Bleeding (red and green kinds), and *Chrysanthemum carinatum*.

Planning a border

If you haven't grown hardy annuals before I suggest drawing drills across the plot 3 ft (1 m) apart in both directions. This gives metre or yard squares, and then parallel drills are drawn with a pointed label within each square.

The straight rows of annuals soon merge into one another as they grow. Straight rows make it easier to identify

the emerging seedlings and it is quite easy to hoe between the rows to kill weeds. Space the rows 6 in. (15 cm) apart for the dwarf growers and up to 18 in. (45 cm) for tall ones.

Some annuals will take several weeks to germinate and with these and varieties you have not grown before, which makes seedling identification difficult, mix a little radish seed in the row. The radish will germinate in a very short time and clearly indicate the rows for hoeing. The line of seedlings

The ever-popular Candytuft is very easy to grow and very free flowering.

will also be seen as they grow a week or two later. Just pull out the radish once they have done their indicating job. Often the annuals can be thinned then.

Where the seed is not sown too thickly there is no need to thin, unless you want really large individual plants with bigger single flower stems for cutting. Thin seedlings to stand a similar distance down the row as between rows, and up to half the eventual height is a good spacing.

Generally speaking rich garden soil is not required. Overfed annuals produce an excess of foliage which in extreme cases masks the flowers. Tall lank growth will tend to flop when heavy with rain and spoil the graded height effect.

Hot, sunny banks and light quick-drying soils are good for eschscholzia (Californian Poppy) and nasturtiums. They revel in the sunshine and thrive in poor soil. Once sown both will self seed and cover the soil for several years with brilliantly coloured flowers.

The nasturtium is especially valuable, the more recent cultivars like 'Red Roulette' carrying flowers well above the leaves. Their bright flowers can be used to colour and give a peppery flavour to salads. Excellent subjects for windowboxes, tubs, hanging baskets and all containers, they are better sown in April or May; earlier sowings can be damaged by cold.

Once germinated and thinned little further cultural treatment is needed. The taller-growing types, reaching over 2 ft (60 cm), may need some support. Twiggy branches, such as prunings from apple trees, should be pushed into the soil as the young plants grow. Flowers and foliage will quickly cover the sticks.

Most plants can be left to self seed if the seedlings will cause no nuisance the following year. The seed pods of some plants, such as nigella, commonly called Love-in-a-Mist, and Poppies, are very useful in dried arrangements.

A number of hardy annuals can also be dried for permanent use. One of the brightest is helichrysum, commonly and aptly called Strawflower because the flowers are brittle like straw. Cut the flowers to dry before the yellow centre shows. Other drying candidates are pink and purple bracts of Clary, rose-pink rhodanthe and rose-purple xeranthemum, which is best cut when just fully open.

All these flowers to be dried are best cut, bunched and hung in a nice drying atmosphere out of strong sunlight.

Godetia deserves to be grown more widely, as it is a colourful plant, and besides being easy to grow it is good for cutting and for filling the flower border.

Love-in-a-Mist is another easily grown annual that comes in a variety of colours.

Once dry and brittle they are ready for arrangement.

Finally a suggestion for the rock and alpine garden. Many of the perennial alpine plants are spring flowering and a sprinkling of seeds of *Brachycome iberidifolia*, the Swan River Daisy, in shades of blue, and leptosiphon, commonly called Stardust because the tiny plants are covered in star-shaped flowers, will bring an extra splash of colour in summer.

BULBS AND CORMS

Many of the spring-flowering bulbs we plant in the autumn, such as Hyacinths, Daffodils and Tulips, have all the leaves and every minute detail of the flower formed within the dry bulbs.

Once established in reasonable garden conditions many of the bulbs and corms increase in number and flower year after year, without special attention. There are many of the smaller-flowering kinds, from aconites, and cyclamen to anemones and scillas, which naturalize under trees. Narcissi are the best to naturalize in grass, while muscari will come up year after year in flower and shrub borders.

The spring-flowering bulbs are excellent partners to late spring and early summer biennials. Combinations such as polyanthus and Double Early Tulips, Wallflowers and Darwin Tulips, bellis and muscari are good examples.

Bulbs can be used more extravagantly in small gardens, and a massed bed of Hyacinths close to the house will fill rooms with their fragrance. Masses of crocus edging

Bulbs are useful for filling gaps in the rock garden. Here Hyacinths have been planted with the multi-headed *Tulipa praestans* 'Fusilier'.

paths and a stately clump of Crown Imperials will bring stabs of colour.

Most of the spring-flowering subjects up to 18 in. (45 cm) in height are good subjects for pots, tubs, window-boxes and patio plant containers. A strawberry pot filled with crocus, *Iris reticulata* and dwarf narcissi can be a real eye-catcher.

Special bulb compost in polythene bags can also be used for bulb culture where space is strictly limited. Choose dwarf kinds because the shallow peat does not provide support for the taller flowers, which are best planted deeper in soil.

While spring bulbs are in full flower it is wise to think of planting the summer flowering kinds. These include large-flowering gladioli, the fragrant near relative acidanthera, galtonia, ismene, lilies, montbretia and tigridia. The lilies are included here because bulbs are often sold in spring, but for best results most will grow away better from an autumn transplanting.

Most true bulbs are not demanding when it comes to soil. Tulips are better in lighter, free-draining soils because slugs can cause damage by eating bulbs in wet, heavy clay. Narcissi will grow better in heavier soils.

A sunny site will give excellent results with most bulbs, but for shade choose aconites, begonias, hardy cyclamen, erythroniums, scillas and Snowdrops. The protection of a south-facing wall is advisable for *Amaryllis belladonna* (not to be confused with the indoor large-flowered 'Amaryllis'), ixia, nerine, and sparaxis.

Sunny banks are ideal for planting groups of spring-flowering bulbs, which seem to appreciate the free-draining site and warm position.

Bulbs such as crocus and Hyacinths are suitable for fertilised peat-filled bags.

Where crocus and narcissi are planted in grass remember it will be necessary to leave the grass uncut until the bulb foliage yellows if the bulbs are to multiply and flower for many years.

Spring-flowering bulbs are planted from August to November. The sooner the small bulbs are planted the better. Left out of the ground they shrivel and the small food reserves are lost. Snowdrops are best moved immediately after flowering while the leaves are still green. Daffodils can be planted as late as Christmas and Tulips even into the New Year if the soil remains unfrozen. Planting as late as this means very short flower stems and not the best of flowers for two seasons.

Summer-flowering bulbs are planted from March to May, with the more tender kinds better planted in April or May, especially in heavy soils. Fertilizers are not really needed as long as the soil has been well dug and well-rotted compost or peat added over a season or two.

Where small numbers of bulbs are planted be sure to group them. It is better to buy a few more bulbs of fewer varieties, then really concentrate the planting to get the best effect. Bulbs for naturalizing are best scattered at random and planted where they drop. When planting among biennial plants, such as Wallflowers, plant these first and then set out the bulbs.

A row or two of narcissi, iris, gladioli and Tulips can be planted in the vegetable garden for cutting. Leave as many leaves as possible when cutting the flowers if the bulbs are wanted for flowering in future years.

Dead-heading
Where possible the removal of dead flower heads will prevent seedpod formation and help to build up the bulbs or corms. You can leave the heads on crocus, chionodoxas, muscari, scillas, Snowdrops and tigridia, because these plants will increase from the falling seeds. Tulip flower heads must be snapped off and removed as the petals start to fall. Left to fall naturally the falling flower parts stick to the leaves and encourage entry of a disease known as tulip fire. Take just the bells from Hyacinths, leaving the plump stalk to help nourish the bulb.

Tidy gardeners sometimes feel tempted to tie the ageing leaves of crocus and narcissi in knots. This is better *not* done, for once the leaves have cracked near soil level, as happens in the tying process, little food will pass to the bulb and the foliage might as well be cut off.

Lifting, Drying and Storing
Try to leave the bulbs and corms until the foliage has died down naturally before lifting, cleaing off old roots and storing in a cool, and for tender subjects, frost-free, place before replanting. Where bulbs like narcissi and Tulips need lifting to make way for summer bedding plants leave them as long as possible. Then lift carefully, retaining the foliage and as much root as possible. These lifted bulbs should then be covered with damp peat or fine soil in a cool spot to dry off naturally.

While most bulbs are best dried slowly and naturally, gladioli are different. Once the leaves start to yellow lift the plants and cut the stems off just $\frac{1}{2}$ in. (1 cm) above the corm. Place in a very warm spot, even over a radiator, and dry quickly. In two or three weeks the husk will be dry and the old shrivelled corm can be twisted off. Then dry again for a week or two before storing in trays and paper bags. Where gladioli are lifted, the stems left on and tied in bunches to dry, the possibility of storage rots developing is much increased.

Small bulbs and cormlets surrounding larger specimens are best discarded unless you are prepared to grow the little ones on separately to flowering size for two or three years.

Some Popular Bulbs
Allium species, the flowering onions, are easy to grow and are rapidly

Smaller Hyacinth bulbs give the right flower size for outdoors. Tall Tulips and Daffodils in growbags need a sheltered site if they don't have the support of soil.

Anemone blanda flowering with winter heathers and blue chionodoxa.

increasing in popularity. Their usually mauve-blue flower heads and subsequent seed heads are popular with flower arrangers. All soils are suitable.

Anemone blanda is a lovely early spring-flowering plant for rock gardens and shady spots. It mixes well with aconites, and Snowdrops. Plant the strange-shaped corms in early autumn.

Do not confuse this with the *Anemone coronaria*, so popular as a cut flower in the double 'St Brigid' and single 'De Caen' form. Cut-flower anemones can be planted in the autumn to flower in the winter under cloches and early spring to early summer for successional flowering outside. Corms 1 in. (2–3 cm) in diameter planted 5 in. (12·5 cm) apart in May give the most flowers. Soak the corms in water for several hours before planting.

Colchicum autumnale, commonly called the Autumn Crocus with its big crocus-like flowers, produces large, broad shiny leaves in spring. The autumn flowers will come from bulbs if placed on the windowsill without soil or water. This bulb is best planted among shrubs to give a splash of autumn colour.

Crocosmia is often found listed with herbaceous plants. It looks like a very large montbretia and has bright orange flowers in July or August. New hybrids are likely to make this plant much more popular. Once established it increases rapidly, even in heavy soil.

Crocus fall into three main groups, and all are planted in the autumn. The true autumn-flowering varieties have small autumn flowers ahead of the

Eranthis hyemalis, the Winter Aconite, is one of the earliest spring flowers. It will spread well under trees once it has become established.

spring growth of foliage. The so-called winter-flowering or species crocus also have small daintily marked flowers, but in February the large-flowered Dutch type in shades of white, blue and yellow as well as bicolors, follow in March.

Cyclamen come in a range of species to give small delicate flowers from July to March. Very popular are *C. neapolitanum*, flowering in the autumn followed by green marbled silver leaves in spring, and *C. coum*, flowering from January to March. Established plants self-seed and it is easier to establish pot-grown plants rather than dry corms. This plant will thrive in quite

Galanthus nivalis, the Snowdrop, also grows well under trees.

dry conditions such as under trees.

Eranthis hyemalis, commonly called Winter Aconite, is one of the earliest plants to flower in spring. Plant in August or September and see that the tubers are kept moist until well established.

Fritillaria are unusual plants. Two quite different types are grown. *F. meleagris*, the Snake's-head Fritillary, 12 in. (30 cm) high, is a good subject to naturalize under trees and in grass. *F. imperialis*, the Crown Imperial, grows to a stately 2–3 ft (60–90 cm) high and bears yellow or orange flower heads in April. This is the plant which supposedly hung its head after Christ passed by in the garden of Gethsemane, and each flower holds 'teardrops' in the base.

Hyacinthus are always popular, and the large-flowered Dutch hybrid Hyacinths are available in colours from white, yellow, orange, red, mauve, to light and dark blue. Choose small bulbs with a 13/14 cm circumference for outdoor use in exposed situations. The smaller flower heads from smaller bulbs stand up better to the wind. Roman Hyacinths are very early flowering and best grown indoors in pots.

Ixia, the Corn Lily, is a very attractive

cut flower. Plant in a sheltered border, preferably under cloches, in October to flower in May.

Iris come in four groups. The earliest to flower are the small species like *I. danfordiae*, yellow, and various blue shades of the sweetly scented *I. reticulata*. These are ideal for rock gardens and windowboxes. Then there are Dutch, Spanish and English iris. The Dutch flower in late May and each flower stem produces two flower buds, one opening after the other, which gives a long cut-flower life. Next to flower are the more slender Spanish iris and then finally the larger flowering English iris open in June and July.

Lilium species need planting while the bulbs are fresh and plump for the best results. Virus diseases are carried by greenfly and reduce the vigour of lilies so remove any ailing specimens. New hybrids free of virus will grow vigorously in most garden soils. Many are stem rooting, so mulch with leaf mould, or well-rotted manure or compost as they come through the soil in spring. New plants can be propagated from bulb scales and from seed. The seed is best sown outside or in frames exposed to frost. Seedlings will develop in the spring and reach flowering size in about three years.

Many lilies grow well in pots, but choose good-sized bulbs and plant one in to a 6–8 in. (15–20 cm) pot. Half fill the pot and plant the bulb in good potting compost. Plunge in peat and once shoots 1 in. (2·5 cm) high have formed remove the peat and fill the pots up with more good compost. *L.* 'Destiny', *L.* 'Enchantment', and *L. regale* are good for pots and can be planted in the garden after flowering.

Lilies can be propagated from the scales. A small bulb forms at the base.

Lilies are attractive plants in the garden as well as grown in pots. 'Destiny' is one of the many good hybrids.

Lilies associate well with azaleas and rhododendrons.

Muscari, commonly called Grape Hyacinth, is a very showy blue spring-flowering bulb. Once established it can become almost invasive. There is no better sight however than a bold patch of this bright blue. It mixes well with dwarf early-flowering Tulips and polyanthus.

Narcissi come in many different flower types forming separate groups, but I would like to make a plea for more miniature species in the rock garden. Watch for the *N. cyclamineus* hybrids like 'Peeping Tom', a clear yellow in colour.

Large trumpet Daffodils generally flower first and the smaller the cup the later the flowering. Plant breeders are changing this by introducing later-flowering big trumpets, but the general rule remains. The bigger the bulb the more flowers it will produce for all varieties. Choose the Pheasant Eye types for the best fragrance.

Where narcissi have grown for years in grass but stop flowering, lift the clumps in late summer, split them up and replant. This allows the bulbs to build up their size to flower again. Soft, rotten bulbs which contain white maggots will be infected with narcissus fly and must be destroyed. Work HCH (BHC) dust around the dying foliage to prevent further narcissus fly attack.

Scilla has two popular species, the early and small *Scilla siberica*, which has bright blue flowers carried on stems 6 in. (15 cm) high in March and April, and the giant Bluebell-like *S. campanulata* with pink, blue and white kinds. The latter is best planted under trees and among shrubs where the bulbs will multiply rapidly if left undisturbed.

Tulipa is another genus containing many groups, which helps to provide a succession of flowering. The dwarf hybrids of *T. fosteriana*, *T. greigii* and *T. kaufmanniana* come first, and are followed by Single Earlies, Double Earlies, the Triumphs (which are good to force for cut flowers), the Darwin Hybrids, Lily-flowered, Darwins, Cottage and then finally Parrot and Fringed Tulips.

Tremendous advances have been made with the dwarf hybrids and many have attractive chocolate markings on the leaves.

Flower size is also increasing, with huge flowers on such Darwin Hybrids as 'Gudoshnik', creamy peach and red, 'Apeldoorn', vivid scarlet, and 'Jewel of Spring', yellow. If you like the fringed and curled edges of the Parrot Tulips be sure to plant them where strong winds will not snap off the brittle stems.

Geraniums, fuchsias and annuals are ideal for all plant containers.

Massed summer colour is easily achieved from seed-raised summer bedding plants. Plan the scheme carefully before planting.

The flagon-shaped flowers of the Lily-flowered kinds are especially good for cutting.

SUMMER BEDDING PLANTS

Seed catalogues and seed packets are scattered with such initials as H.A. (hardy annual), H.H.A. (half-hardy annual), H.B. (hardy biennial), H.P. (hardy perennial) and H.H.P. (half-hardy perennial). If you compare several catalogues there will be contradictions because the lines between these different groups of plants are somewhat blurred.

The lovely blue brachycome can be sown outside in spring in the warmest parts of Britain, and yet it needs raising indoors as a half-hardy annual in colder areas. The continuous flowering *Begonia semperflorens* is raised and bedded out for one season as a half-hardy annual when in fact it is perennial and, protected from frost, will flower for several years. Lobelia, salvias, verbena and some Stocks can also be grown as perennials, but the half-hardy annual treatment is much more common.

Summer bedding plants is the term I prefer to use to describe all those plants which are raised from seed indoors in early spring. The seedlings are pricked off singly into seedboxes or pots and then slowly hardened to outdoor conditions before planting out in early summer to fill the garden with colour.

They are most striking grouped in formal bedding schemes and surrounded either by neatly mown lawn or cleanly swept paving. While a useful means of filling gaps in mixed borders,

their other main use is in plant containers. Tubs, troughs, window-boxes and every kind of outdoor plant pot can be filled with them.

The cost of raising the slower-growing kinds which need sowing very early in spring in quite high temperatures, 60–70°F (15–21°C), means they are often best left to commercial growers. The cost of heating propagating frames and greenhouses to these temperatures early in the year for begonias, impatiens, lobelia, salvias and verbena is more than buying the plants.

Faster-growing types like alyssum, aster, Marigold and tagetes can be sown later, in early April, and with more heat from the sun become an economic proposition.

Whether growing your own or buying plants it is worth remembering bigger plants spaced more widely will give the best show. Some nurserymen cram up to 60 seedlings in a small tray. While these might look cheaper at the outset they will not give the value for money achieved when a lesser number of larger plants are bought for the same or slightly higher price.

A sure indication of well-grown bedding plants is uniform height, and nice bushy plants with strong dark green leaves. Plants grown too quickly, in temperatures that are too high will have soft growth and a pale green, 'drawn up' appearance. Soft plants like this will not take kindly to being planted outdoors.

Should you wish to raise your own bedding plants and not have indoor heated conditions then hardier plants like alyssum, Pansies and Stocks can be raised under cold-frames from an April sowing. Another possibility is to sow in early autumn when the soil is warm and overwinter under frames. Antirrhinums, Pansies and East Lothian Stocks respond well to this treatment.

Where you have broad windowsills it is also worth overwintering *Begonia semperflorens*. Before the autumn frost, water the beds of begonias well and lift good plants with a fair ball of soil – about the size of a fist. Pot these plants up in 5 in. (13 cm) half-pots (the sort year-round pot chrysanthemums are grown in). Either a good loam-based potting compost or proprietary peat composts are suitable for this. Cut back the top growth by about half and bring the potted plants indoors. In a few weeks new growth will be flowering.

The varieties with red flowers make good Christmas flowering plants. These overwintered plants can be put out in the garden again the following May or June.

Once we have well-grown young plants, whether in boxes or singly in pots, the critical time is transplanting outside. Even where the soil is well prepared, planting too soon can mean destruction by frost, and planting too late can mean shrivelling up in the heat of the sun. Single pot-grown subjects will have a bigger root-ball and are therefore better able to withstand late planting.

Generally I prefer to plant on the early side, with frost less of a problem in sheltered city and suburban gardens and in coastal areas. If your garden is in a hollow where cold frosty air gathers,

The perennial Gloriosa Daisy is usually treated as a half-hardy annual.

Hybrid African Marigolds have huge yellow and orange flower heads. Also in the picture are alyssum, ageratum, asters and French Marigolds.

and in cold areas, it is wiser to delay and to use more pot-grown plants.

Water all plants well before planting out. I like to add liquid fertilizer before transplanting to give the bedding a flying start. All plants will flower better with the dead flower heads removed. This is important for dahlias, Livingstone Daisies, Marigolds, nicotiana, petunias, salvias, Stocks and zinnias, but not really practical with alyssum, ageratum and lobelia. The F_1 hybrid *Begonia semperflorens* never sets seed and is perfect for sun and shade.

Sunny spots are ideal for petunias and all the Marigolds, whereas antirrhinums, Pansies and Stocks will withstand the rain. Watch for slugs in wet weather, especially just after planting out. Greenfly can be a problem with nicotiana and petunias in dry weather, but one spray will soon clear this pest.

Hoeing through the beds early in the season will be necessary to control weeds but once the bedding plants cover the ground they need little attention. Where spring bulbs and

BEDDING PLANT CHART				
Plant	Height	Space	When to plant outside	Flower from
Ageratum	low	6–8 in.†	from late May	June
Alyssum	low	6–8 in.	from mid April	May
*Antirrhinum	low–tall	10–14 in.	from late March	June
*Aster	med.	8–10 in.	from early May	Aug.
Begonia semperflorens	low	6–10 in.	from late May	June
*Carnations (F)	med.	10–14 in.	from early April	Aug.
*Dahlia	med.–tall	12–15 in.	from late May	Aug.
Lobelia	low	6–8 in.	from early May	June
*Marigold African	med.–tall	8–12 in.	from late May	July
Marigold French	low–med.	6–12 in.	from late May	July
Mesembryanthemum	low	8–10 in.	from early May	June
Nemesia	low–med.	8–12 in.	from early May	July
Nicotiana (F)	med–tall	12–15 in.	from early April	July
Pansy	low	8–12 in.	from late Feb. to Oct.	April
Petunia	med.	10–12 in.	from early May	July
Phlox drummondii	low–med.	8–10 in.	from late April	July
Salvia	med.	10–12 in.	from late May	July
*Stock Ten Week (F)	med.	10–12 in.	from early April	June
Tagetes	low–med.	6–12 in.	from late May	July
*Zinnia	low–tall	10–12 in.	from late May	July

* Provide flowers to cut (F) fragrant.
Space – larger plants spread wider when transplanting.
When to plant – hardiness guide for average British conditions.
†8 in. = 20·3 cm

Sempervivums and sedums grow well in sink gardens.

bedding such as polyanthus are slow to finish flowering, summer bedding can be planted in between. The French Marigolds do a good cover-up job in this case. Spring-flowering Daffodils covered with summer-flowering seed-raised penstemons is also effective.

ALPINE AND ROCK PLANTS

Where lack of space curtails your gardening activities the small-growing alpine and rock plants really come into their own. Large gardens, too, can accommodate them in more grandiose schemes with carefully designed rock faces that give a mountainside feel. Big rock gardens can take a lot of maintaining, however, so be careful not to construct more than is easily weeded.

A modest raised rock garden up to 15 ft (5 m) across is one possibility and small raised gardens within dry stone walling another. The narrow cracks between paving slabs and stone sink gardens, either on the flat or raised 2 ft (60 cm) or so from the ground are other possibilities.

Where the situation is somewhat shaded then gardens built with peat blocks and inverted heather turves as retaining wall are recommended. If you have none of these options then glazed sinks can be adapted and terracotta strawberry pots brought into use.

Excepting the peat beds, all alpine planting needs to be on free-draining soil. Add plenty of coarse gritty material to heavy soil. Ideally make up a mix of two parts good soil, one part

Tumbling masses of *Alyssum saxatile*, which is easily raised from seed, dwarf phlox and aubrietia cover terrace walling most effectively.

peat and one part coarse grit – rather like a good seed compost – for rock plants.

You will need a good heap of soil even for the 15 ft (5 m) rock garden and it is best to prepare this in advance of construction. See that the rocks are placed in position first, working the soil mixture into the crevices as the rock garden is being constructed.

Even when planting sink gardens, after putting some coarse material at the base for drainage, position rocks first and then infill. Remember to place the sink in its final position before filling – the empty sink can be heavy enough without rocks and soil!

Quite small rocks are heavy and when building even a small feature in a suburban garden several tons of

Even where space is limited, there is room for a few alpines. Sink gardens offer one very attractive solution to this problem.

natural stone are needed. For most of us a small raised bed supported by a dry stone wall is the easiest to handle and, set at the right height, the edge makes a convenient place to sit.

It is important to have soil back up to the wall for satisfactory growth. Just removing the odd brick in a wall and attempting to fill with with compost is not satisfactory. Many alpines have fine searching roots which penetrate some depth in hot, sunny weather.

Seedlings often develop in the tiny crevices between paving. Take advantage of this natural occurrence and brush alyssum, thyme and similar seeds into crevices where you want plants to grow.

Natural stone sinks have become very expensive and are not easy for gardeners to obtain. One possible alternative is to put a rough veneer over a discarded glazed sink. Scratch over the surface first if possible, then apply one of the weatherproof, all-purpose glues. Once the glue is tacky cover with a $\frac{1}{2}-\frac{3}{4}$ in. (1·5 cm) layer of cement mix. This needs to be one part cement, one part sand, and one part fine peat mixed with water to a doughy consistency.

Where the sink is very shallow and in other planting sites with very little soil, include different kinds of sedum and sempervivum, commonly called House Leeks. The Americans call sempervivum Hen and Chicken because the one larger plant is surrounded by young offspring. They have a special place in the rock garden because of their neat rosette shape, the many different coloured forms and large flower heads. A strawberry pot planted up with a collection of these plants can look most attractive.

The rich blue lithospermum flowers for weeks in the rock garden.

The Drumstick Primula, *P. denticulata*, is easily raised from seed or root cuttings. It needs a bold rock to provide sensible proportions.

Select and plant your rock feature over a whole season to get the longest flowering period. Spring is the time when many different types flower but there are the summer-flowering pinks, the continuously-flowering blue lithospermum and autumn-flowering *Gentiana sino-ornato*, to mention a few.

Where the chosen rock and/or soils are alkaline, then aubretia, arabis, *Alyssum saxatile*, dianthus and saxifraga are safe bets. On acid soils then gentiana, lithospermum and even the prostrate heathers like the late winter-flowering *Erica carnea* 'Springwood White' come into their own.

Peat beds supported by peat walls are best for plants requiring acid soil conditions, but remember to soak the peat blocks in water before building and keep the blocks damp to prevent cracking and crumbling. Should peat blocks be unobtainable, natural timber branches can be used effectively to retain soil.

Many gardens have banks and terrace walls to divide split-level gardens. All too often these are peppered with reject concrete and sundry stone. Where such material has

been used then good plant growth can cover a multitude of unsightly objects.

Aubretia, alyssum, helianthemum (Rock Rose) and arabis will do a good cover-up job in spring and early summer. Remember to trim these subjects back after flowering to keep the growth neat and vigorous. Aubretia cut really hard back after flowering produces a beautiful mound of new growth which will be smothered in flower the following spring.

Good value for money plants are aethionema, which flowers for weeks, and the tough ajuga with several different coloured leaf forms. Choose campanulas for good blue colouring and an easy nature almost regardless of soil type. Then there are the masses of white flowers on iberis, interesting Edelweiss (leontopodium), the bright mimulus, and lovely pink rock phlox with carpets of flower. There are so many delights in this group of plants.

Don't be put off by lack of space, a collection of 40 or more can be grown in less than a square metre surface area. Even between paving slabs it is possible to build a collection with *Thymus* species, which are good in this

Early summer cottage gardens just would not be the same without the flower and fragrance of Brompton Stocks, which are most useful biennials.

situation because their crushed leaves are nicely fragrant. Try to keep the planting from areas which are very heavily trodden, however, as there is a limit to the punishment plants will take. The very flat platinum-coloured growth of *Raoulia australis* is also attractive in paving.

There are dwarf shrubs like fuchsias and potentillas, deciduous and evergreen dwarf trees to give height and scale to the garden. Where these woody subjects are used a reasonable depth of compost and sufficient summer moisture for attractive growth is needed.

Do not overlook conifers, for there are many suitable true dwarfs that will add much in the form of shape and texture to a rock site. The chapter on conifers will provide ideas.

BIENNIALS

Much of the early summer flower colour comes from seed-raised biennials. All too often we are so busy in late spring and early summer that these plants, which are sown one year to flower and die the next, are forgotten.

It might be rather a long time to wait from sowing to flowering in comparison with annuals, but if you need

convincing that these plants are worth growing just think of Double Daisies, Honesty, Forget-me-nots, Stock, Sweet William and Wallflowers. Even in those bitterly cold areas where leafy plants will not overwinter unprotected, biennials are worth growing in pots under glass.

The most common use of this group of plants is as spring bedding in association with spring-flowering bulbs. Wallflowers and Forget-me-nots with Tulips, Polyanthus and Pansies with muscari are some of the popular combinations.

Several are worth growing to fill gaps in the herbaceous and mixed flower borders. Good examples for this are Iceland Poppy, Honesty and verbascum. It is also worth growing a few Canterbury Bells, Iceland Poppies, Stocks and Sweet William separately for cutting.

Sowing

All the biennials mentioned can be sown outside in the open ground during May or June. Sowing at this time needs a little care because hot sun can shrivel up tiny seedlings. Find a partially shaded site and see that the

soil is thoroughly moistened before allowing the surface to dry and starting to sow. It may well be necessary to give several really good waterings in hot weather to get the seedlings established.

Very fine seed like Iceland Poppy and Polyanthus are safer sown in pots of seed compost but see that the pots are kept cool and moist. Stock and Wallflower seedlings are likely to be attacked by flea beetle, which eats neat round holes in the young leaves. Dust the seedlings when damp with HCH (BHC) to prevent damage.

Nicely established seedlings can be spaced out either in seedboxes like bedding plants, or outside in nursery rows possibly on the vegetable plot. They are easier to look after in nursery rows and need final transplanting to the flowering position in early autumn.

Leafy plants like stocks and wallflowers will need a little protection from cold drying winds in exposed gardens. A few bushy twigs or low netting will give protection.

In early spring go round and refirm plants which have been rocked about by wind and lifted by frost. Then hoe a little general fertilizer in around them.

After flowering the plants are usually pulled up and rotted down on the compost heap. If the dead flowers are cut off stocks, especially East Lothian Stocks, they will often produce a second flush of flower. The same can be said for Foxgloves and if the heads are cut off before the seed falls millions of self-sown seedlings will be avoided. If you keep pinching off the dead flower heads from Pansies they will flower all summer.

It could be argued that Pansies,

Polyanthus and Primroses produce large fragrant flowers in a good colour range.

Pyramids of pink, blue and white flowers are produced by Canterbury Bells in May.

Lunaria or Honesty has simple pale purple or white flowers but when the seed pods split they leave silver heads popular in dried flower arrangements. Watch out for the strain with attractive cream and green variegated leaves. A good plant to grow under trees and in shade.

Myosotis, the Forget-me-not, is so free seeding you are hardly likely to overlook it. All soils and sites are suitable and the dwarf forms make good pot plants.

Pansies and violas are really perennials, but are also treated as annuals from an early spring sowing. By far the best results, however, are obtained from sowing outside in a shady spot in late July. Set the plants outside in their flowering position in early autumn and the size and quality of flower the next year will be unsurpassed.

Papaver nudicaule, the Iceland Poppy, is one of the most productive cut flowers. Cutting just as the bud splits to show the petal colour and burning the cut ends, either in boiling water or a flame, to prevent milky white sap flow, is the key to longer life once cut. It is easier to sow the seed and raise in boxes to plant out in the flowering site in the autumn. In very cold areas overwinter in the boxes in frames and plant out in early spring.

Polyanthus are also perennial but the best flowers are obtained by sowing

Bellis perennis or Double Daisies make excellent spring edging plants.

very early in spring. Prick out into nursery beds in early summer and remove any premature flowers. Large plants will be made by September when they can be placed in the flower beds to give huge blooms and trusses the following spring.

Protect the developing flower buds from birds.

Stocks are often treated as annuals, but the Brompton kind are best treated as biennials. While some kinds of Stock can have the double-flowered plants selected by their pale green seedling leaf colour, the Bromptons are not easily selected in this way. They have a good colour range and fragrance.

Wallflowers are justly popular. The tip here is to get dwarf bushy plants.

violas and Polyanthus should be grouped under the perennial heading but they do best if treated as biennials.

Some Good Biennials
Bellis perennis, commonly called the Double Daisy, has a massed small-flowered type and a large-flowered one. For the best plants sow under glass in March or April. One of the earlier spring flowers, it shows colour from March onwards. It is a good edging plant.

Calycanthema, the Canterbury Bell, is available in lovely shades of blue, pink and white. There is a double and a cup-and-saucer form; the latter has a flower shape just like a cup and saucer. Space the taller growing kinds at least 12 in. (30 cm) apart.

Cheiranthus allionii or Siberian Wallflower has bright orange, fragrant flowers on rounded plants with prostrate foliage. It can be sown August or September, and the smaller plants can be transplanted more easily.

Dianthus barbatus, the common Sweet William is a very prolific plant, perfect to grow for cut flowers. There are self colours and the bicoloured 'Auricula-eyed' varieties. When grown for cutting just sow thinly where you want the plants to flower. Space rows at least 12 in. (30 cm) apart.

Digitalis, the Foxglove, can hardly be called common with modern strains of D. 'Excelsior Hybrids' having huge spikes, and the stems are encircled with flowers, unlike the single row up the stems of the wild plant. Lovely colours from white and cream to deep pink and purple.

Tulips and Wallflowers give colour and fragrance to early summer flower borders. The purple shrub is Berberis thunbergii 'Atropurea Nana'.

Buy the low-growing bedding strains and pinch out the growing tip once seedlings are 4–5 in. (10–12 cm) high, to encourage bushiness.

HERBACEOUS PLANTS

Whether you know these plants as perennials, hardy border flowers or herbaceous plants is not important, their value for colour, for cutting and garden decoration is undisputed. Stately gardens in the past had borders 12–20 ft (4–7 m) wide and 300 ft (100 m) long, banked by hedges.

Smaller gardens demand less extravagant uses, and island beds and much smaller borders are the order today. Many modern cultivars have shorter, stronger stems and compact growth.

The term herbaceous describes perennial plants which grow, flower and seed in a season but do not die. The rootstock is hardy and perennial, producing new shoots in spring and new foliage and flowers every year.

While herbaceous borders are carefully planned and planted in new gardens, for most people it is more a continuing process. A mixed flower border is inherited, old and unwanted types are removed and new plants introduced. Both ways, soil preparation is important.

Thoroughly dig the soil before planting, removing all perennial weeds. Where perennial grass and convolvulus weed roots run through the soil it is better to plant annuals for a season or two until the soil is clean. Let these weeds get among phlox, asters and the like at your peril. Be careful that a 'friendly neighbour' doesn't give you a helping of twitch in with some hardy plant divisions!

Hosta ventricosa 'Variegata' (top), *Filipendula ulmaria* 'Aurea' and ajuga.

Try to plan your herbaceous border to provide good contrasts. Here astilbe in the foreground contrasts with the flower and foliage of a polygonum.

Mix plenty of well-rotted compost or peat into the soil when digging. Some plants, like Paeonies, will flower for years without transplanting, so once again there is only one chance to get the soil foundation right.

Position vigorous plants together to avoid the slower growing and finer specimens being smothered. Arrange taller plants carefully to the back, the centre or to one side of the bed. Try to get a sequence of flowers, from spring doronicum to autumn aster. Try also to achieve contrasts in foliage, the rounded green leaves of euphorbia against silver anaphalis and purple *Sedum maximum* 'Atropurpureum'.

Most of these plants are at their best in the second and third summer. It is for this reason that regular splitting up of old stock and propagation of new is recommended.

The process can go on almost the whole year round. Some plants, like Paeonies, are best split in early autumn, others, like Scabious in April. Root cuttings of anchusa and phlox need to be made in the winter, and *Iris germanica* and pyrethrum are best split after flowering in summer.

A whole range of varieties can be raised from seed sown indoors in spring and in the open ground in early summer. The Christmas Rose grows easily from seed sown outside in the autumn to germinate in spring.

Young plants not only grow better but they also divide up and provide more free-rooting cuttings. If you're producing low-cost plants from seed, grow a good number of seedlings, select the best forms and propagate these vegetatively.

It is worth increasing really good forms of delphinium for example. Take cuttings in early spring when the shoots are 3 in. (7·5 cm) high. See that there is a piece of the old hard root on the base of each cutting. Put $\frac{1}{2}$ in. (12 mm) of sharp sand in the base of a glass jar, add 1–2 in. (3–5 cm) of water and put the cutting in this. If placed on a north-facing windowsill roots will form in a few weeks and the cutting can be potted up in any potting compost and planted out once established.

Stately spikes of yellow verbascum and steel-blue eryngium against a background of conifers.

Bright contrast between white and yellow *Chrysanthemum maximum* and copper helenium. The 'Day Lilies' (*Hemerocallis* right) flower from June to August.

When propagating new plants by division always select vigorous young shoots from the outer edge of each clump. The best way is to tease one or two such divisions off with a fork or trowel. Plant them, then when they are well established the old parent plant

Michaelmas Daisies are colourful autumn plants that attract butterflies.

can be dug up and discarded.

A good dressing of general fertilizer hoed into the surface each spring will give much better growth and flowers. Where big single spikes are wanted on plants like delphiniums, lupins and phlox, reduce the shoots in spring.

Space plants at least 12–15 in. (30–38 cm) apart in groups with the groups of different kinds 18–24 in. (45–60 cm) apart. Five plants per square metre is a good average density, the small kinds closer, the larger more widely spaced. Work out group plantings to keep filling gaps – for example when the lupins go over and dead heads are cut off, adjacent salvia flowers can provide continuity. Really good value plants give months of flower and *Polygonum bistortum*, *Anemone japonica* and potentilla are but three candidates.

Plants growing over 18–24 in. (45–60 cm) high will need some form of support, especially in windswept gardens. There are several methods, with either single stakes or groups of three canes for each clump being the most common. Larger beds can be sup-

ported by erecting large mesh net horizontally over the plants. Drive two stout stakes, the width of the net apart, every 10 ft (3 m) along the border, shorter stake to the front, taller to the back or centre. As the plants develop so the net can be raised, securing the sides of the net to the stakes. There are proprietary circular mesh supports on three wire legs which do a similar job for single plants.

Another good system is the use of bushy branches. These are pushed in around each plant and the tops broken over and inwards to help support the stems which grow up through the twigs.

Most herbaceous plants grow well in a wide variety of soils. Where the site is open and sunny growth will be strong and the need for support less. There are a number suited to more difficult soils.

Damp shaded soils are suitable for astilbe, dicentra, epimedium, hosta (especially the variegated leaf forms) and lythrum.

Hot sunny soils are suited to hemerocallis, *Iris germanica*, nepeta and sedum.

A number will give good ground cover and once established smother out weed. Early spring flowering *Bergenia*, the taller *Geranium* 'Johnsons Blue' and silver-leaved *Stachys byzantinus*, are examples.

Flowers to cut are provided week after week by pyrethrum, *Chrysanthemum maximum* and *Scabious*. Several can be cut in flower and dried for winter arrangement; the yellow *Achillea eupatorium* and steel-blue *Echinops ritro* are popular for this use.

Where the roots are thick and

Begonia × *tuberhybrida*, especially the smaller multiflora cultivars, are useful for bedding outside. The tubers can be stored for another year.

Carnations

Perpetual-flowering Carnations are hardy and will stand some frost. They are best grown under glass, however, and with a minimum winter temperature of 45°F (7°C) will flower all the year round.

Carnations can be grown direct in the greenhouse border soil but are susceptible to soil-borne disease and it is safer to grow in flower pots filled with John Innes potting compost No. 2.

Cuttings root easily in high summer in bright light and warm temperatures. It is best to start with well-rooted cuttings in 3½-in. (9-cm) pots in spring. Pot on into 5-in. (13-cm) pots and eventually on again into 8-in. (20-cm) diameter containers.

Plants will grow and flower well for two years and then are better replaced with new cuttings. When young plants are 8–10 in. (20–25 cm) high, snap out the growing tip to encourage branching out from the base.

Good single blooms on each shoot will only come where all but the central bud are removed, what is called disbudding. Snapping the growing tip from some of the side shoots will delay flowering and space it more evenly.

Keep the greenhouse glass very clean and the house well ventilated whenever temperatures allow, to encourage good sturdy growth. Regular sprays with malathion are needed to control aphis, red spider and thrips.

succulent a little winter protection may be needed, especially on wet, heavy soils. Wrap straw around the leaves of newly planted kniphofia in the autumn to provide frost protection.

SPECIALIST FLOWERS

Some gardeners are especially attracted to certain plants and where the specialist enthusiasm is common, groups and societies are operated to further the cultivation of that genera. Each of the seven following flowers have their devotees and all are worth including in the average garden.

Begonias

The large, fully double flowered begonias grown from tubers dominate this group, though other species are grown as bedding plants and houseplants. Worthwhile plants can be raised from seed sown early in the year in heat, but the best stock is vegetatively propagated from named varieties.

Tubers sold in shops in spring are seed raised, most of them from Belgium; whilst these are good value for money, they will be slightly variable in flower form. Warmth and moisture are needed to start the tubers into growth in spring. One method is to put the tubers in a polythene bag of damp peat in an airing cupboard. Once roots and shoots are seen, pot up singly in an all-peat potting compost.

Large tubers with more than one shoot can be cut in half. Alternatively cut off stout shoots to root as cuttings but retain a piece of the old corm on the cutting.

The Gloxinias, which are botanically known as *Sinningia*, require the same treatment to start them into growth, and when sprouted before potting are less likely to be planted upside down.

Begonias grow very well in fertilized peat-filled growing bags, but if any plants are allowed to dry out the flower heads will drop. Trailing varieties are very attractive in hanging baskets. They are good subjects for shady sites.

Chrysanthemums

Hardy early-flowering chrysanthemums can be left in the soil overwinter to produce stems of spray,

Lovely fragrant carnations can be grown successfully in a cool greenhouse.

grown much the same as Michaelmas Daisies. Much better results will be obtained, however, where cuttings are taken from new basal shoots each spring. Certainly cuttings need to be taken annually for large single blooms and plants to flower under glass.

The cultural sequence starts late autumn and early winter when chrysanthemums have finished flowering and dormancy has started. Single plants are cut back and lifted from the soil or pot. Most of the soil is then shaken off and all green shoots cut off at soil level. If you leave 2–3 in. (5–7 cm) of woody stem on each root, usually called a stool, it can be handled more easily.

Place the stools in trays 3–4 in. (8–10 cm) deep, pack potting compost around the roots and water them in. Place these trays in a cold-frame overwinter and bring into warmer conditions in early spring. Once new green shoots 3 in. (8 cm) long develop take softwood cuttings. Rooted cuttings are potted on into 3½-in. (9 cm) pots. If you have no heat to root cuttings then using new shoots with roots already attached will give passable results.

Early-flowering varieties are planted outdoors in April and those kinds to be flowered under glass repotted in sequence to 5½-in. (13-cm) and ultimately 8–10-in. (20–25-cm) pots.

Once well established, young plants have the growing tip pinched out to increase the number of flowering shoots. If the tip is taken out when plants are 10–12 in. (25–30 cm) in height an average of six to eight flower stems are likely. If you want to grow really big single exhibition flowers then reduce the number of flower stems to two or three.

Potted, later-flowering varieties are taken outside once in their largest pot. Standing the pot on sand or ashes helps to reduce the amount of watering.

Each plant will need one or more canes and several ties to support the flowering stems as they develop. Where a number of flowers are required on each stem, for a cut spray perhaps, little disbudding is necessary. Some spray varieties will flower more uniformly if just the lead centre bud is removed. All but the top lead bud must be pinched out where one large flower on each stem is required.

Quite a number of the outdoor early-flowering cultivars will produce good disbudded single blooms and, if fed and watered after they are cut, will

Late-flowering spray and single bloom chrysanthemums in pots under glass. Choose early flowering varieties for outdoors.

produce a second flush of attractive spray flowers.

Mid and late flowering varieties grown in pots need to be taken under

Dahlias are equally attractive as cut flowers or as garden plants.

glass in the autumn before the chance of severe frost. Ventilate the greenhouse as much as possible after housing to reduce the chance of mildew fungus forming on the leaves and botrytis wet rots forming on the flowers.

Commercial growers root cuttings quite late into July and plant these cuttings straight into the border soil to run one or two flowers per cutting.

Dahlias
Dahlias are one of the most prolific of summer and early autumn flowers. Plant either tubers in spring or well rooted cuttings after the chance of frost in early summer.

They grow rapidly and need good reserves of moisture and plant food, so prepare the soil well before planting. Many grow quite tall and produce heavy leafy plants. Allocating one stout stake with at least 3 ft (1 m) out of the ground is necessary if late summer and early autumn damage from wind is to be avoided.

Lower growing, bedding types are

Fuchsias are good plants for tubs, either mixed with other plants or used alone. Plant pendula varieties to trail over the side of a container.

cultivation. Many of the varieties will overwinter if given a little protection. The top growth dies right back rather like herbaceous plants and new shoots come from the base in spring.

Plants in containers should be dried off somewhat in the autumn. If the compost is kept slightly moist and the plants given the shelter of a shed or cold greenhouse overwinter, they will often survive.

The best way to replace stock is to root softwood cuttings in summer and overwinter young plants. Where a temperature of 50°F (10°C) can be maintained the young plants will continue to grow. More softwood cuttings can then be taken in spring to increase the stock of each variety.

Standard forms with the head grown on a 2–3 ft (60–90 cm) trunk are best grown from cuttings taken July or August. If you can find cuttings with leaves in threes rather than pairs up the stem, they will make more freely branched and bushier plants. Keep these cuttings growing right through the winter. Pinch out all the side shoots to push the growth upright, and tie the single stem to a cane. Once the growing tip has reached the length of stem you require, pinch out the growing tip to develop a bushy head.

All young plants will need the growing tip pinching out twice to produce shapely plants. This is especially the case for pendulous varieties grown in hanging baskets.

Gladioli
While there are early and late flowering varieties, the best way to get a

Plant gladioli fairly deep to help support the heavy flower stems.

raised from seed but the better cut flower kinds, whether cactus, decorative, pompon, anemone-flowered or collerette are better propagated vegetatively.

Once frost has cut back flowers and leaves lift the whole plant and cut off the top, leaving 6 in. (15 cm) of stem. Some of the stems are so thick they need cutting with a saw. Where a good long growing season has occurred, plump tuberous roots will be found.

Shake the soil from these and stack them upside down to dry out in a greenhouse or frame. They will take a week or two to dry so keep the lifted tubers warm and free from frost.

Once dry and all the soil has been shaken from the roots, I like to store them in dry peat.

In early spring the tubers can be boxed up like chrysanthemum stools to produce cuttings, or the tubers can be replanted. Big tubers, with several stems, will often divide up before planting to increase the numbers.

Dahlia cuttings need to be taken young; once the cuttings get large and the stems hollow they are more difficult to root. If you can cut off the cutting in such a way that you leave behind two immature leaves more cuttings will come from the axils of the two leaves.

Cuttings rooted in late spring and early summer can be kept in 3½-in. (9-cm) pots all summer to produce pot tubers. The root restriction produces neat plump tubers rather like those bought in polythene prepacks in spring. Pot tubers dried off naturally in the autumn are easier to overwinter than those grown in open ground.

Fuchsias
There are few plants to equal the fuchsia for pot, tub and hanging basket

succession of blooms to cut is successional planting and the use of big and small corms of one variety. Plant corms once the soil conditions are not too wet and cold, from mid March to late April or early May.

Smaller corms (8–10 cm circumference) are usually cheaper and flower later than large corms (14 cm circumference upwards). When planting late in free-draining soil it is worth surrounding the corms with damp peat. This not only encourages rooting but also makes cleaning easier when corms are lifted in the autumn.

Corms are better planted fairly deep, 4 in. (10 cm) on heavy soil to 6 in. (15 cm) on light sandy soil. The soil gives the stem support and reduces the need to stake. Many of the smaller ruffled flower types, called Butterfly gladioli, produce two or three spikes per corm and are good for cutting.

Sweet Peas

There are different types of Sweet Peas growing naturally from 4–6 in. (10–15 cm) high to over 6 ft (2 m). All Sweet Peas will do best from a late September or early October sowing under cloches or cold-frames.

Spring sowing, both under glass and in the open, will give acceptable results, but where hot weather comes before the spring seedlings are well established, the season is shortened.

Try to cultivate the soil thoroughly, mixing well-rotted compost into the second spit in early autumn. Sweet Pea seeds can then be sown direct where the plants are to flower and covered with cloches in the winter.

Naturally-trained Sweet Peas with lovely long stems, from an autumn sowing. For exhibition blooms, the cordon system of training is usually used.

Pinch the tip from Sweet Pea seedlings to encourage strong side shoots.

It is advisable to pinch the growing tip from all seedlings once six leaves have formed. Strong side shoots will then develop.

Taller growing varieties, including the very popular Spencer types grown for exhibition, can be supported on twiggy sticks, canes and nets. The best flowers, however, will be cut from cordon trained plants.

For cordon training, seedlings are spaced 8 in. (20 cm) apart and each one tied to an 8 ft (2·4 m) cane. All the tendrils on every leaf are pinched off while young and all the side shoots, which spring from between each leaf and the main stem, are snapped out. The plants are supported by a loose tie at every second leaf. A really good flower will then be produced at every leaf and with regular watering and feeding blooms can be cut from June to September. Once the plants have grown to the top of the canes they can be untied, the stems layed along the ground and the growing tip turned up another cane 5–6 ft (1·5–2 m) down the row. If the cordon Sweet Peas are grown in a double row the first six plants can be untied and the seventh plant untied and its tip re-tied to the first cane. Then the eighth to the second cane, and so on right down and round the row until the first six plants are tied to the last six canes.

Cordon training is also suitable for Sweet Peas grown under cold glass. Here they start flowering earlier and string is a cheaper means of support.

Spray regularly to control greenfly, which spread virus disease. Sweet Peas infected with virus develop a twisted growing tip to the plant and the leaves yellow. Infected plants are better destroyed to prevent this disease spreading.

Houseplants

The sight of plants indoors brings pleasure to everyone, and most of us get satisfaction from seeing a living plant in our care thrive and increase in size and beauty. To achieve success, however, calls for a careful choice of subjects.

Many of the plants we choose to grow indoors are far from their natural habitat and climate, but if you choose with care and select the right plant for the right conditions, the risk of failure is considerably reduced.

One of the most common and most popular indoor foliage plants is the Rubber Plant, *Ficus elastica*, a native of tropical jungles. Amazingly, it will be quite happy in our homes on a light, warm windowsill in summer, although it is unlikely to grow fast in the winter if night temperatures drop close to freezing. Give it the right conditions, however, and eventually it will outgrow the space available.

Modern, light, centrally heated offices provide ideal conditions for the Rubber Plant and other similar foliage plants that in nature would have tropical conditions. And such plants bring life to what can otherwise be stark surroundings. Indoor plants can, in fact, contribute more than beauty. They trap dust and give off moisture, which can improve the dry atmosphere created by central heating. And they make excellent natural screens in open-plan offices and showrooms.

Windows overlooked by neighbours can be screened effectively with light foliage plants in pots on the sill and with climbing or trailing subjects hanging from the pelmet. There are many attractive plant-pot holders.

Where a tall free-standing plant display is needed there are various pole and cane supports which hold both 3½ in. (9 cm) and 4½ in. (11 cm) pots. It is often cheaper to use several plants in this way rather than to buy one large and expensive specimen.

The Grape Ivy, *Rhoicissus rhomboidea* is a robust houseplant, easy to grow.

Pot covers almost always enhance the appearance of a plant. A variety of antique containers can be used, from copper kettles to small, timber, half barrels, as well as the wide variety of specially made covers.

Don't be afraid to use flowering plants as attractive centrepieces. Many such plants raised from seed die after flowering and it makes sense to place them in full view rather than to extend their life for a few days but not see them to such full effect. Good flowering pot plants are often cheaper than cut flowers, and give excellent value for money in comparison.

LOOKING AFTER YOUR PLANTS

Plants have six basic requirements, whether grown indoors or out – light, air, warmth, moisture, a rooting medium, and food. Light is by far the most critical of these for houseplants.

Light

During the winter, both the length of day and the brightness of daylight are insufficient for ideal growth. That is why many foliage plants benefit from being moved close to a window during the winter.

The stronger and brighter light of summer allows many plants to grow adequately even when positioned quite well into the room. This is because the light penetrates well into the room and is reflected off light surfaces such as white ceilings and walls. Some plants are naturally able to withstand shady conditions better than others. As a general rule, the variegated forms with less chlorophyll in the leaf tend to need more light.

Although light is good, there can be too much, and on occasions sunlight on south-facing windows in high summer can cause leaf scorch. This only happens where net curtains trap the heat, where plants are given insufficient water, or where particularly susceptible, fleshy-leaved subjects like African Violets are put in these positions. Generally, lack of light is a far more serious problem.

Symptoms of insufficient light are long, thin stems with wide spaces between leaves, yellowing of older leaves, and pale green young leaves and growing tips. When the temperature is high, encouraging fast growth in poor light, these symptoms are worse.

Where plants like Geraniums are being overwintered on a windowsill and the lack of light gives thin, pale green growth, a back reflector of kitchen foil will improve things.

Almost any plant grown in a really shady position (where it is almost too dark to read), will need to be given periods in the light to recuperate. The growth of some plants in dark sites can also be improved with artificial light from bulbs and tubes. The African Violet, for example, can be grown very successfully in artificial light. It is important to remember, however, that with some plants artificial light can cause problems if it upsets the natural length of day; the production of flowers on Christmas Cactus and of the red bracts on Poinsettia will be inhibited.

Air

Plants absorb carbon dioxide from the air in daylight to convert into plant food, and release oxygen, and in this way they make a significant contribution to our environment. In the past we were concerned with fumes from town gas fires and stoves damaging houseplants, but today natural gas releases more carbon dioxide, and this helps to improve growth. In fact, it has been suggested that any improvement in growth that comes from speaking to your plants each day results from the extra carbon dioxide exhaled while talking!

Generally, however, we have no need to worry about *air*, as there is plenty in every situation. It is only cold draughts that cause concerns, or a dry atmosphere. Both are easily overcome.

Warmth

With regard to temperature, it is a matter of finding plants suited to the room – extra heat or less heat is unlikely to be provided just for the plants. Fortunately, there is a wide choice, from hardy items like Ivies and Daffodils, which withstand frost, to Mother-in-law's Tongue and cacti, which relish hot, arid conditions.

It is easier to get plants which need warmth settled in the home position in late spring or early summer. Then by reducing the water in winter they can

By using special hydroculture techniques it is possible to grow plants without soil. Watering and feeding becomes much easier with this system.

Weighing is an accurate method of determining water need (see text).

be kept just ticking over through the dark cold months. They start to grow again quickly when light and temperatures increase.

Watering

This is the one area where we exert total control. There is little we can do if the sun doesn't shine, but when it comes to watering everything is in our hands. And it is important to remember that it is not only water at the roots that is vital. Air moisture, or humidity, is also extremely important. Plants grouped together will provide humidity for one another. Syringing the foliage occasionally will also help to improve humidity around the plants and freshen them up. This is especially important in centrally heated homes. Hot air rising continuously from radiators and heaters is of great comfort to the pest red spider, but of little benefit to plants. To see for yourself watch the leaves of plants tremble continuously if placed over a radiator.

Most water is, of course, absorbed through the roots, and the best way to check water requirements for pot plants is to pick them up and feel the weight. Wet plants will be heavy, then as the water dries up the pots will become lighter. To convert this to foolproof terms, seek the advice of an experienced grower; if he says a plant is just nicely damp, pop it on scales, make a note of the weight, and water whenever weight loss is recorded. Just add water until the original weight is gained.

Most plants grow best by drying out somewhat and then being watered. This is better than keeping plants constantly wet.

Capillary watering is another foolproof method. One way to achieve this is with a saucer of fine silver sand. Wet the sand, place the pot firmly on this, water once from the top and then just keep the sand damp. The plant will then draw up the water it needs.

Pot plant wicks are a variation on this theme, with the water needed by the plant being drawn up through a wick which goes through the drainage hole in the base of the pot and up into the compost.

When watering remember less is needed when growth is slower in winter, and if you water by weight it means a weightwatcher's diet through the winter months.

Hydroculture is a special method of growing plants without soil, and with this system all the rules about watering are broken. The plants are grown in sand or heat-expanded clay granules and the pot stands in a constant depth of about 1 in. (2·5 cm) of water.

Compost

The days when gardeners made up potting composts to special recipes to suit each individual plant have long since gone.

Whether John Innes compost or one of the peat-based mixtures is used doesn't matter for most plants, though a few have a definite preference for one or the other. But don't be tempted to use ordinary garden soil. It is unlikely to have a suitable structure for pot plants and will probably contain pests, diseases and weed seeds.

Loam-based composts are less critical when it comes to watering and feeding. Errors with over or under watering and feeding are more easily

Groups of houseplants usually look better than isolated plants.

corrected. However, the surface does tend to dry into a hard white crust and needs pricking over (like hoeing outside) to keep the compost looking fresh and well aerated.

All-peat composts are especially suited to some groups of plants like ferns and begonias but can be a little light in weight. One useful tip is to use wide-based containers and see plants do not outgrow the pot.

Most plants can be grown in the proprietary all-peat potting composts, but where peat-sand mixes are used we get the extra weight. Peat and sand is an ideal mix for rooting cuttings.

It is necessary to use specially formulated *seed composts* for seed raising and rooting cuttings, and *potting composts* for growing on all plants.

Plants can be grown without any compost, but this is a special technique known as hydroculture, which was mentioned previously. In this case the sand or granules serve primarily to anchor the plant.

Feeding

It must be remembered that the compost in a small pot cannot contain sufficient food to keep a plant growing healthily for very long – it must be supplemented with a liquid fertilizer.

It is best to use one of the plant foods sold specially for houseplants, as it is much easier to mix small quantities.

It is difficult to give rule-of-thumb instructions on frequency of feeding. First read the instructions carefully on houseplant food containers. Do not exceed the dosage rates and remember that in winter when many plants' growth rate slows and nearly stops, little if any feeding is required.

Plants growing rapidly will need

more regular feeding and large plants in small pots may need a dilute liquid feed at very nearly every watering. The response to fertilizer is quite rapid when needed, and with careful observation and experience you will soon get the measure of each plant's needs. Brown tips to the leaves is a common sign of excessive feeding and lack of moisture increases the concentration of plant food to aggravate the situation.

Where flowering plants make masses of leaves to the point of covering the flowers, reduce the fertilizer. Very slow growth, and small leaves which are lighter green than normal probably indicates insufficient plant food.

MATCHING PLANT TO PLACE

If a houseplant is positioned in a situation that doesn't suit it, there is bound to be an uphill struggle to keep it healthy. Success is far more certain if you decide the kind of environment you can offer your plants and choose accordingly. The sections below have been arranged to help you select those plants that will suit the various conditions you may be able to provide.

Plants Which Need Warmth

Many of today's popular houseplants come from subtropical and tropical regions. Introducing these plants to our homes in late spring, summer or early autumn gives them a chance to become acclimatized before the onset of shorter days and colder nights.

Varieties grown for their attractive foliage such as *Begonia rex*, *Codiaeum* (Croton), *Dieffenbachia*, *Ficus*, *Maranta* and *Monstera* are good examples.

Ivies can make an interesting collection, with their different leaf forms.

Campanula isophylla is a delightful plant if kept in good light to prevent it becoming too straggly. There is also a white form, *C.i.* 'Alba'.

Flowering kinds include *Aphelandra* (which also has attractive striped leaves), *Columnea*, *Hypocyrta* and *Saintpaulia*.

Plants to Withstand the Cold
A number of hardy garden plants can be grown indoors in pots. Ivies are the perfect example, with many variegated leaf forms of *Hedera helix*, the small-leaved Common Ivy, and *Hedera canariensis* the Canary Island Ivy. If you have Ivies which have become drawn up, woody and leafless at the base they will often recover completely if planted outside.

It will be appreciated that their total hardiness means they will survive indoors when the heating goes off at night in winter. There are several other plants in this category, from aucuba with cream spotted leaves to fatsia, sometimes called aralia.

The bigeneric cross between *Fatsia* and *Hedera*, × *Fatshedera*, makes a good indoor plant. If you really want to have fun, try running a stem of × *Fatshedera* up and then bud Ivy on to the top to form an attractive indoor weeping tree.

Flowering shrubs also come into this hardy category with Japanese Azalea, camellias, cytisus, fuchsias and hydrangeas being good examples. Where these plants have been forced into early flower with heat, be sure to expose slowly to the cooler temperatures before putting them in the garden.

Although camellias are quite hardy be careful when you bring them indoors. If the air is too hot and too dry there will inevitably be premature flower bud drop. These plants are perfect to bring colour into an unheated sun lounge, porch or cold greenhouse in winter.

Easy Plants
If indoor plants have the habit of dying in your care start with the easy-to-grow types first. Ivies, chlorophytums (the Spider Plant), cissus, *Philodendron scandens*, rhoicissus and tradescantia can be recommended. All these are not only easy to grow but they are easy to propagate as well – the Spider Plant from runners, the rest from cuttings. Several will root from soft young shoots placed in a glass of water on a light windowsill.

Plants for a Dry Atmosphere
Central heating and the dry atmosphere in large office blocks and stores requires special plants. Some plants are much better equipped than others. The bromeliads, which include the pineapple, will stand the dry air but require light. Several, like *Neoregelia carolinae* retain a pool of moisture in the central brightly coloured vase of leaves. Keep this topped up to keep them happy in dry conditions.

Aechmea, the Greek Vase or Urn Plant, is another bromeliad; it is one of the longest flowering plants and has attractive silver leaves. Other plants which tolerate arid conditions are sanseveiria (Mother-in-law's Tongue), which eventually produces fragrant white flowers, and the almost indestructible aspidistra.

Plants for Wet Soil
As a general rule plants should be allowed to dry out somewhat before watering again, and it is not good practice to leave them standing in saucers of water. There are, however, a few plants which will quite happily stand in water all the time.

These exceptions are caladiums with their brightly coloured leaves and commonly called Angel's Wings, *Astilbe* and *Cyperus*, commonly called Umbrella Grass. These will come to no harm if stood in a saucer of water.

Plants for Bottle Gardens
A small sealed world within a bottle can be ideal for some plants. Even if the top

Try experimenting with containers. This fittonia is in a wine bottle.

106

is left uncorked the need to water will be much reduced. Plants, especially ferns and the small-leaved Ivy and snake-skin fittonia, will thrive even in green glass bottles, but remember darker glass means less light.

Avoid placing planted and sealed bottles in full sun in midsummer because this can cause leaf scorch. While flowering plants like saintpaulia, African Violet, can be grown in glass jars it is difficult to remove dead flowers which if left start rots in the humid atmosphere.

Choose a peat-based compost or a weak sterilized loam-based potting compost for bottles. Too rich a compost and too much fertilizer will produce excessive growth which just overfills the container.

See that the compost is just nicely moist and fill into the jar through a paper funnel. Once planted just water round the glass to clean it and dampen the plants down.

Where condensation forms on the inside of the glass remove the stopper and leave the bottle to dry for a few days before resealing. You may need to do this several times before the glass clears.

Use small rooted cuttings and watch them grow like the proverbial ship in a bottle. Goldfish bowls and large brandy glasses also help to provide the humid conditions saintpaulias appreciate. Planted in these it is easy to remove dying flowers.

Other plants suitable for all bottle gardens and terrariums include *Asplenium nidus, Begonia rex, Cryptanthus bivittatus, Ficus pumila* and scindapsus.

AN A–Z OF PLANT CARE

Achimenes A very free-flowering plant in summer, it requires treatment similar to tuberous begonias and sinningia (gloxinia). Plenty of warmth is required to start the tubers into growth, and during the growing season the compost should be kept nicely damp. The plants are better out of strong, hot sunshine, especially as water droplets on the leaves would cause brown spots.

Anthurium The scarlet bract on this plant lasts very well in water if cut. It is difficult to grow conventionally, demanding an open orchid-like potting compost, but now they are more easily grown in the hydroculture style.

Aphelandra If you let this plant become dry and wilt the shiny white and green leaves will not come up again. It is grown for the yellow flower bracts as well as the attractive leaves.

Araucaria (Norfolk Island Pine). This very elegant houseplant is quite easy to grow, being virtually hardy. It will stand some shade and eventually grows 6 ft (2 m) tall.

Azalea indica (Indian Azalea). Although this plant can be forced into flower for midwinter to early spring sales, it is not hardy. The tip for watering is to see that a 1 in. (2·5 cm) high damp mark exists up the stem from compost level. No damp mark means the plant needs watering. More than 1 in. (2·5 cm) means the compost is plenty wet enough.

To keep the plant for another year, plunge the pots outside all summer and keep watered, then bring indoors in winter to flower again.

Begonia This is a large group of plants, and the main types are described below.

Fibrous rooted kinds are raised from seed and the F_1 hybrids continue to flower the year round. Plants used outside for summer bedding can be lifted in the autumn before the frost and will continue to flower in pots right through the winter. If outdoor and indoor plants have become rather tall just prune them back to a few inches (5–10 centimetres) above the pot.

Europa and Reiger types have masses of flowers, either large singles with yellow stamens or double flowers. Scarlet 'Fireglow' is very popular and looks well under artificial light. Use a systemic fungicide to control mildew which is more of a problem where the growing conditions are too cold. Tall plants can be cut back and they will soon grow away again and continue flowering.

Beloperone (Shrimp Plant). Trim this easy-to-grow plant back by half, preferably in late spring or during the summer if the branches get leggy and short of leaves at the base.

Capsicum Easily raised from seed, the plant has colourful fruits in winter. See that plants are well fed as the fruits swell and colour to prevent leaf fall.

Chrysanthemum The year-round pot varieties are of little use once they have flowered. Plants bought in flower in spring may flower again in the autumn if planted in the garden but this is very much a gamble. When purchasing flowering plants in winter see that the flowers are fairly well open. In the bright days of summer plants purchased in bud will last longer.

Cyclamen Light cool conditions and

This magnificent specimen of the Bird's Nest Fern, *Asplenium nidus*, is growing and thriving in the author's home.

a humid atmosphere are ideal for cyclamen. The bathroom and kitchen are often good spots.

If you want to flower the corm a second year keep watered and fed until May, then place the pot on its side to dry out. In early autumn stand the pot upright and start watering. When new growth starts, a little old compost can be scraped from round the top of the pot and replaced with new. Water and feed as normal and the plant should flower indoors in late winter.

Plants grown the second and subsequent years are often easier to keep.

Euphorbia (Poinsettia). Where the cyclamen requires cool conditions and leaves yellow and wilt in too much heat, the popular scarlet, pink or white-bracted poinsettia requires warmth. If you keep the plant on a light warm windowsill, and the compost just damp, the coloured bracts will stay on the plant for months.

While it is not possible to equal the nurseryman's quality a second year, it is still worth trying to flower them again. Dry the plant in late spring by leaving the pot on its side. In early autumn cut the branches back to 2–3 in. (5–7.5 cm) above the pot. Burn the cuts with a match to stem the loss of white sap. Then water and feed as for other houseplants. If you keep your specimen out of artificial light red bracts will form again in late winter.

Ferns There are obviously many ferns to grow, but those below are among the most attractive and reliable. True ferns will stand shady sites and some withstand cold.

Asparagus plumosus, while not a true

A well-grown Spider Plant in a macramé hanger in the author's home.

fern in that it is raised from seed best sown in April, is a very popular and easy houseplant with long trailing stems once well established.

Cyrtomium falcatum, the Japanese Holly Fern, is one of the toughest ferns to grow, and will withstand draughts and smoke better than most other kinds. Water well in summer, but only sparingly in winter.

Pteris types are easy and very attractive, with divided leaves which are variegated in some species.

Asplenium nidus (Bird's Nest Fern) and *Adiantum* (Maidenhair) are better given slightly warmer conditions. Old leaves and leaves on plants subject to checks from cold temperature produce masses of brown spores on the underside in early spring. New leaves

soon grow to replace the older ones.

Fuschia Flowering plants brought home and taken indoors from the greenhouse in summer often drop flowers. This is usually caused by a shortage of water. Keep the plants well watered with dilute liquid feed and new flower buds will soon form.

Hibiscus Do not be afraid to prune this indoor flowering shrub hard back in spring. New flowering shoots will soon form.

Hydrangea Plants forced into early flower will survive subsequently in the garden in a mild climate. Do not take forced plants outside until the chance of frost has passed. Some pink varieties produce blue flowers in acid soil.

Palms There are several types suitable for indoors, from the small Parlour Palm, *Neanthe bella*, to the taller Kentias *(Howea forsteriana)*, and the eventually tree-like *Phoenix canariensis*. All will survive shaded positions but need warmth and a damp compost. Sponge the leaves and see that they get some light, especially in winter.

Pelargonium The zonal pelargonium, commonly called Geranium, is a most popular houseplant. Easy to root from cuttings in summer it is best kept a bit on the dry side. Prune long leggy plants hard back in early spring.

Pelargonium × domesticum is the Regal Pelargonium, a big showy early summer-flowering plant. Take cutting of new shoots after the main flush of flower in early summer.

To repot a plant, first knock it out of the old pot and tease out a few roots.

Use the old pot as a mould and pack fresh compost between the two pots.

Firm the root-ball, making sure there are no air pockets, then water thoroughly.

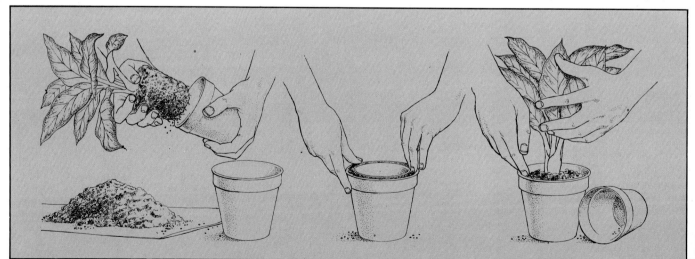

Saintpaulia (African Violet). A very popular plant which grows and flowers well under artificial light. If you have plants which produce plenty of leaves but no flowers, let the compost dry out somewhat for 3–4 weeks. Flower buds will soon form and routine feeding and watering can be continued.

Solanum (Christmas Cherry). An attractive member of the tomato family but definitely *not* edible.

Stephanotis A sweetly scented white-flowering but tender climber. Water with lime-free water – either rainwater or fridge condensate.

FLOWERS FROM BULBS

A number of our spring-flowering bulbs grow well in pots and, given a little warmth once well rooted, can be forced into early flower. The secret of success is to pot up early and keep outside and cool until well rooted. Most of the potting composts are suitable but avoid the fertilizer-rich kinds like John Innes 2 and 3.

Crocus, Hyacinths, *Iris reticulata*, Narcissi, Snowdrops and Tulips need 2–3 in. (5–7·5 cm) shoots above the pot before bringing indoors. I like to leave Crocus, iris and Snowdrops outside until the flower buds are visible. Give these three bulbs too much heat too soon and they produce all leaves and no flowers.

Amaryllis is a very popular bulb and the large flowers, often coming before the leaves, are very dramatic. Pot up the bulb in any good potting compost, then give bottom warmth of about 68 °F (20 °C), a good place being over a radiator or hot water tank. Once

Cacti and succulents are popular, trouble-free plants. They usually look best grouped together in the home.

growth starts the temperature can be lowered to 55–60 °F (13–15 °C) and the plant moved to a light windowsill.

After flowering keep watering and feed occasionally to build up the bulb. Although the bulbs can be kept growing I like to put the pot on its side in late summer to dry the plant off. Start into growth again in winter. Do not be in a hurry to repot, once every three years is usually sufficient. Root-bound plants flower well given a liquid feed in spring.

Cacti and succulents

This group of plants is said to be the most popular in Britain, perhaps because the true cacti do manage pretty well on neglect. Most will stand the cold of winter indoors as long as compost and air are dry.

Water in spring and they swell up, flower and grow at an alarming rate. Quite modest rooting, they do not need repeated repotting and grow satisfactorily in pots seemingly too small.

Succulents need treatment more akin to general houseplant care but drying off a little helps flower bud formation.

Most popular of all are the leaf cacti – *Schlumbergera gaertneri*, the Easter Cactus, and *Zygocactus truncatus*, the Christmas Cactus. Both are pro-

pagated easily from plump leaf pieces.

They make most growth during the summer when they need watering and feeding freely. A rest period either outside in summer or on a cool windowsill will soon produce the red buds which develop into flowers. Keep the plant on a light windowsill and well watered once flower buds have formed. After flowering it is no bad thing to rest the plants for 3–4 weeks by easing off the watering, before encouraging new growth once again.

PROPAGATION

The majority of indoor ornamental plants can be raised from either seed or soft tip cuttings. The methods used for this are identical to all indoor seed and softwood cutting raising, from vegetable and bedding plants to shrubby subjects. Even cacti can easily be raised from seed if sown fresh, ideally within two years of gathering.

Aerial layering

Extra-large houseplants like *Ficus elastica*, (the Rubber Plant) and *Monstera deliciosa*, (the Swiss Cheese Plant) can be propagated by an aerial layer. Here the top 9–15 in. (23–38 cm) are rooted on specimens which have outgrown the space available for them. There is the added bonus that once the

Crocus look best indoors if special crocus bowls are used for planting.

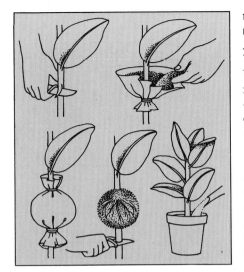

The Rubber Plant is suitable for aerial layering. The method is described below.

top has been taken out, the original plant will often shoot out below the cut to produce new branches.

Choose the warm months of the year when plants are growing well and there is good light for aerial layering. Select a clean piece of stem and make a slanting cut about 2 in. (5 cm) long up the stem and a little less than half way through. Tuck damp sphagnum moss or moss peat into and around the cut. Hold this in place with a sheet of polythene.

Cutting the base of a polythene bag open and slipping the tube over the plant is the easy way to wrap the cut. Tie the bottom of the tube around the stem of the plant, put the moss in place and then secure the polythene tube at the top, twisting and wrapping to hold the rooting medium in place.

Once roots are well formed the rooted tip can be cut right off and potted up into potting compost, but keep the leaves well syringed for several days. It is advisable to keep the potted cutting out of hot sun and covered with a polythene bag for several days until well established.

Milky sap will flow from the cut Rubber Plant stem but this will dry and seal in time.

Leaf and Stem Cuttings

The beginner to indoor gardening can start propagating by placing the young growing tips of plants like coleus, fuchsia, Grape Ivy and tradescantia in a glass with 1 in. (2·5 cm) of water. The shoots should be 2–3 in. (5–7·5 cm) long. If placed on a light, warm windowsill roots will soon form and the rooted cuttings can then be potted up singly.

If you require a greater challenge

then mature leaves with 1–2 in. (2·5–5 cm) of sound stem taken from an African Violet will root in damp peat. Warmth and covering with a polythene bag will speed rooting. It is advisable to remove the bag for half an hour or so each day to let the rather hairy leaf dry off and reduce the chance of soft rots causing damage.

Even more skill is needed to root the 1-in. (2·5-cm) square sections cut from leaves of *Begonia rex* and the 1-in. (2·5-cm) wide sections of sansevieria and streptocarpus leaves. Lay the begonia pieces like postage stamps flat on the compost and the streptocarpus end up slightly in the compost for best results. Light, warmth and humidity is all that is required to grow new plants from such small pieces of plant.

Pips, Stones and Tops to Grow

Try growing indoor plants from citrus pips, date stones, avocado pear seed, fresh peanuts and even pineapple tops. While it is possible to get the peanuts to produce a few nuts, and after several years 3-ft (1-m) wide pineapple plants will fruit, the chances of other plants cropping is remote.

Where the citrus are kept in small pots and the roots restricted, some seedlings will flower and very occasionally plants will set fruit.

All these plants need plenty of warmth to get them growing. Once roots start to form they can be moved to a light warm windowsill and treated like other houseplants.

An easy way with pineapple is to take a fresh fruit with all the leafy top intact and just snap the top out. Remove a few smaller lower leaves and place the top in a jamjar. The base of the leafy shoot

Orange and lemon trees are easily grown from pips, kept in a warm place.

must be just covered with water. If placed over a radiator or boiler for warmth, roots soon form and the top can then be potted up and grown on.

Mature plants can be encouraged to flower by placing them close to ripe fruit. The ethylene gas given off by all ripe and rotting fruits, for instance apples, speeds the formation of the pineapple fruit spike.

Roots and Tubers

Begonias and gloxinias grown from tubers, and the swollen roots of climbing lily – *Gloriosa rothschildiana* – and caladium, need plenty of warmth to start them into growth. I like to place these in damp peat in a polythene bag in a very warm place like an airing cupboard, then pot them up once shoots and roots start to form.

Division

A few plants like the aspidistra and sansevieria can be propagated by division. It is best to wait until the mother plant is well grown and the pot full of roots before cutting off a shoot with roots from the outside edge. The offsets can be potted up singly.

PRUNING

Many houseplants need no pruning, but the more rampant growers will need the tips pinched out and branches cut back to restrict their size and encourage long spindly stems to branch out.

All the young Ivies, cissus and rhoicissus, for example, are better with the growing tips pinched out to produce more bushy specimens. Where these growing tips are 2–3 in. (5–7·5 cm) long they can be used as cuttings to produce more plants.

Woody plants like hibiscus and hydrangea can be pruned hard back in spring – the hydrangea after flowering – and strong new growths will develop from the stump. Azalea, on the other hand, needs no more than a very gentle trim after flowering to retain shape.

Yellowing and browning leaves are best removed. In the case of cyclamen and similar succulent plants be sure to remove the leaf stalk cleanly. Old pieces of stalk can rot back and damage the whole plant.

Cyclamen leaves are cleanly removed by rolling the leaf stem between finger and thumb through 180° and then plucking it away from the corm.

Miniaturized trees, usually called bonsai – which translated from the Japanese means tray-grown – can be kept small by pruning the roots. Once tree seedlings are established in pots the old, gnarled appearance is obtained by root restriction.

Keeping the plant rootbound in a small container, and twisting and shaping the young branches achieves the aged look. The branches can be wired to hold the desired branch shape until the wood hardens and stays in position naturally.

Cleaning

All plants grow better and look more attractive with clean leaves. Regular syringeing with water keeps plants fresh and helps wash off dust. Occasionally, however, it is necessary to wipe all shiny leaves over with a damp cloth. A rather tedious job with small-leaved Ivies but well worth the effort.

Extra shine can be brought to glossy leaves either by sponging over with milk and water or spraying with proprietary leaf-shine oils. Give this cosmetic treatment very occasionally to prevent the leaf shine materials building up on the leaf too much.

PESTS AND DISEASES

The best way to limit pest and disease problems is a strong, healthy plant. Ailing specimens are the first to become infected.

Greenfly are everywhere and sooner or later every home is likely to attract this pest. There are many sprays that can be used to control all aphids; and the systemic kinds which are taken up in the plant sap and remain effective for several weeks are best.

Insecticides based on resmethrin are quick-acting and safe to use in the home. This chemical will also control *whitefly* if four sprays at three-day intervals are given. If whitefly are sprayed just once more eggs hatch and quickly reinfect the plant. Fuchsias, impatiens and pelargoniums are all very susceptible to whitefly. Cineraria and calceolaria attract greenfly.

Hot, dry conditions are ideal for *red spider* to increase. The symptoms are yellowish-bronzed leaves. Severe attacks have cobwebbing over the leaves and myriads of the tiny red insects. A moist atmosphere, which means syringeing regularly with water, reduces the chance of attack. Sprays with derris will help control, although badly infected plants are difficult to clean even with diazinon and systemic insecticides. Ivies, Roses and crotons are susceptible to red spider attack in hot, dry conditions.

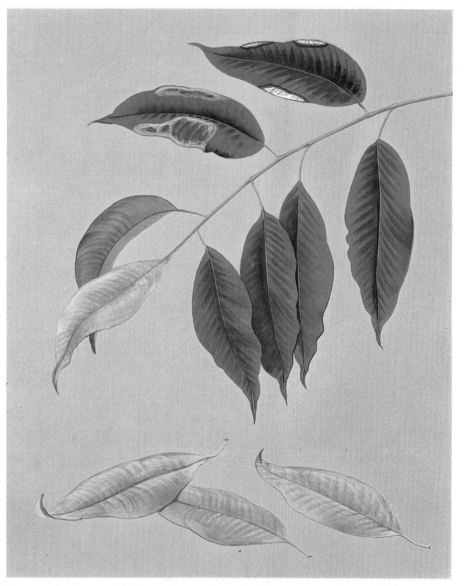

Leaves yellowing and falling prematurely can be due to too much or too little water. Brown leaf edges are often caused by too much fertilizer.

Mealy bugs, insects rather like tiny woodlice covered with waxy-white hairs, occur on cacti and a number of houseplants. These are best removed with cotton-bud sticks, or cottonwool on the end of a match dipped in either methylated spirit or dilute malathion.

Scale is a small brown or greyish brown limpet-like creature found on the undersides of leaves, usually against the mid-rib and under branches close to the main stem. It can be removed with the point of a knife and controlled by spraying with malathion and systemic insecticides.

Sciarid fly is a tiny black fly with white grubs which eat plant roots. This pest has increased with the greater use of all-peat composts. Water the compost with diluted malathion.

Be sure to read the instructions carefully on all proprietary chemicals.

Some plants are damaged by certain materials, ferns and hydrangeas being especially susceptible.

When applying dilute sprays to remove scale and mealy bug, wear rubber gloves, and with obnoxious-smelling insecticides take the plant outside to spray. Better control will often be achieved where the plant is placed inside a large polythene bag during spraying. The plant should be kept sealed in the bag for a few hours to achieve a complete kill. Keep sprayed plants out of hot sunshine for a few hours.

Two diseases – the soft brown rot caused by botrytis and the white felty growth of mildew – are the most likely to be encountered indoors. Systemic fungicides containing benomyl will give control on many plants. Begonias are especially susceptible to mildew.

YOUR GUIDE TO HOUSEPLANTS

Name			Recommended Min Temp indoors	Flowering Period	Description	Cultural Hints
Achimenes Hot Water Plant	M	❋	18°C (65°F)	June–Oct.	Upright or trailing plants with purple, blue, violet, pink or white flowers.	Keep in a light place, but shade from hot sun. Need warmth and humidity. Likes a peat compost.
Adiantum Maidenhair Fern	M	❦	10°C (50°F)		Delicate soft green fronds on wiry black stems.	A cool damp atmosphere in summer is best, in a light position.
Ananas Pineapple	M	❦	18°C (65°F)	Fruits late summer	Grown for their attractive, strap-like foliage.	A light position is required. Spray leaves with water occasionally.
Anthurium Flamingo Flower	D	❋	10°C (50°F)	Most of the year	Unusual red flowers rather like an opened-up Arum.	Grow best in an all-peat compost. Surround pot with damp peat.
Aphelandra Zebra Plant	M	❦	13°C (55°F)	July–Sept.	The green leaves are boldly striped with white. Flowers yellow.	Warmth and evenly moist, not wet, compost are important. Once leaves wilt they will stay down.
Araucaria Norfolk Island Pine	E	❦	5°C (41°F)		An easy houseplant, with pine-like branches.	Will withstand some shade, and most room conditions.
Aspidistra Cast Iron Plant	E	❦	10°C (50°F)		A tough foliage plant. There is a cream and green variety.	Will tolerate shade and a dry air, but best in light shade.
Asparagus Asparagus Fern	E	❦	7°C (45°F)		These 'ferns' have dainty foliage. Easy to grow.	Will tolerate shade. Need plenty of water; regular feeding helps.
Asplenium Birds Nest Fern	M	❦	13°C (55°F)		Rich green blade-like leaves that grow in a rosette.	Require a light position out of direct sunshine. Use a peat compost.
Azalea Indian Azalea	M	❋	13°C (55°F)	Nov.–April (forced)	Popular gift plants. Very floriferous.	Keep in a light position and always well watered. Use lime-free water.
Begonia Rhizomatous	M	❦	15°C (60°F)		Most popular are the B. rex and Iron Cross foliage begonias.	A light position out of direct sunshine is required.
Tuberous	M	❋	15°C (60°F)	Summer	Large camellia-like flowers. There are trailing kinds with smaller flowers.	A temperature of 21 °C (70 °F) is required to start the tubers. Remove single female flowers.
Fibrous	E	❋	18°C (65°F)	May–Jan.	Often used for bedding, but are also excellent pot plants.	An occasional liquid feed keeps them growing vigorously.
Beloperone Shrimp Plant	E	❋	7°C (45°F)	March–Nov.	Pinky-orange shrimp-shaped flowers over a long period.	Thrives on a sunny windowsill. Cut back straggly plants in spring.
Calceolaria Slipper Flower	E	❋	7°C (45°F)	Feb.–May	Soft velvety pouched flowers, in red, yellow or orange.	Avoid high temperatures. Give a position on a light windowsill.
Camellia	E	❋	Hardy	Jan.–April	Exotic waxy flowers, in shades of red, white and pink.	Plunge pots outdoors during the summer. Keep cool and well watered indoors.
Campanula isophylla Star of Bethlehem	M	❋	10°C (50°F)	July–Aug.	A plant of trailing habit, with masses of pretty blue or white flowers.	Pinch out growing tips in spring to produce compact plants. Root soft green shoots.
Capsicum Pepper	M	❧	10°C (50°F)		Grown for attractive winter yellow to purple fruits.	Keep well fed and moist. Discard once fruits shrivel.
Chamaedorea Parlour Palm	M	❦	13°C (55°F)		A small palm, growing to 1 m (3 ft).	Best in indirect light. Sponge leaves occasionally with water.
Chlorophytum Spider Plant	E	❦	7°C (45°F)		Long narrow leaves and plantlets produced on the ends of stems.	Grow best with good light and with plenty of water. Very easy.
Chrysanthemum	E	❋	10°C (50°F)	All year	Well-known dwarfed versions of the garden chrysanthemum.	A light position and cool temperature will keep them flowering.
Cissus Kangaroo Vine	E	❦	7°C (45°F)		A climber with glossy green leaves.	Will survive in subdued light but grows better in good light.
Codiaeum Croton	D	❦	15°C (60°F)		Foliage plants, usually with red, yellow, orange and green variegation.	Avoid fluctuating temperatures. Keep in good light. Syringe in summer.
Coleus Flame Nettle	M	❦	15°C (60°F)		Popular foliage plants, with leaves in many varied colours.	Good light is needed for well-balanced growth.
Cryptanthus Earth Star	M	❦	13°C (55°F)		A star-shaped rosette of variegated leaves.	Very easy to grow. Keep on dry side in winter.
Cyperus Umbrella Grass	M	❦	13°C (55°F)		Grass-like leaves arranged like umbrella spokes on a long stalk.	Place in good light and keep constantly moist.
Cyclamen	M	❋	10°C (50°F)	Aug.–May	Well-known flowering pot plants popular as gifts.	Needs a steady temperature and water supply and light position.
Dieffenbachia Dumb Cane	M/D	❦	13°C (55°F)		Striking foliage plants with variegated leaves, usually cream and green.	Feed monthly through summer. Keep out of direct sun in summer but place in light position in winter.
Dracaena Dragon Plant	D	❦	13°C (55°F)		Variegated strap-like leaves.	A light position is required for strong leaf colour. Feed every two weeks in summer.
Erica gracilis Heather	M	❋	5°C (41°F)	Sept.–Jan.	Pink, white or purple 'heathers'.	Best in all-peat compost. Avoid high temperatures and keep moist.
Euphorbia pulcherrima Poinsettia	M	❋	13°C (55°F)	Nov.–Feb.	Bright red bracts, though there are pink and white forms.	Keep moist but not over-wet, and keep in a light position

Name			Recommended Min Temp indoors	Flowering Period	Description	Cultural Hints
X Fatshedera	E	foliage	4°C (40°F)		Glossy hand-shaped green leaves. Perfect foliage plant for a cool situation.	Will thrive in light or more shaded conditions. Plants that have grown too tall can be cut back in March.
Ficus Rubber Plant	M/D	foliage	15°C (60°F)		Besides the popular Rubber Plant, F. elastica, there are species with foliage of different shape.	Variegated kinds need good light, but not direct summer sun. The Creeping Fig, F. pumila, which trails, will survive 7°C (45°F).
Grevillea Silk Oak	M	foliage	7°C (45°F)		Feathery light green foliage.	Keep well watered while growing actively. Provide light conditions.
Hedera Ivy	E	foliage	Hardy		Besides the common ivy, there are kinds with attractively shaped and variegated foliage.	Will grow well in shade, but variegated kinds need brighter conditions.
Hippeastrum Amaryllis	E	flowers	13°C (55°F)	Dec.–Aug.	Massive, spectacular flowers, carried on a strong stem.	A bottom heat of 2°C (70°F) is advisable to start growth.
Hydrangea	E	flowers	13°C (55°F)	May–Aug.	Popular plants that can be forced into flower by bringing plants into the temperature given from January onwards.	Blue varieties need lime-free compost. Plant outdoors after flowering, or place pot outside until time to force again. Feed regularly.
Kalanchoe	E	flowers	5°C (41°F)	Feb.–March	Heads of small bright red flowers, contrasting against glossy green foliage.	Feed occasionally. Best stood outdoors for the summer, but do not allow to dry out.
Maranta Prayer Plant	M	foliage	15°C (60°F)		Striking, variegated leaves, those of M. leuconeura folding together at night.	Keep in quite shady conditions. A moist atmosphere is required.
Monstera Swiss Cheese Plant	M/D	foliage	13°C (55°F)		Large shiny green foliage; big holes and gashes develop in older leaves.	Direct aerial roots into the compost or moss-wrapped supporting stakes, to improve growth.
Peperomia	M	foliage/flowers	13°C (55°F)		Compact houseplants with a variety of leaf shapes, forms, and textures.	Moist, warm conditions are best. Position in good light but out of direct summer sun.
Philodendron	M	foliage	13°C (55°F)		A group of foliage plants with a variety of interesting leaf shapes.	Sponge leaves occasionally. Climbing forms should have a piece of cork bark or a moss-filled cylinder to take the aerial roots.
Pilea cadierei Aluminium Plant	E	foliage	10°C (50°F)		Green leaves with silvery markings.	Kept moist this is one of the easiest plants to grow.
Platycerium Stag's-horn Fern	M	foliage	10°C (50°F)		A most dramatic fern, with broad forked leaves shaped like a stag's horn.	Grows well in a peat-based compost. Syringe or sponge occasionally. Keep atmosphere moist.
Primula	E	flowers	7°C (45°F)	Jan.–May	Pretty spring-flowering plants, the popular species being P. obconica and P. malacoides.	Keep damp at all times. Is best in cool conditions.
Saintpaulia African Violet	M/D	flowers	13°C (55°F)	Almost year round	Profusion of flowers carried over neat, hairy leaves for a long period.	Warmth and a light position are both important. While the plants are flowering keep compost nicely moist.
Sansevieria Mother-in-law's Tongue	M/D	foliage	10°C (50°F)	Very occasionally flowers	Large, variegated tongue-like leaves.	Best in full sun. Be careful not to overwater in winter.
Saxifrga stolonifera Mother of Thousands	E	foliage	7°C (45°F)		Small variegated rounded leaves, and tiny plantlets produced on runners.	Keep well watered throughout the year. Place in good light out of direct summer sunshine. Feed occasionally.
Schlumbergera gaertneri Whitsun Cactus	M	flowers	10°C (50°F)	April–May	A 'leaf cactus' with leaf-like stems and bright red or pink flowers.	Put outside during the summer. Commence watering when the red pips are seen at the stem tips.
Senecio cruentus Cineraria	E	flowers	7°C (45°F)	Dec.–May	Daisy-like flowers in a wide range of colours. A valuable winter-flowering plant.	A light, cool position is required. Water carefully. Raise from seed annually.
Sinningia Gloxinia	M	flowers	18°C (65°F)	June–Sept.	Large trumpet-shaped flowers and thick velvety leaves.	A temperature of 21°C (70°F) is required to start the tubers. Use an all-peat compost.
Solanum Winter Cherry	E	fruit	7°C (45°F)		Bright red berries in December and January.	Spray flowers with water to help set the fruit. Once set, feed fortnightly.
Tradescantia	M	foliage	7°C (45°F)		Popular foliage plants, with striped leaves.	Pinch out all green shoots to preserve variegation. Provide a light position.
Vriesia Flaming Sword	D	foliage/flowers	13°C (55°F)	May–July	Attractive banded leaves and long-lasting red bracts.	Use an all-peat compost and water freely in summer. Need warm damp atmosphere.
Zebrina	M	foliage	13°C (55°F)		Trailing plant with silver, purple and green leaves.	Keep pinched back to avoid straggly plants. Feed fortnightly during summer months.

Key
- foliage — grown for its attractive foliage
- flowers — grown for its flowers
- fruit — grown for its colourful fruit
- E — easy to grow
- M — medium-difficult to grow
- D — demanding to grow – usually requires much warmth, especially at night

Roses

Modern roses provide one of the cheapest and easiest forms of flower gardening. Even where space is limited, there are dwarf kinds and miniatures to be grown and enjoyed. And vigorous young plants set out carefully will give from 20 to 50 years of flowering.

While to the purist roses are best seen on their own, quite satisfactory plant partnerships can be made. Planting daffodil bulbs among the stronger-growing yellow bush roses works well. Many yellow roses have fresh green leaves which go nicely with the daffodil flowers, and as they go over the rose foliage covers the dying bulb leaves. Bright red tulips contrast with the copper shoots of many red roses.

Shrub roses and climbers supported by poles can be planted among other shrubs to very good effect.

TYPES OF ROSE

Although there are thousands of different varieties of rose, they can be easily classified into five main groups: hybrid tea; floribunda; miniature; climber; and shrub roses.

The first three groups above can be budded or grafted on to a tall single stem to produce a standard, or what the Americans quite aptly call a tree rose. Where you need to bring added height to a bed or to displays of roses, then standards fill the bill.

Weeping standard roses are produced by budding rambler varieties on to tall stems.

Hybrid Tea Roses

Most popular of all are the bush hybrid tea roses, which have large shapely flowers borne either singly or in twos and threes on a long single stem. Keen rosarians growing for exhibition and flower arrangers growing blooms to cut will disbud (remove any smaller buds below the one main flower) to get perfect single flowers.

The best-known hybrid tea is 'Peace', a large yellow, edged pink, with rich dark glossy green leaves. Popular for many years, it is now being superseded by less spreading bushes like the rich yellow 'King's Ransom'. When we think of roses we usually have fragrant red varieties in mind and 'Alec's Red', 'Ernest H. Morse' and 'Fragrant Cloud' are popular in this group.

Vigour of growth, disease resistance and number of flowers are being increased with the continual introduction of new varieties, and the white 'Pascali' is a good indication of these developments. Unusual colours from near brown to the silver-lilac and fragrant 'Blue Moon' add to the variety now available.

Floribunda Roses

Where a mass of colour rather than single bloom quality is the requirement then the floribunda varieties should be chosen. Sometimes we come across the name polyantha rose within the group and this refers to small rounded flowers

There are roses which grow from 12 in. (30 cm) to several metres high. Some vigorous climbing roses such as 'Mermaid' will grow 20–30 ft (6–10 m) in height and spread. Others like 'Golden Showers' make nice 6 ft (2 m) high pillars of growth.

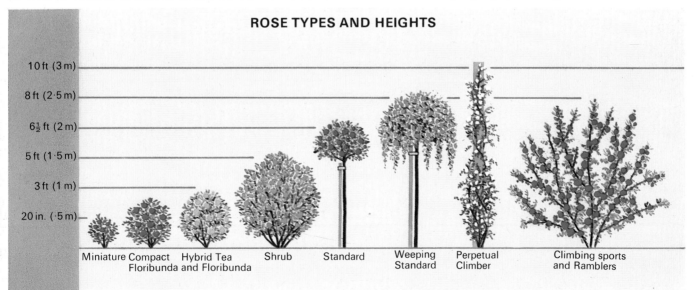

ROSE TYPES AND HEIGHTS

10 ft (3 m)
8 ft (2·5 m)
6½ ft (2 m)
5 ft (1·5 m)
3 ft (1 m)
20 in. (·5 m)

Miniature Compact Floribunda and Floribunda   Hybrid Tea   Shrub   Standard   Weeping Standard   Perpetual Climber   Climbing sports and Ramblers

Prune the occasional old branch right out at the base of climbing roses.

up to 20 in. (50 cm) are gaining in popularity both for bedding out and to use in smaller gardens. Good examples are crimson-scarlet 'Marlena', orange-scarlet 'Topsi' and pink 'Tip Top'.

Miniatures

Even smaller are the true miniature roses, growing eventually to 1 ft (30 cm) high. Purchasing these can be somewhat confusing because plants of the same variety grown from rooted cuttings are smaller and take longer to reach their ultimate size than bushes propagated by grafting or budding the variety on to a more vigorous rootstock.

Today we have varieties with very neat, shapely flowers in great profusion in a good range of colour. Popular kinds include orange 'Darling Flame', 'Gold Pin', 'Mr. Bluebird', white 'Pour Toi', and red 'Weeman'.

Climbers and Ramblers

There are three divisions within this group although once again the dividing lines are merged by continual crosses made by plant breeders.

Ramblers, as a general rule, have long arching branches which are smothered with clusters of small single and semi-double flowers in early summer. One terrific flush of colour and they are finished. Good and popular examples are salmon-pink 'Albertine', 'Crimson Showers' and creamy-white 'Alberic Barbier'. The pale pink 'New Dawn' is more perpetual flowering than other varieties.

It is the continuous flowering habit we seek, and modern climbing roses will flower from early summer to the frost. Many climbers used in the past were sports (a sudden freak growth from H.T. and floribunda varieties)

of polyantha pompons (these were the forerunners of hybrid polyanthas and then the modern floribunda hybrids).

It was the famous rose breeder

Large single hybrid tea blooms remain popular in gardens and for cutting.

Poulsen of Denmark who introduced the hybrid tea-polyantha rose cross in 1924 to bring us the modern floribundas of today. The more breeders continue their work, the more H.T.s and floribundas merge, with roses like the tall-growing rich pink 'Queen Elizabeth' being referred to as a grandiflora in America.

Good examples of varieties with shapely flower buds massed on a strong stem are the white 'Iceberg', the scented pink 'Dearest' and the vivid red 'Evelyn Fison'. Colours, flower shape and plant habit are continually changed by the introduction of new varieties and the 'painted' flowers of single-flower floribundas like 'Picasso' are a good example.

The majority of varieties in these two groups will grow 2–3 ft (60–90 cm) and more high. A recently introduced group of compact floribundas growing

Miniature roses are ideal for raised beds and windowboxes.

Modern floribundas, such as 'Orange Sensation' generate a mass of colour.

Shrub roses are at their best in June and July. They blend well into a mixed border of other shrubs and herbaceous plants.

spotted by nurserymen and reproduced by budding.

Climbing sports of vigorous varieties like 'Peace' and 'Super Star' made masses of growth and little flower. Some exceptions, usually from weaker-growing bush varieties like pale pink 'Madame Butterfly' and rich copper 'Mrs. Sam McGredy', perform well in the garden.

Generally speaking, however, the modern truly perpetual flowering climbers are best in today's gardens. Masses of beautiful flowers are produced by 'Danse du Feu', scarlet, 'Golden Showers', 'Pink Perpétue', 'Handel', a cream and pink, and apricot-orange 'Schoolgirl'.

A special note should be made of the well-proved 'Mermaid'. A large single rich yellow flower, fragrant and borne against attractive shiny green leaves. It grows very well on walls and is vigorous but rather fiercely thorned.

Shrub Roses

Once again two clear divisions can be seen – the true species roses with Latin names, and the modern shrub roses with more ordinary names. Most of these roses need room and are at their flowering best for a few weeks at midsummer.

Rosa moyesii reaches over 6½ ft (2 m) and is grown for the early blood-red flowers and large orange-red hips. *Rosa rubrifolia* has pale pink flowers and red hips but its great beauty is the blue-grey over rich copper foliage. It needs pruning back regularly to get the best leaf colour on new growth. *Rosa* 'Frau Dagmar Hastrup' is often seen along the German main roads and as a dense ground cover planting in Holland. It has large single carmine-pink flowers followed by masses of scarlet hips.

The old cottage garden feel can be brought to your shrub border with flowering shrub roses like double pink *Rosa* 'Constance Spry', creamy yellow *Rosa* 'Fruhlingsgold', and repeat-flowering white *Rosa* 'Nevada'.

Alternatives to Formal Beds

While the formal rose beds with bush and standard forms are most popular, there are many alternatives. Miniature roses are fine grown on the windowsill in pots, in windowboxes, troughs and tubs, as well as in the open garden.

The more vigorous ramblers and climbers are attractive sprawling up through old trees, over tree stumps, trellis and unsightly sheds, oil storage tanks and fences. Perpetual-flowering climbers are best up poles and over pergolas, especially when mixed with large-flowering clematis. They are ideal to train against walls and the stronger growing kinds can be widely spaced and trained horizontally on wires to form a low hede or divide.

A large well-grown standard rose can become quite a feature in small gardens where there is no space for trees.

Shrub roses will produce a good screen with the more fiercely thorned keeping out unwanted trespassers. Tall upright varieties of roses like 'Queen Elizabeth' make good informal hedges and screens.

Site and Soil

Roses grow well in very nearly every garden. On very light sandy soils, on very chalky alkaline ones and on heavy clay, the incorporation of well-rotted organic matter and peat in quantity will considerably improve growth.

Avoid planting roses where roses have been grown before, because a condition called replant disease may reduce growth considerably. Where an ailing rose in a group needs replacing introduce some fresh soil to the planting area. Any other plant will follow roses without any problem, so soil can be exchanged with another part of the garden, such as the vegetable plot, where a rose replant is unavoidable.

Where the planting site is very heavily overshadowed by trees rose growth will be drawn and thin. It is best to use non-flowering evergreens in such situations.

On most garden soils digging the area over to one full spade's depth and mixing in organic material as you go

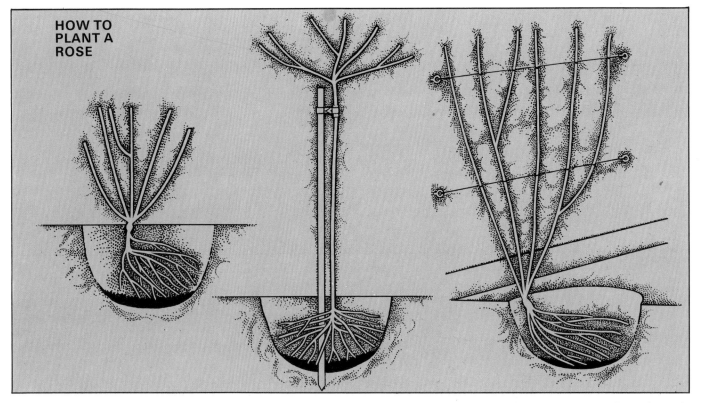

Plant with the rounded, swollen part of stem just below soil level. Secure the *top* of a standard rose to a stout stake. Some form of wire support will be needed to train climbing roses against walls or fences.

will be sufficient for 20 to 30 years' strong growth. If you want the very best roses try to dig some peat and compost into the sub-soil. Where the sub-soil is very heavy clay, be sure to leave this in position, just improve it somewhat by adding plenty of organic material.

It is advisable to cultivate two spades' depth against walls before planting climbers. See that plenty of water-retaining organic matter is worked into the lower soil to provide moisture in summer. Climbers against walls which are dry at the roots become susceptible to mildew disease.

I prefer planting in groups of one variety for the best effect. Where different varieties are mixed be sure to arrange the taller and stronger growing types either to the centre or back of the group. The spacing between plants will depend on the type and vigour of the variety.

Pot-grown and container-grown roses can be planted at any time of the year. Be especially careful when transplanting freshly potted container roses in spring. For these, it is best to cut the base off the container, place in position and then cut off the container side, filling in with soil as you go to keep root disturbance to a minimum.

Plants well rooted in the container and growing strongly are sure to grow away quickly. All containers need watering well before planting. Equally, 'bare root' roses which can be planted in frost-free soil any time from October to March inclusive need damp roots when being planted.

Where roses arrive with roots looking dry, soak the root and up the stem as far as is practical in water for an hour or two before planting. Very shrivelled rose bushes can often be plumped up again by totally burying in the soil for a week or two.

MINIMUM PLANTING DISTANCES BETWEEN PLANTS	
Miniature Roses	1 ft*
Compact Floribunda Bush Roses	1½ ft
Hybrid Tea and Floribunda Bush Roses	2–2½ ft
Hybrid Tea and Floribunda Bush Roses. Very strong growing varieties	2½ ft
Low Growing Shrub Roses	3 ft
Standard Roses	from 4½ ft
Weeping Standard Roses	from 6 ft
Strong Growing Shrub Roses	6 ft
Perpetual Climbing	8 ft
Climbing Sports and Ramblers	10 ft

Bush roses should not be planted closer than ½ their planting distance from the edge of bed or border.
*1 ft = 0 3 m

Should 'bare root' bushes be delivered before you are ready to plant and when soil conditions are too wet or too frosty, either pack damp peat round the roots or dig a trench and bury the roots in soil until everything is ready.

Prune off any damaged roots when planting, and with 'bare root' bushes I like to reduce the top growth down to 12–15 in. (30–38 cm). Full pruning can then be undertaken in March.

While it is not to be generally recommended, bush roses will often survive lifting and transplanting outside the recommended season. It is, of course, necessary to cut off all flowers and buds and keep the plants well watered. Very good establishment will also come from transplanting in late September, stripping off all leaves and cutting the bushes back by at least one-third. New roots are made before winter and the plants grow away very strongly the following spring.

PRUNING

While heated discussion continues on the best time to prune roses, experience has taught me a simple code which works. The once-flowering ramblers are best with old, flowered wood removed in summer after flowering. Shrub roses can be given similar treatment, although the cutting need not generally be so harsh. The

HOW TO PRUNE A HYBRID TEA ROSE

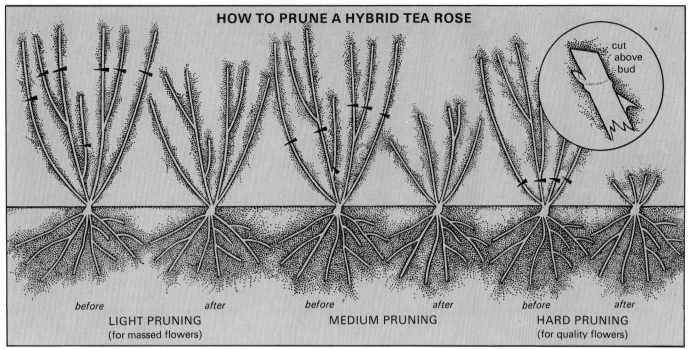

cut above bud

before   *after*
LIGHT PRUNING
(for massed flowers)

before   *after*
MEDIUM PRUNING

before   *after*
HARD PRUNING
(for quality flowers)

perpetual-flowering shrub roses need no more than careful thinning in March.

All other roses need pruning around the third week of March. The only qualification to this is reducing the top growth of bush and standard roses by up to one-third in late autumn to reduce resistance to strong winter winds. If all the top is left on, the plants rock in high winds and this opens a hole in the soil round the base of each plant. This hole can fill with water, and the waterlogged conditions can damage roots, in an extreme case killing the plant.

The third week of March pruning is one of the most important and one of the easiest and most satisfying of cultural operations. You can certainly see where the job has been done and it gives a really tidy appearance to the garden. New growth and flower is so much better as a result of the pruning, and the prunings burn easily to provide potash-rich ash for the soil.

Taking the job in stages, the autumn cut-back coupled with a complete rake up and removal of leaves does much to reduce disease attack. Then in March prune out all thin, old and diseased branches.

It is easy to do this with a good sharp pair of secateurs and gloves. The good strong young branches can then be cut back from 15 in. (38 cm) to 8 in. (20 cm).

Remember, the harder you prune the stronger the new growth will be. Very hard cutting back means less flowers but each one will be so much bigger. Lighter pruning means more flowers but each flower somewhat smaller.

It is best to prune back to a few branches 8 in. (20 cm) above ground for big exhibition hybrid tea blooms and 15 in. (38 cm) for floribundas to give a mass of flowers.

Do not be afraid to cut bush roses – invariably a skilled gardener would cut out more, however hard you feel you have pruned. Try to leave straight single branches sticking up from the crown of the bush. Where the branch ends in a series of short stumpy branches it seldom produces worthwhile flowers.

The perpetual-flowering climbers are pruned in much the same way except we keep the main branches, and cut all the side shoots coming from

Spray with tar oil in winter if you have any left over from fruit trees.

them, back to 2–4 in. (5–10 cm). Every now and then an old branch can be cut right back to encourage new branches to shoot out from the base.

Where new supple branches are tied over horizontally it encourages the development of a flowering side shoot from the bud at the base of every leaf. Once these flowering shoots have started to grow, the branch can be tied up vertically again if necessary.

New growth will sprout from the oldest, blackest, hard barky-looking wood. Ideally cut just above the line caused when a leaf falls. If you can't see this then prune virtually blind and cut off the old snags as soon as the new shoots are seen sprouting out.

The only other pruning needed is to cut out any badly diseased foliage and old flower heads as the petals fall. Dead-heading is most important if more flowers are to be encouraged. When you remove the dead blooms don't just snap them out. Look down the stem to a good leaf with plump bud between leaf and stem. Cut above this and a flowering shoot will develop.

FEEDING ROSES
Where masses of wood is being cut out annually, roses will need feeding to encourage strong renewal growth. Ideally work a good dressing of proprietary rose fertilizer into the surrounding soil after pruning. It is well worth giving all perpetual-flowering roses another top-dressing of fertilizer after the first summer flush in July to help maintain good flower

production. Water this fertilizer in well if the soil and weather is dry.

A light dressing in early autumn will also see that the plants are well nourished ready for the burst of growth next spring. Small, poorly coloured leaves, weak spindly growth, and small flowers with few petals are sure signs of insufficient plant food; foliar feeding as well as the soil application will help improve growth.

SUMMER CARE

After pruning and feeding in March, it is wise to apply a 2–3 in. (5–7·5 cm) mulch of peat, compost or similar material to retain moisture and help smother weeds during the summer. This is especially valuable on light, quick-drying soils. Where these mulches are used be sure that burning cigarette ends are not carelessly dropped because if the peat or litter smoulders around roses it can kill them.

An alternative weed control is to water clean soil in early spring with a selective weedkiller based on simazine. This will give weed-free soil for a year if left undisturbed. Where light cultivation is used to keep soil clean and tidy, just hoe the surface. Rose roots come close to the top and cutting them with hoe, fork and spade encourages unwanted suckers to grow.

Watering

Watering is not generally needed, as roses root deeply and are generally well able to fend for themselves. However, where they are growing in very light soil and mildew is a problem, give the soil an occasional very thorough soaking with water in summer.

Coping with Suckers

Most roses today are propagated by budding (occasionally miniature roses are grafted) on to specially selected vigorous rootstocks. The old *Rosa canina* stock, while producing roses of very long life, tended to throw up many suckers from below ground.

Modern stocks like *R. laxa* do not have the same suckering weakness but occasional suckers will occur. There is no absolutely foolproof means of identifying suckers. They always come from below the knobby point where the budded variety joins the rootstock.

Usually they are much lighter green and smaller leaved than the cultivated variety. Once you are sure it is a sucker – and not a lovely new branch growing up from the base – pull it away. Get

Some common rose pests: *a* rose leafhopper; *b* leaf cutter bee damage; *c* cockchafer (the rose chafer is a green and red beetle); *d* tortrix moth damage; *e* frog hopper; *f* thrip damage; *g* red spider mite attack; *h* typical caterpillar damage.

hold of the sucker as low as possible and then tear it out. If possible put your foot against the bush to support it while pulling the sucker away.

Sucker shoots sprouting from standard rose stems just need rubbing off while green and tender.

Propagation

The more vigorous varieties of roses, especially ramblers and floribundas, can be propagated by taking hardwood cuttings. Select shoots of the current year's growth as it starts to harden in September. Insert these outside in sandy soil and they will be rooted and ready to transplant in 14 months' time.

More reliable results will be obtained where the required variety is budded on specially selected rootstocks in June or July, but this is a job for the nurseryman or very keen amateur.

Miniature roses can be grown from seed, but not special varieties.

ROSE TROUBLES

There are three diseases of roses which occur quite commonly and chemical sprays are needed to control their spread. Most widespread is powdery mildew, a fungus which produces greyish-white spots on the leaves and flower buds, eventually spreading to cover complete shoots and branches.

Mildew is usually widespread in dry seasons and on roses suffering from lack of moisture at the root. Some varieties like rambler 'Dorothy Perkins' and the glorious red floribunda 'Europeana' are more susceptible than others. Mildewed shoots are best pruned out, especially early in the season, and protective sprays applied.

Black-spot is the most aptly named fungus disease and under mild, damp, clean air conditions spread can be very rapid. The first sign of attack is small black spots on the leaf, the spots being edged yellow. The spots enlarge and increase in number, causing leaf fall.

Some varieties are more susceptible than others; those with hard, shiny leaves are usually more resistant. The disease is less of a problem in smoky, polluted areas.

See that all old leaves are cleared up and burned in winter where infection has occurred. Spray over the bushes and ground in winter with tar oil to get a clean start. Mulching will also help prevent reinfection from overwintered spores in the soil.

Spray the plants during growth with either protective or systemic fungicides to prevent infection of the new growth or kill germinating spores as they grow into the leaf.

Rose rust is the most serious of the three diseases and severe attacks will cause the death of bushes. The first signs are small clusters of orange pustules on the underside of the leaves. These eventually turn black in August, then the leaves fall. Sprays of maneb and zineb will protect leaves from further infection by rust and black-spot.

Fortnightly sprays with chemical combinations like maneb and dinocap will control all three diseases. New systemic fungicides which are taken up in the plant sap and actually kill these diseases are now available to amateurs. The use of those based on bupirimate and triforine promise to make disease control easier and more effective.

The main pest of roses is greenfly, in severe attacks covering the leaves with a black sooty mould. There are many suitable insecticides to control them; those based on pirimicarb will leave beneficial insects such as lace-wings and ladybirds unharmed. Spray twice at 3–4-day intervals to get a complete kill.

Prune out shoots severely infected with mildew and spray with a systemic fungicide to clean up such infections.

There are a number of other minor pests of roses which we see from time to time. Some of these are best described in pictorial form, and these should be fairly easy to identify from the coloured illustrations shown on the opposite page.

Caterpillars of several kinds of moth are best killed by pinching them when seen, or by using sprays based on trichlorphon. The same spray will control leaf-rolling sawfly, rose slug-worm, cuckoo spit and leaf hopper (small yellowish insects which leave behind tell-tale empty white skins).

Leaf cutter bees will remove quite a large part of leaves from roses and beech but this creature is worth the damage it does for the interest it causes. If found the nests can be destroyed to prevent further damage but control is not usually necessary.

Dusts of HCH (BHC) around the base of roses will help prevent damage by cockchafer, rose and garden chafer.

While this may appear a formidable array of pests and diseases, in practice roses will grow and flourish for years without sprays and regardless of the many pests. An occasional combined fungicide and pesticide spray will help produce the perfect blooms keen gardeners desire.

Choosing Roses

There are so many really good roses it is very difficult to choose the best for our gardens. I cannot recommend enough visits to rose nurseries and garden centres at the time when the roses are in flower in order to be sure that the growth, colour and fragrance meets with your approval.

Orange pustules on the undersides of leaves are typical symptoms of rust.

Black-spot usually brings early leaf fall on infected plants.

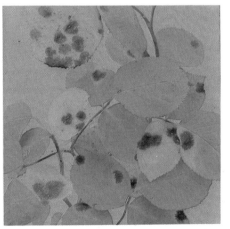

Fruit

Contrary to widespread belief you do not need a lot of space to grow a selection of fruit crops. Even an area as small as 12 ft × 7 ft (3·5 m × 2·3 m) can support a surprising amount.

Cropping in a small area naturally calls for careful planning, but a plot the size mentioned can support two rows of strawberries, three rhubarb plants, three rows of raspberries, a couple of blackcurrants, a redcurrant and a gooseberry, a loganberry, blackberry, and an apple tree. It will be necessary to thin out some of the soft fruit as the different kinds grow and demand more space, but this is no more than is often done commercially.

The cropping plan shown on the following page is only one of countless fruit combinations which can be used, but it offers a framework from which to start. The tree is best placed to the north of the plot, and although it could be a plum or pear, an apple on dwarfing roots is likely to be easier to handle.

In some respects a small garden has advantages for fruit growing. Where the plot is fenced on one or two sides it is an advantage when it comes to netting for protection against birds.

Vines, cane and cordon fruits can also be planted against fences. Grapes, however, require warm conditions for quality fruit so cane fruits would be better in colder northern districts.

Strong cold winds in spring can be a real problem for fruit growers, and again suburban gardens fenced and hedged provide protection.

Fruit trees and bushes do not need much regular attention, apart from some pruning and occasional spraying.

When replanting do not plant another apple where there was apple before. Rotate with pear and stone fruits. Crop rotation is not practised to the same extent with fruit as it is with vegetables, but on an intensively cropped plot it will be necessary to scrap strawberry plants after three or

Raspberries growing in part of the author's 12 ft × 7 ft fruit plot, showing how even a small area can produce worthwhile yields.

four years. The area cleared of strawberries could either be taken up by the increasing size of soft fruit bushes or be replanted with rhubarb. It may be possible to replant a few strawberries where rhubarb crowns were lifted to force.

Light is important on densely planted plots. Raspberries and soft fruits would need to be kept well pruned and canes tied in to allow light to get through to the strawberries.

Growing the redcurrant and gooseberry bushes on a stem 2–2½ ft (60–75 cm) high would provide more space for strawberries and rhubarb.

BUYING FRUIT TREES
It is vital to start off with healthy stock. Trouble will soon spread in an intensively cropped area, and virus diseases in unhealthy plants will considerably reduce yields and cannot

be cured by garden sprays.

All the advice given on buying shrubs applies to fruit bushes too, but additionally pay attention to the leaves of soft fruit such as raspberries and strawberries – avoid any that are showing unnaturally yellow, mottled, contorted or stunted leaves.

Rootstocks
Rootstocks are a vital consideration when buying top fruit such as apples or pears. A Bramley apple can have a spread of 16 ft (5 m) or 30 ft (9 m), depending on the rootstock.

All stone fruits (cherries, plums etc.), and apples and pears are better grafted on to special roots rather than produced as plants on their own roots. A suitable rootstock can significantly affect ultimate tree size, and also induce earlier fruiting. There are other factors such as disease resistance with

Dwarfing rootstocks keep apple trees small and easily managed but need secure stakes.

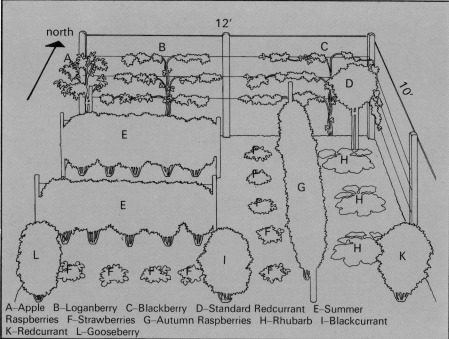

A–Apple B–Loganberry C–Blackberry D–Standard Redcurrant E–Summer Raspberries F–Strawberries G–Autumn Raspberries H–Rhubarb I–Blackcurrant K–Redcurrant L–Gooseberry

One possible cropping plan for a 12 ft × 10 ft (4 m × 3 m) fruit plot.

certain cherry and grape stocks, and pest resistance in some apple stocks.

The new dwarfing stock for cherries – Colt – will make cherry growing in gardens more practical. A dwarfing stock for plums and gages called Pixie will also be valuable in small gardens.

Apple Rootstocks

Thanks to the work carried out at East Malling and Long Ashton research stations, there is a range of good rootstocks available for apples.

M 9 (Malling 9) is a very dwarfing stock suitable for good soils. It is essential to keep trees on this stock *securely staked* for the *whole* of their life.

M 26 (Malling 26) is a more recent introduction and is slightly stronger growing than M 9. It will need secure staking in poor sandy soils but like M 9 will start fruiting in the second and third year from grafting.

MM 106 (Malling Merton 106) is described as semi-dwarfing because on good soils it provides medium-sized trees and on poor soils dwarf trees. MM 106 is the best all-round stock for gardens.

MM 111 (Malling Merton 111) is vigorous, producing excellent bush trees. It is resistant to drought and is the best for really poor soils.

Trees on MM 111 stock will fruit several years later than the dwarfing stocks, but will produce heavier yields.

M 9 and M 26 are ideal for cordons and dwarf pyramid apples, while MM 111 is most suitable for bush and standard trees.

The chart (right) gives an indication of bush tree diameters for some representative varieties on the various stocks. These will provide a guide to planting distances.

Pear Rootstocks

The stock recommended for general garden use is EM Quince A (East Malling Quince A). This stock produces trees 12 ft (3·6 m) across.

EM Quince C has a more dwarfing effect but it needs to be used with a vigorous variety and on good soil.

Plum Rootstocks

Dwarfing stock Pixie, which is a new kind, requires good soil. The one best suited to the average garden is St. Julien A. Brompton is more vigorous and should be used where heavy cropping varieties are grown well for maximum yield.

St. Julien will produce trees 12–15 ft (3·6–4·6 m) across, while Brompton produces trees 18–20 ft (5·5–6·1 m) in diameter.

APPLES

Bush trees are usually the most popular, but look for specimens which have a trunk a little taller than usual.

These are sometimes called 'bush-on-leg'. They are shorter than a half-standard, and do not get too high for picking, but have sufficient clear stem to make cultivating beneath the branches easy.

Dependable Varieties

Varieties should be selected with both flavour and pollinators in mind, for cross pollination is necessary for consistent and heavy crops. The apple selector chart indicates those which flower at the same period. If you only have one tree, there is a good chance of a suitable pollinator in a neighbour's garden.

The following are some of the varieties that are worth considering.

'Arthur Turner' (cooking). This has greenish-yellow fruit and beautiful pink flowers.

'Blenheim Orange' (cooking and dessert). Large orange-yellow apples of good flavour. Can be cooked. Makes a large tree and is slow to fruit.

Approximate guide to diameter of some typical trees on selected rootstocks.

SELECTED ROOTSTOCKS			
Rootstock	'Bramley' (strong growing)	'Discovery' (medium)	'Cox's Orange Pippin' (less vigorous)
M 9	16 ft (5 m)	12 ft (3·6 m)	10 ft (3 m)
M 26	20 ft (6·1 m)	15 ft (4·6 m)	11 ft (3·3 m)
MM 106	25 ft (7·5 m)	16 ft (5 m)	12 ft (3·6 m)
MM 111	30 ft (9 m)	20 ft (6·1 m)	15 ft (4·6 m)

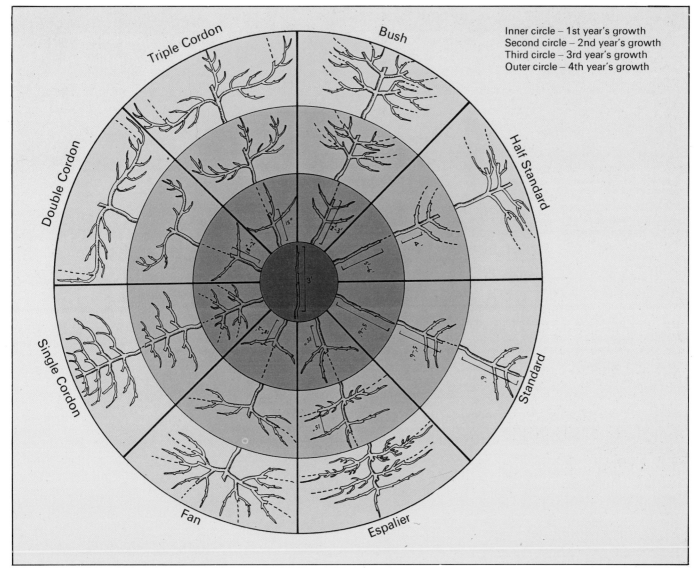

Starting with a maiden tree (centre), it is possible to produce many different tree shapes by careful pruning and training. Each ring of the circle represents one year's growth.

YEAR ROUND FRESH FRUIT

Fruit	Jan	Feb	Mar	April	May	June	July	Aug	Sept	Oct	Nov	Dec
Apricot								●●	●			
Apple ('Early Victoria' or 'Grenadier')							●	●●●	●●●	●		
Apple (mid-season, e.g. 'Lord Derby')									●	●●●	●●●	●
Apple (late, e.g. 'Idared')	●●	●●●●	●●●	●●●	●●●	●						
Blackberry								●	●●●	●●●	●●	
Cherries							●●●	●●●	●			
Currants						●●●	●●●					
Gooseberries					●●	●●●	●●●					
Grapes									●●	●●●	●	
Loganberries							●●	●●	●			
Peaches								●●●	●●			
Pears (early)								●●	●●			
Pears (late)										●●	●●●	●●
Plums							●●	●●●	●●			
Raspberries						●●	●●●	●				
Raspberries (autumn-fruiting)									●●●	●●●		
Rhubarb		●● FORCED	●●●	●●●	●●●	●●●	●					
Strawberries				●FORCED●	●●●	●						
Strawberries (perpetual-fruiting)								●	●●●	●		

125

'Spartan' is a useful late dessert apple for a small garden. It also tends to be hardy and disease resistant.

If planting more than one tree, select two varieties from the same group, to increase the chances of good pollination. Those marked 'T' are triploid varieties, which do not provide viable pollen, so plant three varieties including the triploid.

The flowering crab 'Golden Hornet' can also be used for cross-pollination purposes.

APPLE SELECTOR

Varieties	★	July	Aug	Sept	Oct	Nov	Dec	Jan	Feb	Mar	Apl	May	June
Early flowering													
Discovery	★		▲	▲▲	▲▲								
Egremont Russet	★			▲	▲▲	▲▲	▲						
Idared							●●	●●	●●	●▲	▲▲	▲▲	▲
Mid-season flowering													
Arthur Turner	★			●	●●	●●							
Blenheim Orange (T)							●●	●●	●▲	▲▲	▲▲		
Bramley's Seedling (T)					●	●●	●●	●●	●●	●●	●		
Charles Ross	★				▲▲	▲▲	▲▲						
Cox's Orange Pippin						▲▲	▲▲	▲▲					
Epicure (Laxton's)			▲	▲▲	▲								
Fortune (Laxton's)				▲▲	▲▲								
Grenadier or Early Victoria	★	●●	●●	●●	●								
James Grieve	★		●●	●●▲	●								
Rev W. Wilks	★		●	●●▲	●●	●							
Sunset (Laxton's)						▲	▲▲	▲					
Worcester Pearmain	★			▲	▲▲	▲							
Late flowering													
Ellison's Orange				▲▲	▲▲	▲▲							
Golden Delicious							▲▲	▲▲	▲▲	▲▲	▲		
Laxton's Superb							▲▲	▲▲	▲▲	▲			
Lord Derby	★				●	●●	●●						
Newton Wonder						●	●●	●●	●●	●●	●		
Spartan							▲▲	▲▲	▲▲	▲▲			

★ Good varieties suitable for all parts of the country   ● Cooking   ▲ Dessert

'Bramley's Seedling' (cooking). Keeps well but makes a very large tree.

'Charles Ross' (dessert). Large and attractive fruit. Compact tree with disease-resistant leaves.

'Cox's Orange Pippin' (dessert). Requires good soil and a warm climate. It is also susceptible to disease.

'Discovery' (dessert). Delicious, juicy fruit, when picked ripe from the tree. Has disease-resistant foliage.

'Egremont Russet' (dessert). Has neat upright growth, and fruits very early in the tree's life. Excellent for small gardens. Resistant to disease.

'Ellison's Orange' (dessert). A variety with a distinctive flavour, and delicious eaten ripe from the tree. Flowers resistant to frost.

'Epicure' (dessert). A pretty striped fruit, of excellent flavour. It makes a small tree and is disease resistant.

'Fortune' (dessert). Has fruit striped red on yellow, of delicious flavour. The variety is disease resistant and crops from an early age.

'Grenadier' (cooker). A good free cropping and disease resistant early cooking apple. It is usually picked green but turns yellow as it ripens.

'Idared' (cooking and dessert). A valuable cooking apple because it keeps from November to June. Although it is a little sharp it can be eaten from February onwards. A watch should be kept for mildew.

'James Grieve' (cooking and dessert). Easiest of all garden apples. Pick early to cook and eat fresh from the tree when ripe. Produces regular, heavy crops but the fruit bruises easily.

'Lord Derby' (cooking). A large apple that turns reddish when cooked. Upright growth and disease resistant.

'Rev. W. Wilks' (cooking). A large pale yellow apple when ripe. Easy to grow and disease resistant.

'Spartan' (dessert). Flowers resistant to spring frost, disease resistant and useful for a small garden.

'Worcester Pearmain' (dessert). Attractive flowers and fruit, and best eaten ripe from the tree. Disease resistant, easy to grow, and suitable for small gardens.

If you do not have enough space for two or three trees, select a 'family' apple and 'family' pear; each will have three varieties grafted on one tree. These will pollinate one another and provide a succession of ripe fruits.

Cultivation

Any well-cultivated garden soil suits apples. Avoid difficult-to-grow kinds like Cox's Orange Pippin in northern districts and on poor soils.

It is important when planting to see that the knobbly section of stem above soil level (the graft) is clear of the earth. If you cover the graft with soil the variety will produce its own roots and the effect of the rootstock will be lost. However, if the graft has been made well above the soil line, it is worth planting deeper – provided the graft is not covered – as this will reduce the need to stake and encourage earlier and heavier fruiting.

Do not plant apples in hollows where cold spring frosts are likely. Choose late-flowering varieties for cold frosty areas.

Keep soil around newly planted trees free of weeds. Competition from weeds in the first year can reduce growth by 50 per cent, and this effect can be continued well into the tree's life.

If a tree produces too many small fruits, or fruits heavily only every other year, thin out in early July.

Harvesting

To pick an apple, hold it and lift up through 90° from the branch. It will come away easily if it is ready to pick. Do not snatch the fruit from the tree as this can break off a spur and remove the next season's flower bud.

The fruit can be stored in trays in a cool, slightly damp atmosphere. Remove the ripe fruits otherwise these will speed the ripening process of the remaining apples.

Pruning

Compact growing varieties such as 'Charles Ross', 'Discovery', 'Early

With spur pruning, wood formed in the summer is cut back to four buds.

Grenadier' is a prolific and disease-resistant early apple. A cooker, it is usually picked green but ripens to yellow.

Victoria', 'Epicure', 'Egremont Russet', 'Fortune', 'Grenadier', 'James Grieve', 'Lord Derby', 'Ellison's Orange', 'Rev. Wilks' and 'Worcester Pearmain' bush trees will crop regularly without any pruning once the initial branch framework has been clearly established.

Generally however, some pruning is advisable, and they can be either spur or renewal pruned. Cordon, fan and espalier trained apples should be spur pruned. All trees are best with the lead shoots of the current year's growth pruned back by half each year.

All shoots showing signs of mildew in spring must be pruned out and burnt before the infection spreads.

Pests and Diseases

Aphids cause leaves to curl, shoots to distort and feel sticky. Use a tar oil winter wash and prune off distorted twigs with overwintering eggs.

Birds sometimes take ripe fruit, while in winter bullfinches can be a nuisance by pecking off buds. Net for protection.

Canker causes dark hollows in the bark which spread. The wood around it then swells, and if girdled the piece of branch above dies. Pare away diseased wood, burn the pieces and paint the wound.

Caterpillars of winter and tortrix moth cause damage by eating leaves in spring. Adults can be caught by applying a band of grease round the trunk from October to March.

Maggots which have entered leaving one neat hole are from the *codling moth*. Trap by wrapping sacking or corrugated cardboard around fairly smooth bark in June. Remove and burn in October. Maggots which eat the surface of fruit before burrowing belong to the *sawfly*. The fruits drop before they ripen, and these should be picked up and destroyed in June to reduce chance of an attack next year.

Mildew looks like a greyish growth over shoots and leaves. Watch out for it when the first leaves develop.

Scab causes brown and blackish spots to appear on the leaves and fruits. Light green patches also develop on the leaves. Rake up and burn all diseased leaves, especially any which fall early.

Woolly aphis have a waxy white covering; this requires forceful spring sprays to penetrate and control.

Harvesting

Bunches of ripe grapes cut with a length of branch can be hung in a cool place where they will keep for several weeks. Be sure to remove any rotting berries so that the rot does not spread.

Pruning

Single rod training is the simplest method for greenhouse and outdoor vines. The rods can be trained up walls, along fences or along horizontal wires supported by posts in the open. Fruit is carried on the side shoots. Stop growth two leaves past a flower truss.

Vines can also be trained by cutting the young plant hard back to 4 in. (10 cm) in the autumn. The following autumn the strong cane that has grown is cut back to two leaf scars (two buds) to provide two strong rods in the second year. One of these is cut back to two buds in the third autumn to provide replacement rods and the second rod is cut back to seven buds to produce fruiting laterals. Rods that have fruited are cut back hard and the new rods tied in their place.

Pests and Diseases

Mealy bug and *scale insects* can be controlled by a tar oil winter wash applied while the rods are dormant.

Mildew is sometimes a very serious disease. Avoid plants becoming dry at the roots, and thin back sub-laterals if the growth becomes too thick. Spray with Dinocap when the shoots are 2–3 in. (5–7·5 cm) long. Another spray may be necessary when the flowers have set.

If any berries succumb to various fungus diseases, pick them off before the problem spreads.

A warm sunny position, and a good season is needed for quality grapes, but good wine grapes can be grown quite successfully outdoors.

OUTDOOR GRAPES

For quality dessert grapes to be grown outside in all but the warmest parts a warm, sunny position and a very warm season are needed. Outdoor grapes will, however, produce grapes that are good for wine, and a cold greenhouse will improve dessert varieties.

Dependable Varieties

Suitable outdoor varieties include 'Riesling Sylvaner', which is especially suitable for wine, and 'Brant', a small black variety with brilliant crimson autumn leaf colour.

Cultivation

Grapes are long lived and very hardy. They are also deep rooting and require a free-draining soil that is not too rich. Even though the roots are very hardy when dormant, some protection is needed in spring as young spring growth can be severely damaged by late frosts.

Prepare the soil by digging two spades' depth, adding compost to improve drainage. Pot-grown vines should be planted 9 in. (23 cm) away from walls and 5 ft (1·5 m) apart for single rod specimens.

Mulch to retain moisture, especially near walls.

Very good quality 'Black Hamburg' grapes can be grown under cold glass, the rods trained either against the wall or the roof.

Although peaches are really only suitable for warm and sheltered sites, they can be very successful if given the right location.

Fan trees are perhaps best purchased from the nursery with the basic branch framework formed. Then it is a matter of pruning the lead shoots of each branch back in early spring. It is best to cut back to a cluster of three buds at one point to get two or three new branches radiating out from the cut.

When the branches have extended to the area available, prune to achieve fruiting. Fruit is produced on the previous year's wood. The plump rounded buds are flower buds, the longer, thinner ones produce growth. Any shoots that grow toward the wall or at 90° away from it should be rubbed out in April while young, soft and green.

Select shoots on top and beneath each branch, and about every 6 in. 15 cm) along and tie to the horizontal support wires, placed 9 in. (23 cm) apart. Pinch out the tip of side shoots when 18 in. (45 cm) long. Each year a strong new shoot should be trained from the base of the lateral and alongside it as a replacement. The fruited branch is cut out in late summer. Surplus shoots can be pinched back to four leaves or rubbed out.

Pests and Diseases

Aphids can be controlled with tar oil in winter or with proprietary greenfly sprays in summer.

Mildew is usually the result of dry soils. If the disease appears, sulphur sprays at 14-day intervals will afford control

Peach leaf curl causes curled leaves with red blisters. Spray with a liquid copper fungicide in January or February when buds begin to swell. Repeat 10 days later and again before the flower buds open and once more as the leaves fall in the autumn.

Peach leaf curl is a very disfiguring disease, spray early to control.

PEACHES

In warm sheltered gardens in favourable areas peaches can be grown outdoors quite satisfactorily as bush trees. If trained as fans against south or west facing walls, they will thrive and fruit even in some of the less favourable areas. But in cold regions they need the protection of a cold greenhouse to fruit with any degree of reliability.

Dependable Varieties

Trees grown from pips will sometimes fruit satisfactorily, but it is best to grow named varieties grafted on to the dwarfing 'St. Julien A' rootstock.

'Peregrine', which is ready in early August, is reliable, while 'Rochester' is a good variety for bush cultivation. All varieties are self-pollinating.

Cultivation

Trees with bare roots are best planted in October or November, or early spring; container grown peaches can be planted at any time.

Choose a well-cultivated soil that is not too chalky. It needs to be free draining but also water retentive in summer. Add plenty of well-rotted compost before planting, especially near walls or fences.

Peaches must be watered well in very dry weather and it is wise to aid pollination by dusting the open flowers midday with a feather or soft paintbrush when dry and sunny. Gently misting with water on sunny days also helps. Once the fruits are the size of a penny single them out, then when the size of a 10 pence piece thin to 9 in. (23 cm) apart for final development.

Harvesting

When fruits start to ripen, tie the leaves back to expose the fruits to sun. Once the flesh is soft to touch around the stalk, gather the fruits. Spaced on tissue in a cool place, they will store for a week or two.

Pruning

Established bush peaches require little pruning apart from cutting out any diseased and dead wood in May. An occasional branch can be pruned back at the same time to encourage new growth from the centre of the tree.

Pears can grow into very large trees on seedling rootstocks but on Quince A stock make compact, early-flowering trees.

PEARS

Although pears need similar treatment and conditions to apples, they generally need a warmer climate.

The vigorous young shoots and leaves are soft and all too easily damaged by strong cold winds in spring. Because they benefit from the protection offered they are often grown as wall trees.

A well-cultivated garden soil should give good results, but avoid chalky soils.

Dependable Varieties

One specialist nurseryman alone offers more than 50 varieties of pear, and this is only a very conservative list.

'Conference' is the best variety to start with. It will produce fruit without pollination, although such fruit may be rather cylindrical in shape. It gives regular heavy crops in all parts of the country and is easy to grow. It is ready to pick in October and can be stored until Christmas.

'Williams' Bon Chretien' is even better quality. This September-ripening variety has upright growth and it can be grown in all parts of the country, even when planted against a north wall.

'Doyenne du Comice' is the most delicious of all pears, and excellent to bottle. If Comice is planted in the warmest position it will help bring flowering forward to overlap with Conference and Williams. The fruit is ripe from November to January.

The majority of bush and trained pears are grown on Quince A rootstock, which produces compact and early fruiting trees. The large trees seen in old gardens are usually on seedling pear stock, and may take 10–15 years to come into fruit.

Cultivation

Spacing between plants will depend not only on rootstock but also variety and pruning. A moderate variety on Quince A can be spaced 12 ft (3·5 m) apart with hard pruning. A vigorous variety on the same stock on good soil but lightly pruned will need 15 ft (4·5 m) between trees.

Pears will grow best where the soil under them is kept cultivated. Mulching with compost in spring helps; as does the application of a general fertilizer at 2–3 oz per sq yd (60–85 g per sq m) in January.

All fruit trees in grass will also benefit from 1 oz per sq yd (30 g per sq m) of sulphate of ammonia in spring.

Where pear trees flourish but fail to set fruit, inadequate pollination or spring frosts are usually the cause.

Harvesting

Pears should be picked when they are ripe but *before* they soften. The fruits should separate easily from the tree when lifted through 90° in the hand.

Both flavour and smell develop better if the fruit is stored in single layers in trays or boxes in a cool damp atmosphere. An established tree is likely to average 20–30 lb (9–13·5 kg) of fruit each year.

Pruning

Pears are pruned in a similar way to apples, although they respond better than apples to really hard pruning. Lead shoots of established trees can be cut back to 2 in. (5 cm) each winter and all laterals to 1 in. (2·5 cm).

The number of fruiting spurs may have to be reduced on established trees if they are not to carry too many small fruits.

Aim for between seven and ten main branches for closely planted bush trees.

Pests and Diseases

Aphis, including greenfly and blackfly, may cause a black sticky mould over leaves and shoots. A tar oil winter wash, followed by a greenfly spray after the petals have fallen, will bring control.

Fireblight is a serious disease which must be reported to your local Ministry of Agriculture office. Symptoms are a sudden total blackening of young

Fruit buds are plumper than the rather triangular vegetative buds.

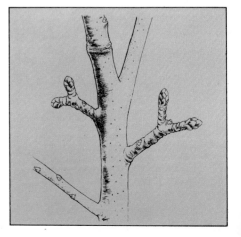

shoots as if burnt by fire; and liquid streaks running down the bark of branches is another sign. All infected wood must be cut out and burned, and the tools used must be sterilized. Cotoneaster, Mountain Ash and pyracantha are also affected.

Pear leaf blister causes pale green or pink blisters, turning brown on the leaves from April onwards. Lime sulphur – which also controls scab – can be applied in late March as the buds begin to open, but it must not be used on the variety Comice. A small attack can be controlled by burning infected leaves.

Pear midge is an occasional pest that once present will reappear year after year until sprayed. Small fruits fail to develop, turn black and fall. White maggots will be found inside fruits. Spray at white flower bud stage with dimethoate.

Pear scab shows itself as black scabs and cracks on fruit. Other symptoms are light green spots on the leaves which turn brown, and blistered and spotted young shoots. Collect and burn diseased leaves and prune out diseased shoots. Spray with captan.

PLUMS, GAGES AND DAMSONS

After a 'family' apple tree, a 'Victoria' plum would be my next choice for a small garden

Plums and gages need a warm sunny site and weather to produce the best fruit. Heavy, wet soils, or those that are very acid, do not suit these plants, and damsons should be selected for areas of high rainfall.

Avoid planting in frost hollows.

Dependable Varieties

The varieties listed here are only a

Plums can make good fruit trees for small gardens, especially if grown on a suitable dwarfing rootstock such as St. Julien A.

cross-section of the many different types. All are self-pollinating but better crops will often be achieved if cross pollination occurs.

'Victoria' is ripe to eat fresh in late August/early September, but is suitable for cooking a little earlier.

'Czar' is a hardy reliable early purple/black plum of upright growth, used for cooking.

'Marjorie's Seedling' is a large

culinary plum ready to eat from the tree in October. A good late variety.

Gages have a distinctive flavour. 'Oullin's Gage' is one of the best gages. It is a golden gage plum suitable for eating or cooking.

The rich flavour of damson is provided by 'Prune Damson' (synonymous with 'Shropshire Prune'). This is a compact upright tree, compared with 'Merryweather', another good variety.

St. Julien A is the best rootstock for most gardens. They will start fruiting after about three years on this stock.

Cultivation

Trees on St. Julien A stock should be spaced 12 ft (3·5 m) apart, those on more vigorous stocks further than this.

A heavy mulch of manure and well-rotted compost will improve the performance of these fruits.

It is worth netting fan trees against walls as protection from birds – and to some extent protect blossom from frosts.

Thin fruits in June or July if necessary, to leave one every 2 in. (5 cm) along the branch.

Many fruits can be trained neatly as space-saving cordons.

Space can also be saved by growing fan-trained trees against a fence.

			When action may be necessary							
Problem	**Fruit Affected**	**Control**	Feb	Mar	Apl	May	Jun	Jly	Aug	**Notes**
Pests										
Aphid (Greenfly)	Apple, pear, plum, cherry	bioresmethrin or dimethoate or formothion or malathion or pirimicarb or pirimiphos-methyl or resmethrin or rotenone or diazinon			••	••	••			Use tar oil Dec–Jan
Woolly Aphid	Apple	HCH or dimethoate or malathion				•	•			Green to pink flower bud stage, before May
Capsid	Apple	bioresmethrin, or fenitrothion or HCH or malathion or pirimiphos-methyl				•	•			
Caterpillar (Winter Moth and Sawfly)	Apple	trichlorphon or fenitrothion or HCH or pirimiphos-methyl				••				Apply grease band September
Codling Moth	Apple	fenitrothion, or HCH or malathion or pirimiphos-methyl					•	•		Same treatment for tortrix caterpillar
Leaf Blister Mite	Pear	5% lime sulphur		••						
Midge Pear		dimethoate or fenitrothion or HCH				••				Apply at white flower bud stage DNOC/pet. February. Not a problem on unsprayed trees as natural predators control
Red Spider Mite	Apple, plum etc.	diazinon, malathion or dinocap or pirimiphos-methyl or rotenone					••	•		
Diseases										
Canker	Apple	liquid copper				••				Spray at half leaf fall, and again at full leaf fall
Leaf Curl	Peaches	lime sulphur or liquid copper or captan	••							3rd week Jan and just before flower buds swell
Mildew	Apple	dinocap or benomyl or thiophanate-methyl				••	••	••	•	7–14 day intervals
Scab	Apple, pear	benomyl or captan or thiram or zineb or thiophanate-methyl				••	••	••		

TOP FRUIT: PEST AND DISEASE CONTROL

Follow manufacturer's instructions on proprietary brands for time between spray and harvest.

Harvesting

For eating fresh the fruit is best picked over several times, selecting only fully ripe fruit. Earlier gathering is acceptable for cooking purposes. Yields will vary from season to season, but a well grown 'Victoria' should yield 40 lb (18 kg) or more each year as a bush tree, 15 lb (6·8 kg) as a fan.

Pruning

Nurserymen usually supply trees which have the basic branch framework established. Leave unpruned in the first year or just tip trees transplanted bare root, and in the second spring (the first spring for container-grown trees) cut the lead shoots which will grow to form main branches back by half.

Subsequently it will only be necessary to shorten back the lead shoots of strong growing varieties like 'Victoria' in spring to avoid producing long weeping branches.

Pruning of mature trees is best undertaken in summer after fruiting.

Cover wounds with a proprietary tree wound paste to prevent silver leaf disease entering.

Much of the training of fan trees will probably have been done by the nursery. Side shoots growing at right angles to the wall should be rubbed out while young and green. Other laterals are tied in to the horizontal support wires and surplus shoots stopped by pinching out the tip after seven leaves have formed. After fruiting prune back the seven-leaf-long shoots by half and cut out any thin and unwanted branches. Very strong upward growing shoots from the centre of the fan should be removed.

Pests and Diseases

Aphids can cause a black sooty mould on leaves and fruit.
Birds can be a major problem. Bullfinches eat dormant buds in winter and other birds peck the ripe fruit. Net for protection.
Silver leaf disease causes a silver colour in the leaves and purplish brown staining in the wood. If pared down with a knife this is clearly seen.

All diseased wood must be cut out, back past the inner staining, by July. The wound will need painting over to prevent reinfection.

BLACKBERRIES

Cultivated blackberries are not to be compared with the wild forms found in our hedgerows. Named varieties are adaptable to virtually all garden situations, crop freely over a long period, and have the advantage of big berries and luscious flavour.

Dependable Varieties

'Bedford Giant' fruits early, in late July to late August. Large sweet fruits on plants of medium vigour.

'Oregon Thornless' is also called 'Evergreen Thornless'. This variety fruits from early September to October. The huge succulent berries have a delicious bramble flavour. Medium vigour; it needs plenty of water to achieve maximum berry size.

132

Cultivation

Even a shaded site or north-facing wall are acceptable though the yield will be less than in more open and sunny sites. The biggest, juiciest fruits will come from good soil to which manure and compost has been added.

Avoid digging around blackberry roots. It is better to hoe the surface lightly to control weeds, and to mulch each spring with well-rotted compost.

Blackberries are ideal trained on wires stretched between stout posts against a shed, wall or fence. The wires should be 2, 3, 4 and 5 ft from the ground.

Plant the less vigorous varieties 6 ft (2 m) apart, vigorous kinds 12 ft (4 m) apart.

Container and pot-grown plants will fruit the summer following planting.

Harvesting

If the stems have been tied in to the wires regularly, picking should be straightforward.

Pruning

At the end of the season cut out at ground level all the stems which have borne fruit. Tie in new stems as they develop, keeping them away from fruiting stems (see page 134). When the fruited stems have been pruned out, the new branches that will produce the next season's crop can be tied in. Bare root plants transplanted between October and March should be cut back to 9 in. (23 cm) above the soil.

Pests

Aphids are easily controlled by spraying with malathion.

Raspberry beetle, which causes small maggots in the fruit, can also be controlled satisfactorily with malathion if used at petal fall.

LOGANBERRIES

The loganberry was raised by Judge J. H. Logan in his garden at Santa Cruz, California, in 1881. The thornless form later came from the same state, and even more recently the East Malling Research Station has produced virus-free stock, or clones, which should be bought whenever possible.

Dependable Varieties

Loganberry 'LY 59', is a very heavy cropper producing thorned canes 8–10 ft (2·3–3·1 m) long. The fruit is long and dark.

Loganberry 'LY 654' is the best thornless strain. It is easier to train and

Cultivated blackberries are far removed from the wild bramble, having larger, more succulent berries. This variety is 'Oregon'.

Loganberries are well worth a place in the fruit garden, adding interest and variety.

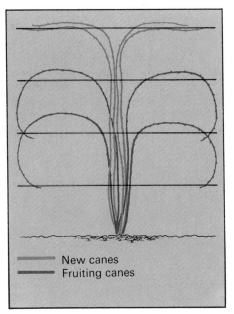

New canes
Fruiting canes

A recommended method of training blackberries and loganberries.

not so vigorous. The large burgundy-red fruits up to 2 in. (5 cm) long are borne in profusion.

Cultivation
Practically all soils and sites are suitable, though slightly acid soil conditions are best. Add plenty of well-rotted compost and manure to chalky soils. Well-rotted compost is also needed on heavy soils to improve drainage, and on sandy soils to retain moisture in summer.

Loganberries require a slightly warmer site than blackberries.

Keep loganberries well watered once the fruits have set to get the largest and most succulent berries.

Harvesting
Once the fruit is ripe, in July and August, hold it between the thumb and first two fingers and gently twist from the stem. It will come away easily.

Pruning
As for blackberries.

Pests and Diseases
Cane spot causes circular purple spots on the stems, leaves and flower stalks in May and June. These spots become larger and the centres turn grey. Cut out diseased stems and spray with a copper fungicide before flowering and again once fruit has set.

Raspberry beetle. It is the small reddish maggots of this beetle that are found in the fruits. Spray with derris or malathion in mid and late June, but not while the plants are in flower to avoid harming bees.

Spur blight symptoms are dark purple blotches which turn silvery grey where leaf joins the stem. Spray the emerging canes with benomyl, followed by two or three successive sprays at 10–14-day intervals, to achieve good control.

BLACKCURRANTS
Blackcurrants are a must for even a small garden. They are one of the most popular soft fruits for jams, tarts, fruit juice and as a flavouring for ice-cream.

A moisture-retaining yet free-draining soil is ideal, but any good garden soil is suitable. A sheltered site will reduce the chances of frost damage to the flowers.

Dependable Varieties
'Baldwin' accounts for most commercial planting; it makes a compact bush on heavy soil.

'Boskoop Giant' ripens early and has very large fruits on each string.

'Malling Jet' flowers late and produces long trusses of fruit.

Cultivation
Plant blackcurrants 4–6 ft (1·2–2 m) apart in October to March for bare root plants, but any time for container-grown bushes.

Apply manure or well-rotted compost as a mulch each spring and general fertilizer at 4 oz per sq yd (120 g per sq m).

Propagate from hard-wood cuttings 8–10 in. (25 cm) long taken in October or November.

Harvesting
Pick dry, when the fruit is black but still firm. An established bush is likely to yield about 6–8 lb (2·75–3·5 kg) of blackcurrants in a reasonable season.

Pruning
Bare root bushes should be cut down to within 1–2 in. (2–5 cm) of the soil after planting. After the first summer (immediately for container grown plants), cut the weakest shoots out to encourage new growth for the following year. The remaining shoots will bear fruit the following summer.

Established, fruiting bushes should have old fruited wood cut out every winter. Always choose the oldest wood, which is very black. Where big bushes have old branches with four or more young laterals, cut back to one lateral to

Space should always be found for blackcurrants; any good garden soil will suit them.

One of the most popular red currants is 'Red Lake', which bears large fruit on long trusses.

White currants are like small white grapes and are delicious in a dessert or eaten fresh.

encourage more new growth from the base, and maintain a balanced plant.

Pests and Diseases

Big Bud Mite causes infected buds to swell up several times larger than normal and are easily seen in winter. This pest spreads virus diseases, which reduce yield. It is best to destroy affected plants and replant with new 'certified' disease-free plants if a virus has been transmitted. Lime sulphur sprayed in March or April when the leaves are the size of a 5p piece will control the mite.

RED AND WHITE CURRANTS

White currants are like small white grapes, delicious eaten fresh as a dessert. Red currants, on the other hand, are eaten as jelly with meat, used with other fruits like raspberries in pies, in tarts, and in preserves.

Dependable Varieties

'Red Lake' has large fruit on long trusses.

'Jonkheer van Tets' is a recent red variety that is vigorous and early.

'Rondom' is a late, heavy yielding variety.

Cultivation

A light, free-draining soil that is not too chalky is best, in a protected position.

Plant 4–5 ft (1·2–1·5 m) apart, allow-ing the wider spacing for more vigorous varieties.

Incorporate plenty of well-rotted compost into the soil before planting, and mulch each spring. Add a high potash fertilizer (possibly one for roses or tomatoes) each spring at 1½–2 oz per sq yd (40–60 g per sq m).

Bushes on a 9–12 in. (23–30 cm) stem are the easiest to grow but where space is limited red and white currants can be trained as single, double and triple-stemmed cordons against a fence, or on a 2–3 ft (60–90 cm) high stem as standards.

Harvesting

Harvest like blackcurrants. An average of 4–5 lb (1·8–2·3 kg) can be expected from an established bush in July.

Pruning

A young bush which has grown for two summers should have the current year's main branch tips cut back by half; the side shoots on both young and established plants can be cut back to 1 in. (2·5 cm) to form fruiting spurs.

Established plants can have an occasional old branch cut out completely to be replaced by new growth. Once branches have reached the required height each season's new lead growth can be cut back to 1 in. (2·5 cm).

Pests and Diseases

Birds can be a problem in both summer and winter. Net to protect the bushes.

Coral spot shows as red spots on the wood. Prune back to disease-free wood and cover the cut with grafting or pruning paste.

Greenfly can cause the leaves to pucker and reddish blisters to appear. Spray with malathion.

GOOSEBERRIES

Gooseberries provide some of the season's earliest soft fruit. They crop over a period of 12 weeks and are useful for many summer desserts. They are also excellent for bottling, making jams and for freezing.

Gooseberries prefer a sunny site, but partial shade will give acceptable yields. In cold areas the more demanding varieties will benefit from the protection of a south-facing fence.

Dependable Varieties

'Careless' is a heavy cropping mid-season green variety that is easy to grow.

'Keepsake' can be picked as early as 'Careless' for cooking, but is late ripening. A strong-growing, pale green variety, it makes large bushes in time and is better protected from frost in cold sites.

'Leveller' produce large succulent yellow fruits when ripe and is the best dessert variety. It requires good soil and is not the easiest to grow.

'Whinham's Industry', is an easily

Gooseberries are a useful summer fruit, and 'Careless' is an easy-to-grow green variety that bears a heavy crop.

more culinary fruit, the remainder left to grow on the bush until ripe. An established plant on reasonable soil should yield from 5–15 lb (2·3–6·8 kg) per bush, depending on season.

Pruning

Cut back the lead shoots by half the summer's growth in winter. If bull-finches are a problem, delay pruning until early spring (to give the birds more buds to go at and reduce the chance of their removing the buds required), or net the bushes.

Prune drooping branches back to an upward growing bud to encourage more upright branches. Once the branches have reached the required height and length, cut the lead shoots back to 1 in. (2·5 cm) or so each winter.

Side shoots can be pruned back to six or seven leaves in July, and cut further back to 1 in. (2·5 cm) in winter. Pruning these side shoots into short fruiting spurs gives larger single fruits of better quality. Where yield rather than quality is the aim, however, prune more along the lines of blackcurrants. Here strong new growth from the centre of the bush is encouraged and the occasional older branch cut out to make space.

Pests and Diseases

American gooseberry mildew coats shoots, leaves and fruit with a powdery white growth which turns felty and brown.

Burn diseased shoots in late August. Spray with a systemic fungicide two or three times at 7–14-day intervals.
Gooseberry sawfly caterpillars can cause problems. These are green with black spots, and they eat all the leaves to the

grown red variety, sweet flavoured and with a hairy skin. One of the most successful on heavier soils.

Cultivation

Improve the soil before planting by adding plenty of well-rotted compost.

A high-potash fertilizer should be worked into the soil before planting, and a spring application made annually at 1–2 oz per sq yd (30–60 g per sq m). A spring mulch of well-rotted compost will help to smother weeds, and retain moisture to increase berry size.

Plant gooseberries 4–6 ft (1·2–1·8 m) apart, the wider distances for the more vigorous varieties. Space single cordons 1 ft (30 cm) apart, double cordons 2 ft (60 cm), and triple cordons 3 ft (1 m).

It makes cultivation and picking easier if gooseberries are grown on a short stem, 6–9 in. (15–23 cm) high. It may be necessary to remove one or two roots and a couple of low branches when planting to achieve this.

Harvesting

Thin the fruits to leave the berries 1 in. (2·5 cm) apart on the stem as soon as the thinnings are large enough to cook, which will be early May. Later every-other berry can be picked to provide

Gooseberries, red and white currants can be grown as cordons against fences, walls or wires. Illustrated are single (left), double (centre), and triple (right) cordons.

leaf ribs during late spring. Control this pest by either picking off the caterpillars or by spraying.

RASPBERRIES

Raspberries are the most rewarding fruit for gardens. Excellent for dessert and culinary purposes, as well as freezing.

Raspberries will grow satisfactorily on all well-cultivated soils, and on most sites, including partially shaded ones, though waterlogged ground must be avoided.

Dependable Varieties

There are two principal groups of raspberries – summer fruiting (June and July) and autumn fruiting (September to frost).

Mid-season varieties include:

'Malling Promise' and 'Malling Jewel'. Both are regular and heavy croppers.

'Glen Clova' starts to ripen earlier and crops over a long period. The large fruits are of good flavour.

'Delight' is one of the largest and heaviest cropping varieties. It is resistant to pests and diseases.

Autumn-fruiting kinds:

'September' is the best known, but 'Zeva' crops longer and more heavily (from July to the frost). The large red fruits are of excellent quality.

'Fallgold' (sweet golden yellow fruit) and 'Heritage' (red) are two American varieties worth considering.

Cultivation

When preparing the ground for raspberries, dig in plenty of well-rotted compost.

Be sure the soil is clear of perennial weeds before planting, which should ideally be in November for bare root canes, though any time from November to late March is all right.

Always plant 'certified' disease-free stock, and plant firmly 15–18 in. (38–45 cm) apart, and if more than one row is planted allow 4–6 ft (1·2–1·8 m) between rows. When transplanting do not allow the roots to become dry.

A heavy mulching with well-rotted manure or compost each spring will help to control weeds. Try not to dig close to surface-rooting raspberries.

Autumn-fruiting varieties are virtually self-supporting, but summer-fruiting kinds may need support. Tie new growth to wires placed 3 ft (1 m) and 5 ft (1·5 m) high, secured to stakes.

Plenty of water and liquid fertilizer as fruits start to swell will increase the

Raspberries, strawberries, black and red currants growing in the author's garden, showing netting protection. The net is supported on plastic containers on canes.

yield and strengthen canes for next season's crops.

Harvesting

When ripe a gentle pull should part the fruit from the 'plug' which stays behind on the cane, though some varieties come away quite easily.

Autumn-fruiting varieties crop over a longer period but do not give such a heavy total yield. It may be worth a lighter crop, however, for an extended season.

Yield from 1 ft (30 cm) of row is 1–2 lb (0·4–0·9 kg).

Pruning

Cut back bare root canes to 6–9 in. (15–23 cm) above soil level after planting. The new canes fruit 15–18 months from planting. Container-grown canes will crop lightly the first summer after planting. Prune out all fruited canes in August and tie new canes to the wires. Tie one new cane every 3–4 in. (7·5–10 cm) along the wires, and then cut out small surplus canes remaining.

Autumn-fruiting varieties planted with bare roots should be cut back after planting. Thereafter they should have fruited wood cut to the ground in *February*. These varieties fruit on the current year's canes, unlike the summer fruiting kinds, which crop on the previous year's growth.

Pests and Diseases
Raspberry beetle causes small maggots in ripe fruit. To control, spray or dust with derris or malathion when the first pink fruit is seen.

Cane spot may be seen in May or June as purple spots which turn grey with a purple edge. Spray with benomyl.

Spur blight shows itself as purple blotches in August. These turn silver and cause die-back. Spray with benomyl.

This disease tends to affect young overcrowded canes worst.

STRAWBERRIES
If the only space you have is a foot or two of windowsill, it is possible to have succulent red strawberries in late April or early May. Outside they can be grown on a paved area in pots, boxes, fertilized peat-filled bags and in tubs or towers. The smallest plot should be able to accommodate a row to produce fruit either in mid-summer or from August to the frost.

There are three main types of strawberry – the ordinary summer-fruiting cultivars, the perpetuals, and the much smaller alpine strawberries.

Dependable Varieties
Summer-fruiting
This is the most widely grown and most popular group, fruiting in June and July. Be sure to buy 'certified' stock – that is guaranteed virus-disease-free plants.

'Cambridge Favourite' is easy to grow and heavy cropping.

'Cambridge Vigour' has good flavour and is good for pot growing.

'Grandee' produces massive berries, crops heavily and has a good flavour.

Perpetual-fruiting
These cultivars carry their crop sporadically over a longer period – from August till October. The so-called 'climbing strawberries' usually belong to this group; the runners need tying up against some form of trellis.

'Gento' is the variety I find most successful. The main plant and its runners crop from August to October. It fruits well into the autumn with cloche or similar protection. Remove the first flowers in May to build up strength for future heavy crops.

Strawberries are always popular, and heavy crops are easily achieved. The berries need the protection of plastic sheeting or straw.

Alpine Strawberries
These are sometimes listed under perpetual fruiters. Varieties like 'Baron Solemacher' carry finger-nail sized berries from June to the frost. The small fruit has rather large woody seeds. Sown in spring it crops the same year.

Cultivation
All well-cultivated soils are suitable, especially if enriched with well-rotted compost. A sunny position is best but they will crop in some shade. Plant in late summer, autumn or spring. Late autumn and spring planted bare root plants will benefit from having the blooms removed in May to build strength for future seasons' crops. Pot-grown runners can be planted later than mid-August and because they suffer no root disturbance will fruit well the following June. Set the plants 12–18 in. (30–45 cm) apart in rows 2 ft (60 cm) apart.

An easy way with strawberries is to plant a single row fairly closely, crop it the first summer, then take at least one good runner from each plant to form a new row, digging the fruited row in afterwards. This prevents perennial weeds becoming established, and masses of runners rooting everywhere. The strawberry then becomes a one-year rotation in the vegetable plot.

Mulching with sheets of polythene is a simple method of cultivation. Strips 2 ft (60 cm) wide are placed down the row. Make two drills in the soil 9 in. (23 cm) each side of where the strawberry plants will go, as if you were sowing seeds, and put the edge of the polythene in the drill and pull back soil to bury the edges. This will give an 18 in. (45 cm) strip, in which you cut crosses where the runners are to be planted.

The strawberries will grow well through the polythene, which suppresses weeds, keeps the fruit clean, stops runners rooting everywhere and gives up to five years of work-free strawberry cropping. Polythene other than black will probably break down in the sunlight after three or four years, but it is inexpensive to replace.

Do not plant strawberries too deeply or too shallowly, but do plant firmly.

Runners on summer-fruiting kinds should be pinched off as soon as they appear unless you intend saving one or two for a new planting. Runners on perpetual-fruiting varieties are left to flower and fruit.

It is beneficial to apply a liquid tomato fertilizer as the berries start to swell to increase fruit size and help build the plant's reserves.

Straw is traditionally used to cover the soil and keep the fruit clean, but polythene sheeting is easier.

Earlier crops can be achieved by using cloches. These offer protection from spring frosts and from birds.

Windowsill growing
If you want to grow strawberries on the windowsill, half-pots of 6 in. (15 cm) diameter are ideal. Use an all-peat potting compost, and pot up runners in early August. Leave the plants outdoors until February, then bring them in and grow like houseplants. Tickle the flowers with a feather when in full bloom to pollinate, then by late April you can be picking ripe berries. Each pot should yield 4–6 oz (100–175 g) of delicious fruit in a reasonable year.

Strawberries are easily propagated from runners, pegged into pots to root. Once rooted and established, the runners can be severed.

Pests and Diseases
Aphids make the leaves sticky.
Botrytis or 'grey mould' causes the fruit to go brown and rotten, the brown subsequently being covered with a furry grey mould. Fungicides like benomyl will achieve control and a polythene mulch reduces damage.
Slugs and snails are sometimes troublesome, but Methiocarb slug pellets will control both these and the strawberry seed beetle, which eats the seeds.

SOFT FRUIT: PEST AND DISEASE CONTROL

Problem	Fruit Affected	Control	When action may be necessary						Notes
			Mar	Apl	May	Jun	Jly	Aug	
Diseases									
Botrytis (grey mould)	Strawberries and cane fruit	benomyl, or dichlofluanid, or thiophanate-methyl, or thiram		●●	●●	●●	●●		
Cane Spot	Raspberries and loganberries	benomyl, or thiophanate-methyl, or thiram		●●	●●	●●			Apply sprays at 14-day intervals
Leaf Spot	Black, red and white currants	benomyl, or thiophanate-methyl, or thiram		●●	●●	●●			Apply sprays at 14-day intervals
Mildew (American gooseberry mildew)	Gooseberries, blackcurrants	benomyl, or dinocap, or thiophanate-methyl			●●	●●	●●		
Spur Blight	Loganberries and raspberries	benomyl, or thiophanate-methyl, or thiram	●	●●	●●				Spray two or three times at 14-day intervals. Start when shoots are ½ in. (1 cm) long
Pests									
Aphis (greenfly)	All soft fruit	malathion or dimethoate or fenitrothion or formothion or rotenone		●●	●●	●●			Spray with tar oil in Dec or Jan, except on strawberries
Big Bud Mite	Blackcurrants	lime sulphur	●●	●●					Some varieties may be damaged by a sulphur spray
Capsid	Currants	malathion or bioresmethrin or dimethoate or fenitrothion or pirimiphos-methyl			●●	●●			
Raspberry Beetle Maggot	Cane fruit	fenitrothion, or malathion, or pirimiphos-methyl, or rotenone				●●			
Sawfly (caterpillars)	Gooseberries	malathion, or bioresmethrin, or fenitrothion or pirimiphos-methyl, or rotenone			●●	●●			

Do not spray with insecticides which may harm bees while the plants are in flower. Otherwise spray at the first sign of attack, when the weather is calm. Dusts are best applied when dew is on the plants as this helps the chemical to stick. It is useful to change the chemicals used each year to avoid a possible build up of resistance in pests and diseases.

Vegetables

The rewards of growing flowers and shrubs are clear to anyone – their beauty and fragrance are enough. Yet vegetables are no less satisfying to grow – a neat, well-kept vegetable plot can do credit to any garden. Many vegetables are attractive enough in their own right, and would not look amiss in a flower border – the foliage of globe artichoke or seakale beet, for instance, is most attractive; even lettuce such as the coppery-leaved 'Continuity' can be effective in a border.

The reason most gardeners grow vegetables is, of course, because they prefer the better taste of home-grown vegetables picked fresh from the garden. The financial gain is an extra benefit.

The wide range of different varieties of vegetable now available to gardeners has also added a great deal to the fun of vegetable growing. Grow new varieties alongside well-proven kinds so that you can gradually assess what best suits your garden conditions and taste.

Few gardeners have perfect site and soil conditions for growing every kind of vegetable, although repeated cultivation and the addition of organic material will do much to improve them. Crops such as potatoes and leeks will also help, in breaking-in heavy soils not previously or recently used for vegetables.

When sowing seed, try to avoid the temptation to sow it too thickly and deeply. Most seeds need no more than a light covering of soil, particularly if the soil is good and moist. In dry conditions, it is worth running some water along the base of the drill before sowing, especially if you are using pelleted seed. Germination depends to some extent on weather conditions and the vegetable in question, but in most cases it takes two or three weeks – longer in cold weather.

No gardener should be deterred

Inexpensive protection can be provided by removing the base from plastic containers.

To make the best use of cloches, plan to grow several suitable crops together.

purely on grounds of space from attempting to grow vegetables – it's quite feasible to grow a selection of vegetables, salads, and herbs in tubs, windowboxes, growing bags and other containers. It is possible to grow a surprisingly wide range of crops that will contribute significantly to the family budget in a plot only 10 ft × 12 ft (3 m × 4 m), as just two items from such a plot show in the table on page 142.

Protected Cropping

Because the greatest saving is achieved by having your own crops ready for picking while the prices in the shops are still high, it is well worth giving some of your plants the benefit of some protection. Cutting your own lettuce for most of the year and harvesting your first beans a few weeks before everyone else also brings its own sense of satisfaction.

Providing suitable protection need not involve much expenditure either – even discarded white and clear plastic containers can make an extremely useful contribution (simply cut out the base, as shown above). These can be used to cover single or small groups of plants, such as radish, but make sure you screw the cut edge into the soil for $\frac{1}{2}$ in. (1 cm) or so to prevent the wind blowing the container away. Remove the cap on the top to ventilate in very hot weather and to apply water. Lettuce grows particularly well under these containers.

Plastic 'tunnel cloches' are inexpensive to buy, and the cost of replacing the polythene covers every couple of years will be well repaid by the increased value of the crops. If you are going to use polythene for garden-crop protection make sure you buy ultra-violet-inhibited polythene sheet. This is usually sold as UVI polythene.

Another simple glass cover can be constructed using a wooden box, merely by removing the base and placing a sheet of glass on top of it. Step up the dimensions and you have a cold-frame. The basis of a frame is just four side walls with a sloping glass or clear plastic-covered roof.

Shelter and protection need not depend on man-made objects – nature provides its own. Hedges and screens positioned in and around suburban gardens naturally break the wind; and the wind-filtering effect of trees, shrubs and hedges is much better than a nearly impenetrable fence (see hedge chapter).

Placing twiggy sticks around early crops such as peas will also give some wind protection, as will wire netting seedling guards.

Crop Rotation

A wise gardener is not content simply to achieve a good crop for a year or two; he looks ahead and by careful planning makes sure his land will stay fertile and disease-free.

It is good, basic gardening practice to rotate crops with one another around a vegetable plot to avoid cropping the same site with the same vegetable or same type of vegetable year after year. Vegetable crops are generally divided into three main groups: root crops, brassicas and the 'others' (see chart). The importance of rotation can be demonstrated by taking greens as an

TYPICAL COST RETURNS

Lettuce		Total Cost
Cost of Seed	0·40	
Peat pots	0·42	
Compost	0·50	
Slug pellets	0·40	Value at retail price 180 lettuces May to November
This crop will require some 'empty container' cloches		

Runner Beans		Total Cost
Cost of Seed	1·50	
Liquid fertiliser	1·50	Value at fresh retail price 18 lb (8 kg) per week
Peat pots	0·42	
Compost	0·50	
Canes	5·00	Value at frozen food price at 0·08 per ¼ lb (120 gms)
(Canes will last at least five years)		

The figures are based on the crop covering a 10 ft × 12 ft (3 m × 4 m) plot and calculated at 1974 prices. The proportion should remain constant today.

example. Greens fall into the brassica group and include broccoli, Brussels sprouts, cabbage, cauliflower, kale and savoy. If these crops are grown year

after year in the same soil, diseases such as club-root will multiply rapidly. If, on the other hand, they are only grown in any one site one year in three, being

Before sowing vegetable seeds break down the soil into a fine tilth.

Use a garden line to ensure that all the drills are drawn straight and neat.

The soil can be removed with either a hoe or a trowel, but avoid sowing deeply.

Always sow the seeds carefully and thinly as this makes thinning easier.

One of the easiest ways to cover the seeds is to shuffle the soil into place.

Firm soil over the seeds by treading and then rake out foot marks.

IDEAL CROP ROTATION

	First Year	Second Year	Third Year
Add compost and/or manure	**OTHER CROPS** Aubergine Peas Beans Peppers Celery Spinach Leeks Sweet Corn Lettuce Tomatoes Onions	Brussels Sprouts Kohl-Rabi Cabbage Radish Cauliflower Swede Kale Turnip Savoy Turnip grown for green foliage Sprouting Broccoli	Artichoke, Jerusalem Beetroot Carrot Chicory Parsnip Potatoes
Add fertiliser	**ROOT CROPS** Artichoke, Jerusalem Beetroot Carrot Chicory Parsnip Potatoes	Aubergine Peas Beans Peppers Celery Spinach Leeks Sweet Corn Lettuce Tomatoes Onions	Brussels Sprouts Kohl-Rabi Cabbage Radish Cauliflower Swede Kale Turnip Savoy Turnip grown for green foliage Sprouting Broccoli
Add fertiliser and lime	**BRASSICAS** Brussels Sprouts Kohl-Rabi Cabbage Radish Cauliflower Swede Kale Turnip Savoy Turnip grown for green foliage Sprouting Broccoli	Artichoke, Jerusalem Beetroot Carrot Chicory Parsnip Potatoes	Aubergine Peas Beans Peppers Celery Spinach Leeks Sweet Corn Lettuce Tomatoes Onions

rotated with the other two groups, the disease is denied its host plant and cannot build up in the soil.

Apart from pests and diseases, the plant food requirements of the various groups of vegetables are different. The peas and beans, technically called legumes, grow with the help of bacteria which take nitrogen from the air and convert it into nitrogenous plant foods. They do this so efficiently that they leave more nitrogenous material in the soil after cropping than was there at the outset. Planting nitrogen-demanding vegetables to follow the legumes allows the full use of this extra nitrogen, thus considerably helping growth as well as saving on nitrogenous fertilizers.

Crop rotation also helps when it comes to applying manure and compost. Crops such as celery, potatoes and runner beans revel in soils which have plenty of freshly dug in, well-rotted animal manure and garden compost. Soils recently enriched in this way are not, however, ideal for root crops such as carrots and parsnips because the roots tend to divide and go several ways in search of the manure. It is much better to allow crops like runner beans to take full advantage of the freshly manured land and then

follow with carrots a season later. Carrots will grow faster and to a larger size in richer and more moisture-retaining soils which contain very well rotted down organic matter.

Although fertilizers can be added to soil at any stage, it is a good idea to apply lime (if it is needed) ahead of brassicas. In a normal rotation scheme this will give the greatest period of time between the application of lime and the planting of potatoes, which are more likely to have their skins marked by scab disease in lime-bearing soils.

As part of good crop rotation, all brassicas should be grown together.

Sowing and Harvesting

When starting to grow vegetables for the first time and at the beginning of each new year it is a help to measure up the plot available and work out where all the different kinds of vegetables you would like to grow will fit. Remember you should rotate the crops, to avoid having one crop in the same position for several years.

It will be necessary to know when each crop will start to require space and when it will be harvested, and this information is given on the chart. For example, if you wish to grow peas and Brussels sprouts, you can see that peas sown in March will be cleared in July, in time to make way for the Brussels sprout plants. This example would also fit conveniently into the basic crop rotation scheme (see previous page), as the pea belongs to the 'other crop' category, while the Brussels sprout is a member of the brassica group of vegetables. Where possible you should try to balance the 'space filling' with the crop rotational requirements.

Apart from its initial use for crop planning, this chart is also valuable at any time of the year as space becomes available in your vegetable plot. If, for example, you have some space in July, running your finger down the sow-outdoors column will show you that you could start off spring cabbage, lettuce, radish, spinach and turnip. Remember, however, that weather can affect crop maturity by a week or so either way.

WHEN TO SOW, PLANT AND HARVEST

Vegetable	Sow outdoors	Sow outdoors under cloches	Sow indoors	Thin	Transplant outdoors	Jan	Feb	Mar	Apr	May	Jun	Jul	Aug	Sep	Oct	Nov	Dec
Artichoke (Globe)	Perennial				April						●	●●	●	●●			
Artichoke (Jerusalem)	Perennial				Autumn or Spring	○○	○○	○○	○○	○○	○			●●●	●○	○○	○○
Asparagus	Perennial				April					●●	●						
Aubergines	—	—	April	—	June								●●	●●●			
Beans (broad)	October	—		—	—						●●	●●	●●				
Beans (broad) (a)	—	—	(a) Jan/Feb	—	(a) March						●●	●●	●●				
(b)	Mar/Apr	—	—	—	—							●●	●●●				
Beans (French)	June	May	—	—	—								●●	●●			
Beans (runner)	May/June	April	—	—	—								●●	●●	●●		
Beetroot	April/June	—	—	May/Jul	—	○○	○○	○○	○		●	●●	●●	●	○○	○○	○○
Broccoli (sprouting)	Apr/May	—	—	—	July/Aug			●●	●●								
Brussels Sprouts	Mar/May	—	—	May/Jun	Jun/Jul	●●	●●	●●						●●	●●	●●	●●
Cabbage (spring)	End July	—	—	—	Sept/Oct			●●	●●	●●	●●						
Cabbage (spring)	Early Aug	—	—	Sept	—			●●	●●	●●	●●						
Cabbage (summer)	—	—	Feb	—	April							●●	●●	●●	●		
Cabbage (summer)	April	—	—	May	—								●●	●●	●●		
Cabbage (winter)	May	—	—	—	July	●●	●●	●●								●●	●●
Cabbage (Savoy)	Mar/April	—	—	—	Jul/Aug	●●	●	●●									●●
Calabrese	Apr/May	—	—	June	—								●●	●●●			
Carrot	Mar/May	—	—	May/June	—	○○	○○	○○	○			●●	●●	●●	●●	○○	
Cauliflower (summer)	Feb/April	—	—	Apr/May	—							●●	●●●				
Cauliflower (summer)(a)	—	Sept	—	—	Mar						●●	●●					
Cauliflower (summer)(b)	—	—	(b) Jan/Feb	—	Mar						●●	●●					
Cauliflower (autumn)	Apr/May	—	—	—	Jun/Jul									●●	●●		
Cauliflower (winter)	May	—	—	—	Jul/Aug				●●	●●							
Celery	—	—	Mar/Apr	—	May/Jun	●									●●	●●	●

Vegetable	Sow outdoors	Sow outdoors under cloches	Sow indoors	Thin	Transplant outdoors	Jan	Feb	Mar	Apr	May	Jun	Jul	Aug	Sep	Oct	Nov	Dec
Celery (self-blanching)	—	—	Feb/Apr	—	Apr/Jun								●	●	●		
Chicory	Apr/May	—	—	June	—	○	○	○	○							○	○
Courgette	—	—	Apr/May	—	June							●	●	●	●		
Cucumber (frame)	—	—	Apr/May	—	June							●	●	●	●	●	
Cucumber (ridge)	—	—	Apr/May	—	June							●	●	●	●		
Kale	Apr/May	—	—	—	Jun/Jul	●	●	●	●	●	●					●	●
Kohl-rabi	Mar/Aug	—	—	As reqd	—								●	●	●	●	
Leek	Mar/Apr	—	—	—	May/Jun	●	●	●	●	●						●	●
Lettuce	Mar/Sep	—	—	As reqd	—					●	●	●	●	●	●		
Marrow	—	—	Apr/May	—	June							●	●	●	●		
Melon	—	—	May	—	June								●	●			
Mustard and Cress	All Year	—	—	—	—	●	●	●	●	●	●	●	●	●	●	●	●
Okra	May	Late Apr	—	June	—								●	●	●		
Onion (spring)	Aug–Spring	—	—	—	—	●	●	●	●	●	●	●					
Onion (Japanese)	Aug	—	—	Mar	—	○	○	○	○	○	●	●	●	○	○	○	○
Onion (bulb)	Aug–Spring	—	—	April	—	○	○	○	○	○	○	●	●	●	●	○	○
Onion (sets)	—	—	—	—	Mar/Apr	○	○	○	○	○	○	●	●	●	●	○	○
Parsnip	Feb/Mar	—	—	May	—	○	○	○	○	○	○					●	●
Peas (round)	Oct/Mar	—	—	—	—						●	●					
Peas (wrinkled)	Apr/Jun	—	—	—	—							●	●				
Peppers	—	—	April	—	June								●	●	●		
Potatoes	—	—	—	—	Mar/Apr	○	○	○	○	○	○	●	●	●	●	○	○
Pumpkin	—	—	Apr/May	June	June									●	●		
Radish	Mar/Aug	—	—	—	—						●	●	●	●	●	●	
Rhubarb	March	—	—	—	—			●	●	●	●	●					
Shallots	—	—	—	—	Jan/Mar	○	○	○	○	○	○	●	●	●	○	○	○
Spinach (summer)	Feb/May	—	—	As reqd	—					●	●	●	●	●	●		
Spinach (winter)	Jul/Sep	—	—	As reqd	—	●	●	●								●	●
Spinach (perpetual)	Apr/Jul	—	—	As reqd	—	●	●	●	●	●	●		●	●	●	●	●
Swede	May	—	—	June	—	○	○	○	○					●	●	●	○
Sweet Corn	—	—	Apr/May	June	May								●	●			
Tomato	—	—	Apr	—	June							●	●	●	●		
Turnip (roots)	Apr/Aug	—	—	As reqd	—	○	○	○	○	○	●	●	●	●	●	○	○
Turnip (leaves)	Sept	—	—	—	—											●	●

Key: ▓ Perennials ▓ Brassicas ●●●● Harvesting
▓ Root Crops ▒ Other Crops ○○○○ Storing

The large central flower bud of globe artichokes should be cut first, using secateurs. Cut when the buds are plump and fully swollen.

ARTICHOKE

Apart from sharing a name and the fact that they are both perennial vegetables the globe and Jerusalem artichokes have little in common and are best considered separately.

Globe Artichoke

The large globe-shaped flower buds produced by these plants are cut to provide a delectable vegetable. The plant produces very attractively divided silvery-grey leaves.

To grow this crop well, choose a

Lift tubers of Jerusalem artichokes as required. 'Fuseau' is smooth-skinned.

sheltered sunny site, dig the soil well, and add well-rotted, compost and/or manure. Avoid heavy, wet soils.

Plant young suckers (the side shoots growing around the main stem) in April, in the cropping site 2–2½ ft (60–75 cm) apart. Firm in well.

Give the newly planted offsets plenty of water in dry weather until they are well established, and hoe occasionally to eliminate weeds. In early winter, when the leaves start to die down, cut away the old flower stems and tie the younger leaves up together before drawing soil up round the stems.

Apply a general fertilizer in spring at the rate of 2–3 oz per sq yd (60–85 g per sq m) and mulch with well-rotted manure or compost to improve growth.

Start cropping established plants in July, when the flower buds are plump and fully swollen and before the scales have hard brown tips. Cut with secateurs, taking the large central, or 'king', globe first.

The best crops occur in the second and third year – after this, plant out more suckers to replace three-year-old plants.

Jerusalem Artichoke

This plant is grown for its tubers, which are like knobbly potatoes. The stems grow 6–8 ft (1·8–2·5 m) high and are perfect for a quick summer screen.

Full sun or sun and partial shade provide suitable sites for this crop, and any soil will yield tubers, although better soils produce heavier crops.

Plant the tubers from February onwards, 3–6 in. (7·5–15 cm) deep, 15 in. (38 cm) apart.

During the season, hoe to eliminate weeds and pinch out tips to prevent flower buds developing.

ASPARAGUS

Select an open sunny site and well-drained soil for asparagus. Light soils tending to be sandy are ideal; add sand to very heavy soils to improve drainage. Dig the soil very thoroughly in the autumn to remove all perennial weed roots, and add as much well-rotted garden compost and manure as you can.

You can raise plants from seed, but it is more common to buy one- or two-year-old seedlings (called one-year and two-year 'asparagus crowns') in April. If you have to delay planting them for a few days, store in damp peat.

Dig out a trench 8–10 in. (20–25 cm) deep and 12 in. (30 cm) wide. Then form a shallow ridge 3 in. (7·5 cm) high at the base. Space the crowns 15–18 in. (38–45 cm) apart with the string-like roots spread over both sides of the ridge. Then cover them with 2–3 in. (5–7·5 cm) of soil and subsequently, when hoeing to control weeds, slowly fill up the trench with soil. Space the rows 4–5 ft (1·2–1·5 m) apart if you are growing more than one row.

Each autumn and spring, earth up the rows by drawing 1–2 in. (2·5–5 cm) of soil each side of the row.

Asparagus crowns should be planted on a slight ridge in a prepared trench.

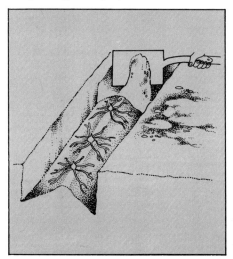

Sprinkle general fertilizer along the row in spring at the rate of 2–3 oz. per sq yd (60–85 g per sq m). Mulch with well-rotted compost after mid-June.

If the greyish grubs of the asparagus beetle are a problem, dust or spray with derris.

A year after planting out, one spear can be cut from each crown. The following year all the spears can be cut over a four-week period, and in the third year (when plants are four to five years old) spears can be cut for six weeks. Stop all cutting by mid-June.

Cut the spears when they are 4–6 in. (10–15 cm) above the soil, and always cut before the tip starts to open into

The Longpod varieties of broad bean are hardy and produce heavy yields.

French beans are popular vegetables that yield a heavy crop – but the beans must be picked regularly to avoid old stringy pods developing.

foliage-producing shoots. Cut about 2–4 in. (5–10 cm) below the surface.

BEANS
There are two main types of broad bean available – White Seeded and Green Seeded. The green seeded are said to be better flavoured, but all are delicious gathered young. These two types can be further divided into two groups, the Longpod types which include the hardy varieties for autumn and winter sowing, and the Windsor type, which is not so hardy and therefore should be sown in spring. The Windsor varieties have only about four beans per pod compared with six to nine beans yielded by the Longpods.

All garden sites and soil will give reasonable results, but try to choose a site sheltered from cold winds for autumn and early spring crops grown without protection.

Sow broad beans 2 in. (5 cm) deep in the open garden in late October or early November, and from February to April. Space 9–12 in. (23–30 cm) apart in double rows with 18 in.–2 ft (45–60 cm) between them. Early sow-

ings not only give earlier crops but often the heaviest yields as well.

The stronger-growing early sown Longpod types may need the support of a few canes pushed into the soil both sides of the row, with string run around to hold up the plants.

Blackfly are often a nuisance on the growing tips in mid-summer, but you can control them by pinching out the growing tips as the blackfly arrive.

Dwarf French Beans
An open sunny site will give the best crops and any well-cultivated garden soil will suit French beans. Dwarf French beans grow well in containers. Try growing them in plant tubs, in growing bags, or in pots on terraces, balconies, back yards and roof gardens.

Time the first sowing so that when the first tender shoots poke through there is no more possibility of frost.

Set the seeds to give five plants per foot of row (16 per metre), and space rows 16 in. (41 cm) apart.

During the season, hoe occasionally to keep down weeds and in hot dry weather water the plants well and also

syringe them from overhead. If flowers fall without forming beans, dryness is the most likely cause.

Runner Beans
Runner beans will grow in partial shade, but an open sunny site is best. They will crop in all well-dug garden soils, but the more organic matter in the form of peat, well-rotted compost and manure dug into the soil to retain moisture, the heavier will be the crop.

Sow the seeds 1–2 in. (2·5–5 cm) deep, where they are to grow, a week or so before the likely date of your last frost in spring. Sow enough seeds to give four plants per 3 ft (1 m) of row. Early beans are produced by raising seeds in pots indoors and planting out after the possibility of frost has passed.

It is possible to grow runner beans unsupported like dwarf beans, if you pinch out the growing tips every time they exceed 12–18 in. (30–45 cm), but beans grown this way trail in the soil and are often curled and splashed with soil when gathered. Where possible it is better to grow them up some form of support. Give strengthening to canes

147

Calabrese is a prolific vegetable, cropped over a long period. Once the central head has been harvested smaller heads develop.

Spinach beet is a hardy vegetable grown for its leaves and not for the root.

and bean poles used to support a double row of runner beans by tying the tops of a few together.

See that these plants never lack moisture. When the first flowers appear, water regularly (every seven to ten days) with dilute liquid fertilizer and cover the surface of the soil with well-rotted compost or peat to retain moisture. Syringing the leaves and flowers during hot weather helps the flowers to set.

Runner beans can be grown in peat-filled growing bags with cane supports.

Runner beans should be picked at least twice a week, when the pods are 10 in. (25 cm) or more long.

BEET
Any site, except those which are heavily shaded, and all well-dug garden soils are suitable for growing beet. It really thrives best, however, in hot, light soils.

Each knobbly piece from the seed packet is in fact a cluster of seeds and not just one seed. Space these clusters 2–3 in. (5–7.5 cm) apart down the row, 1 in. (2.5 cm) deep with 9–15 in. (23–38 cm) between the rows. Sow at regular intervals till early July to provide a succession of young roots.

Take care when selecting varieties for sowing before April, and choose bolt-resistant varieties like 'Avonearly' and 'Boltardy'.

Single out the seedlings if more than one grows at each station, otherwise just hoe to keep down weeds.

BROCCOLI
In the past broccoli was the name used to describe the more hardy forms of white winter cauliflower as well as sprouting broccoli. The current practice is to restrict the name to the sprouting forms. Kales have been linked with broccolis because the more recent types are similar in their growing habit and culinary use.

While green, purple and white sprouting broccolis and kale all require similar cultural treatment, it is the green sprouting broccoli (also called calabrese and commercially sold in frozen form as broccoli spears), which starts off the cropping from midsummer to winter. Varieties are coming which can be sown in late September to crop the following May or June. The kales then take over and survive the toughest weather to provide fresh green vegetables through the winter and spring, to be followed by the white, the early purple and the late purple sprouting broccoli, which may be picked from early spring to early summer.

When looking for kale in the seed catalogues, also look out for its other names – early kale and borecole.

The kales will stand very exposed conditions but choose a more sheltered site for the broccolis, and remember they form very large plants. Good, well-cultivated soils are best, but avoid freshly dug soil when planting out in early and mid-summer.

Sow in shallow drills ½–1 in. (1–2.5 cm) deep, 6–9 in. (15–23 cm) apart in April and May. Plant out the resulting seedlings in the cropping site when they are big enough to handle, 20–30 in. (50–75 cm) apart. Rows should also be spaced . 20–30 in. (50–75 cm) apart. You can plant out calabrese more closely if you want to produce an abundance of small spears for freezing.

Stout growth is needed to withstand winter weather, so be sure the plants are well firmed to achieve this. When dibbing out, put the plant stems well down in the soil – this will improve the plant's anchorage and help it to withstand strong winds. The only other cultural treatment necessary is occasional hoeing to control weeds, and watering in dry weather.

All these plants are very easy to grow and are generally trouble-free, but club-root and cabbage root fly are possible problems. You can achieve chemical control of these by dusting the plant roots with calomel for club-root and by dusting the soil with either bromophos or a similar soil pesticide for root fly. Pick off by hand the green caterpillars of cabbage white butterfly should they occur, or spray the plants with derris.

BRUSSELS SPROUTS

The key to producing quality crops of this popular winter vegetable is to select hybrid varieties to grow on fertile soils, from which you pick sprouts while they are small and firm.

Sow under cover very early in spring for the earliest crops which will be ready from September onwards. Follow this with the main sowing outdoors in shallow drills 1 in. (2·5 cm) deep and 6 in. (15 cm) apart in March or April. The cropping chart shows how the season can be extended by careful selection of varieties.

Water the seedlings well before lifting and transplanting into the cropping site from May to early July. Hoe occasionally to destroy weeds until the leaves cover the soil and naturally smother weed growth. During very dry weather help growth by watering well and giving liquid fertilizer.

If whitefly are a problem, spray the plants with an insecticide. Pick off the green caterpillars of cabbage white butterflies or spray with derris.

CABBAGES AND SAVOYS

Cabbages and savoys are very easy crops to grow, but it is very important to select varieties from the right group for any one time of year, and the cropping chart overleaf will make this easy.

Most sites and just about all garden soils are suitable. In the very poorest soils and heavily overshadowed sites, cabbages may not produce very good hearts. Dusting the soil with lime for cabbage and other brassica crops is advisable on all but chalky and limestone soils.

Be guided by the cropping chart for sowing times – even if your particular variety is not mentioned you will know from the seed packet or catalogue when it should mature and you can work back from there.

Perfect stems packed with sprouts are normal on F_1 hybrid varieties of Brussels sprouts. Such varieties require fertile soils and plenty of water.

BRUSSELS SPROUTS CROPPING CHART

Variety (Cultivar) Examples		Sowing Date	Aug	Sept	Oct	Harvesting Nov	Dec	Jan	Feb	Mar
Early	Peer Gynt, F1	Sow under glass February Transplant April	●	●	●					
Mid to Late	Prince Askold, F1 Vremo Inter	Sow under glass early March and outside late March Transplant April/ May				●	●	●		
Late	Fasolt, F1	Sow early April outside Transplant May/June Also sow direct, no transplanting early May						●	●	●

(1) For the longest cropping period choose early, mid-season and late varieties (as per examples given above). Seasonal conditions will affect the cropping period and most varieties crop beyond the stated period.

(2) Where grown for freezing stop the plants by pinching out the growing tip when basal sprouts are ½ in (1 cm) diameter. This will help all sprouts to mature at once and allow ground to be cleared. Do not stop after September.

Sow about ½ in. (1 cm) deep, in beds or drills as advised on the packet.

The tender early plants raised under glass for summer use are soft and will need careful planting with a trowel. Dib in the outdoor raised plants as for other brassicas. Space summer-maturing plants 18–24 in. (45–60 cm) apart with the same distance between rows.

You should aim to get the young spring-maturing plants well estab-

Work a little fertilizer into the soil around spring-maturing cabbage plant.

CABBAGES AND SAVOYS CROPPING CHART

Variety Examples	Sowing Date	Planting Out	Jan Feb	Mar Apr	May Jun	Jul Aug	Sept Oct	Nov Dec
*Celtic Cross F1,	May	June–July	● ●	●				
Savoy Ormskirk	April/May	June–July	● ●	●				
*Wheelers Imperial (Spring maturing cabbage can also be cut as greens during this period.)	Late July	September			● ●			
Golden Acre (round) Greyhound (pointed)	Jan/Feb under glass	March–April				●		
*Gold Acre (round) Greyhound (pointed)	Early April	Thin out when ready				●		
Golden Acre (round) Greyhound (pointed)	Late April	Thin out when ready				●		
Golden Acre (round) Greyhound (pointed)	Mid May	Thin out when ready					●	
Winnigstadt	Late May	Thin out when ready					●	
*Christmas Drum Head	April	June/July						● ●

Sow 10–14 days earlier if plants shown to be thinned out are transplanted.
*Cultivars equal to these 4 sown at these times will provide cabbage the year round.

lished before the onset of winter. Spacing 6 in. (15 cm) apart in the row allows you to cut every second and/or third plant while still immature as 'spring greens'. Space the rows 15–24 in. (38–60 cm) apart.

Space winter-hearting cabbages 15–24 in. (38–60 cm) apart in the row, the rows 18–24 in. (45–60 cm) apart. Firm planting is advisable for these winter-hearting cabbages.

Caterpillars should be dealt with as described for broccoli.

Swollen knobbly roots are caused by the disease club-root. Attack can be reduced by dipping the plants in dust or paste of calomel. Alternatively raise plants in pots of sterile potting compost and plant out with root-ball intact to grow acceptable crops.

The small white maggots of the cabbage root fly may eat the roots. Pull up plants that wilt in hot weather, and if you find these white maggots, destroy the plants. If you know this pest occurs in your garden treat the roots with calomel dust or dip before planting them out.

You may notice neat round holes in the first two seedling leaves, caused by flea beetle, which is easily controlled by dusting the seedlings with BHC (HCH).

Control aphids and whitefly as soon as you see them by spraying with resmethrin.

CARROTS

Only very heavily shaded sites cause difficulties in growing carrots and all garden soils will yield reasonable crops, although ideally the soil should be light and sandy for the straightest roots.

Sow the earliest crops under cloches in February, and follow with outdoor sowings as soon as soil conditions are suitable. It is better to delay sowing than to sow when the soil is cold, wet and too sticky. Sow in shallow drills ½–1 in. (1–2·5 cm) deep and just cover the seeds with soil. Space the rows 9–12 in. (23–30 cm) apart. Make several regular sowings from March to July, to give a succession.

Thin the seedlings to stand 1 in. (2·5 cm) or so apart. When they are large enough to handle, this will allow you to pull either every other, or every two-in-three, carrots from the stage when they reach finger thickness. Leave the remaining carrots to reach maincrop size. Hoe regularly between plants and rows. If your carrots do not grow as quickly as you would like, water the foliage with a foliar feed from time to time.

Carrot fly is the only problem you are likely to experience. The adult flies lay eggs in May and June and a second brood in July and August. The eggs hatch to produce small maggots which tunnel into the roots. Wilting leaves and the change of leaf colour from

Carrot shapes – from l. to r. top row: Round, Slender Nantes, Amsterdam Forcing, Autumn King, Intermediate, Long; bottom: Larger Nantes, Early Nantes, Chantenay.

green to reddish shades are signs of attack. Guard against carrot fly by working bromophos or diazinon granules into the soil at sowing time.

CAULIFLOWER

The name broccoli was traditionally given to white hearting cauliflower cultivars which were hardy enough to grow outside through the winter. Standardization of names has now brought all except purple sprouting broccoli under the name cauliflower.

Seed catalogues list a quite bewildering range of varieties, and the cropping chart below will simplify the job of selecting cauliflowers for all seasons. However, in all except the warmest, virtually frost-free areas, December- to March-maturing varieties are best avoided.

Select an open, sunny site for all except the winter and early spring maturing kinds (these need some shelter from cold winds). Well cultivated soils, which you can further improve by adding plenty of well-rotted organic matter, give rapid growth and good-sized 'curds'. If the soil is not chalky and alkaline, give it a dusting of lime.

For sowing times, be guided by the cropping chart below and by instructions on the seed packet.

Plant out early varieties in the

Cabbage root fly cause brassica crops to wilt in hot weather and die.

cropping site 18 in. (45 cm) apart from March onwards. If cold, uncomfortable conditions cause a check to growth, turning the plants bluish-green, apply liquid fertilizer or hoe in nitrate of soda or sulphate of ammonia at the rate of 1 oz per sq yd (30 g per sq m).

Transplant late varieties to the cropping site in June or July. Leave 20–24 in. (50–60 cm) between plants and between rows. As the curds develop break the mid-rib of a few

large leaves and fold these outer leaves over the cauliflower head to keep it beautifully white.

The problems are generally the same as those under CABBAGE, but in addition a shortage of boron occasionally occurs in soils, causing the leaves to grow narrow and turn brown. The cauliflowers will be bitter. Correct this by hoeing a dusting of borax into the soil. The correct proportions are 1 oz to 60 sq yd (30 g to 50 sq m).

CELERY

Most garden sites are suitable for celery, but a deeply dug, rich soil is needed for the best results. Cultivate plenty of well-rotted organic matter into the soil ahead of sowing celery. This is especially necessary for blanched types; the self-blanching types are not quite so demanding.

Ideally all types should be sown under glass in spring, preferably in mid-March or April. Make two sowings, one early and one late, to extend the cropping period.

Sow in seed compost, in a temperature of at least 50 °F (10 °C). When seedlings are just large enough to handle transplant them into boxes filled with potting compost. Once established you can grow them under cloches, for transplanting into the cropping site in May or June.

All self-blanching kinds can be planted in a square block of several rows. The inner plants will become more blanched and better to eat than those growing in the outside and in single rows. The smaller plants are when transplanted the less likely they are to run prematurely to seed. Set out plants 9–12 in. (23–30 cm) apart in both directions. Once established, hoe in a general fertilizer at 1 oz per sq yd (30 g per sq m), and water well in dry weather.

Varieties which need blanching should be planted in trenches, setting the plants 6 in. (15 cm) apart in the base of the trench in May or June.

Celery varieties which need blanching can also be grown on the surface of the soil without trenching, either by earthing-up like potatoes or by placing a wooden board on each side of the row and filling with peat.

You can begin blanching when the leaves are 12–15 in. (30–38 cm) high. Always leave the green leaves exposed and increase the height of blanching up the stem in stages over several weeks.

Brown spots on the leaves are caused by celery leaf spot fungus, which can be

CAULIFLOWER CROPPING CHART

Variety Examples	Sowing Date	Planting Out	Jan Feb	Mar Apr	May Jun (Harvesting)	Jul Aug	Sept Oct	Nov Dec
Winter Hardy Varieties								
St George, Summer Snow, Late Queen*	May–June Outdoors	July–August		●	● ● / ● ●			
Early Varieties Summer Maturing								
Dominant	Sow under cloches early October	March Sow direct				● ●		
Snowball*	Sow heated glass in Jan	April					● ●	
Le Cerf	March under glass	April/May				● ●		
Autumn Maturing (Australian Cauliflowers)								
Kangaroo*	Outdoors April/ May in succession for extended cropping	June/July					● ●	●
Snowcap							●	● ●
December–March Maturing for Coastal Areas and Sites with Mild Winters								
Roscoff Cauliflower								
Angers No. 2	Mid May	August	● ●					
St Hilary	Mid May	August	● ●	● ●				●
* Three varieties to give cauliflowers from late April to November.								

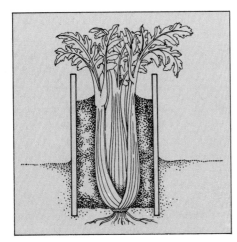

Blanching celery by filling between boards with peat keeps stems clean.

controlled with sprays of Bordeaux mixture or maneb or zineb.

Celery fly or leaf miner may cause trouble and you can identify these by brown blisters which appear on the leaves from May. Pick off infected leaf parts and pinch to destroy the small larvae which tunnel between the two surfaces of the leaves. Where attacks persist spray with malathion.

CELERIAC
Celeriac, or 'turnip-rooted celery', considerably extends the fresh celery season as it may be lifted and stored well into the winter.

Sow as for celery, or alternatively plants may be bought in May or June.

Draw out a deep drill and plant out in the base 9–12 in. (23–30 cm) apart. The drill makes subsequent watering easier as growth and succulence is dependent on ample moisture. Space the rows 15–18 in. (38–45 cm) apart. Hoe to control weeds, and remove side shoots which may develop.

CHICORY
The plump, cream and white forced shoots of chicory, called 'chicons', provide succulent, crisp salad in winter.

Any site is suitable provided it is not in heavy shade, and any well cultivated soil will grow chicory. The F_1 hybrid varieties are easier to force.

Sow in rows in the garden in April or May, just covering the seed with soil. Single out the seedlings to 2–3 in. (5–7·5 cm) for F_1 hybrid varieties, and 6 in. (15 cm) for 'Witloof', as soon as they are large enough to separate easily. Space the rows 15–18 in. (38–45 cm) apart.

The F_1 hybrids such as Normato (early), Mitado (mid-season) and Tardivo (late) are worth trying. The smaller roots of the F_1 hybrids allow the closer spacing of 2–3 in. (5–7·5 cm).

Hoe occasionally to kill weeds and in very dry weather give a few heavy waterings to help to swell the roots.

When the leaves start to turn yellow

Celeriac is also known as turnip-rooted celery. It can be stored for use throughout the winter.

in October or November and before there is a hard frost, lift the roots. Holding the root in one hand twist off the leaves with the other and cut or snap off the thin root end to give plump roots 8 in. (20 cm) long. Store these in a box of dry peat or sand in a cool, frost-free place.

From December to March put five or six roots upright in an 8 in. (20 cm) diameter flower pot, packing damp sand, light soil or peat around the roots. Invert a size larger pot and cover the holes. Keep the soil moist, and in a temperature of 50°F (10°C) and every root will form a chicon in approximately three to four weeks.

Witloof roots need covering with several inches of sand rather than the inverted pot.

CHINESE CABBAGE
Chinese cabbage flourishes in similar sites to other cabbage crops, but a soil improved by the addition of well-rotted organic matter is essential to retain moisture.

Sow direct in the cropping site in early July, just covering the seed with soil. Thin the seedlings to 9–12 in. (23–30 cm) apart, in rows spaced 12–15 in. (30–38 cm) apart.

Make sure the plants do not lack moisture at the roots during hot weather. Otherwise just hoe occasionally to control weeds. This crop grows well in polythene-covered greenhouses.

Good firm heads will be ready in late autumn. The heads may be boiled in the same way as cabbage, but they have

The forced shoots of chicory are known as chicons. The roots before forcing can be seen in the foreground. Chicons are produced in three or four weeks.

Chinese cabbage is becoming better known. It has a milder flavour than cabbage.

a much milder flavour. Alternatively, the leaf ribs of outer leaves may be cooked like asparagus or seakale and the hearts may be shredded and used raw for salads.

CUCUMBER

The long smooth-skinned cucumbers sold in the shops all the year round are varieties only suited to growing in a greenhouse or frame. For outdoors, look for seed marked 'Ridge Cucumber' or 'Outdoor Cucumber'. Gherkins are grown in just the same way as ridge cucumbers.

A well-rotted compost heap in a sheltered, sunny position is ideal for ridge cucumbers. Alternatively plant in a sunny sheltered site and in soil which you have improved by adding plenty of well-rotted organic matter.

Sow outdoor varieties in pots indoors in April or early May, or outside under cloches in the cropping site in mid-May or early June. Plant out 3–4 ft (1–1·2 m) apart in late May or early June, after any danger of frost if cloche protection is not available.

Let the plants run and give occasional liquid feeds and plenty of water in dry weather. Although it is not essential, it is best to stop the main stem at six to eight leaves, thus encouraging the side shoots to develop.

Be sure to retain the male flowers on ridge cucumbers. Cross pollination is essential in these plants and some hand fertilization (i.e. taking the male flower, removing the petals and placing the pollen-bearing parts in the mouth of the female flower) will help to set fruit.

Indoor varieties of cucumber can be grown in pots on the windowsill. Choose short jointed all female varieties, like 'Fembaby' F_1, for this.

Put a piece of glass or wood under developing cucumbers to keep them clean.

ENDIVE

There are two main types of endive – the Batavian type, which resembles a cos lettuce, and the curled type, which has divided and curled leaves.

All garden sites and any well-cultivated garden soils are suitable.

Take a chance on sowing in April to provide a summer crop, but choose one of the curled-leaf varieties. You will, however, obtain more successful crops from sowings of the hardy Batavian type in late June to early August to mature in the winter. Sow in rows 12–15 in. (30–38 cm) apart, where you want the crops to mature.

Thin the seedlings to stand 12–15 in. (30–38 cm) apart. Hoe occasionally to control weeds and apply a top dressing of nitrogenous fertilizer or liquid feed to encourage rapid growth.

When the plants are well developed either cover with an upturned flower pot or place a square of light board over the centre of the plant. This blanches the leaves over a period of three to six weeks according to speed of growth and makes them more succulent and less bitter to taste. Winter crops can be covered with black polythene tunnels.

Endive Moss Curled and Seakale Beet (left) which crops well into the winter.

Leeks are a useful winter vegetable and are quite easy to grow. The fibrous roots also help to break up heavy soil.

KOHL-RABI

Pretty well any site is suitable for kohl-rabi, as long as it is not too overshadowed or dry. Any well-cultivated garden soil will suit.

Sow any time from March to early August, and for a succession of crops sow two or three batches over this period.

Dust acid soils with lime before sowing. Other than this just hoe

The attractive roots of kohl-rabi are best eaten while still small.

occasionally to destroy weeds and water well, ideally with some liquid fertilizer, in very dry weather.

Club-root can attack these crops and control is the same as for cabbage.

LEEKS

Most sites, except those which are heavily shaded, and all well-cultivated soils are suitable for leeks.

Sow early in the year, in February or March, under cover to get the earliest and largest blanched stems. An outdoor sowing in March or April will provide adequate crops, however. Transplant early seedlings into the cropping site in May, and the outdoor raised plants in June. Space plants 9 in. (23 cm) apart in the row, and the rows 12–15 in. (30–38 cm) apart.

When transplanting, use a dibber to make a good hole 1 in. (2·5 cm) or more in diameter and 6–8 in. (15–20 cm) deep, drop the young plant into this and water it in. There is no need to fill back any soil.

Water with a dilute liquid fertilizer in dry weather. When hoeing, draw soil up round the stem a little at a time to lengthen the blanched stem. Cut back big old leaves by half as this will encourage a greater length of blanched stem.

Should orange dusty spots occur on

the leaves, lift plants and destroy leaves (the stem will be edible).

LETTUCE

There are four main groups of lettuce varieties – the rounded cabbage types which are further subdivided into soft leaved or butterhead; the curly crisp types; the upright cos lettuce; and finally the open-hearted cut-leaved or oak-leaved types. All require similar cultural conditions although many varieties have specific seasons for sowing and harvesting which are best followed for assured crops.

Seed catalogues will list many varieties, which may appear bewildering. If in doubt, try the varieties listed in the chart on the opposite page.

Whichever kind you grow, dig all the organic matter you can obtain into the soil. As they are shallow-rooted plants it is not necessary to dig the compost deep into the ground. Avoid sites which are heavily shaded by trees overhead and where there is competition from tree roots for moisture.

By careful selection of varieties and sowing at suitable times, and with some protection available, it is possible to harvest lettuce for most of the year. The cropping chart opposite should be your guide to the sowing time for each kind.

It is important to sow summer varieties little and often. Try to avoid transplanting lettuce in mid-summer.

Final spacing depends to some extent on variety, but 8–12 in. (20–30 cm) apart is about right for most kinds.

Cabbage lettuce Butterhead (top), Cos lettuce (centre), Oak-leaved lettuce (bottom).

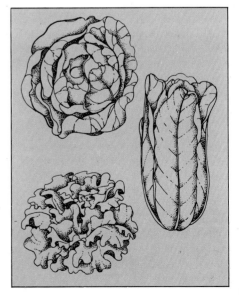

LETTUCE CROPPING CHART

Type/Variety Examples	Sowing Date	Harvesting	Jan Feb	Mar Apr	May Jun	Jul Aug	Sept Oct	Nov Dec
Cabbage Butterhead								
Cobham Green, Suzan	Sow indoors mid January/February	Plant out under cloches/tunnels			• • •			
	Sow every 14 days in March–May outside				•	• •		
Amanda, Dandie	Sow under polythene in October			• •	•			
Avondefiance*	Sow from June to mid August outside	Protect with cloches in early winter to extend crop				•	• •	•
Kordaat*, Kloek	Sow and grow in heated greenhouse end September–October			• •	•			
				• •	•			
Cabbage Crisp								
Windermere*	Sow outdoors under cloches in October	Sow indoors mid January–February			• •			
Great Lakes, Windermere	Sow outdoors March–mid June				•	• •	•	
					•	• •	•	
Avoncrisp	Sow outdoors in mid June–mid August	Protect crop in early winter				•	• •	•
Cos								
Winter Density*	Sow mid September–October under cloches	Sow outside April–mid July			• •	• •	• •	•
Lobjoits Green	Sow outside mid March to mid June					•	• •	•

* These varieties will give year round cropping.

Thin cos type so that they are 9 in. (23 cm) apart and with 12 in. (30 cm) between the rows.

Water the plants well in dry weather, giving them an occasional good soaking, rather than repeated light waterings. Give liquid fertilizer in dry weather to speed growth.

Most cos lettuces need no special treatment, but very large-leaved kinds like the 'Lobjoits Green Cos' will form the densest blanched hearts if you tie in the outer leaves with raffia or string.

Slugs and birds can be major problems at certain times – but slug bait for one and black cotton stretched between twigs for the other should afford protection.

MARROWS AND COURGETTES

One of the easiest and perhaps one of the fastest-growing of our garden vegetables is that known as summer squash to Americans, marrow to the British, and when cut very young courgette to the French.

Sunny sites and those with partial shade are suitable for marrow although too much shade is bad. An open soil containing plenty of well-rotted compost and manure to retain moisture is the ideal.

These plants will also grow very well planted on the top of well decomposed compost heaps or heaps of rotted down leaves or lawn mowings.

Sow seed in 3½ in. (9 cm) pots – two to a pot – in early May. Single out the seedlings as soon as possible and transplant the young plants to the cropping site in early June when there is no more likelihood of frost.

An alternative method is to sow three seeds direct in each cropping site in late May, so they are timed to emerge immediately after any possibility of frost.

Keep the plants very well watered in dry weather. These plants produce

Marrow 'Green Bush' is prolific and young fruits can be cut as courgettes.

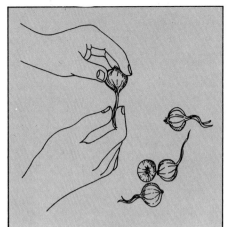

Twist off the strawy tip before planting onion sets, to stop birds pulling them up.

male and female flowers and if you cross-pollinate them by hand, it will increase cropping.

Watch out for slugs and put down slug bait if this becomes necessary.

Cut courgettes when the fruits are 4–5 in. (10–12·5 cm) long. Nearly all of the marrow varieties are best harvested while still young. Test them for tenderness by pushing your thumb nail into one rib of the marrow close to the stalk. If your nail slips in easily the marrow is still young enough to eat.

ONIONS AND SHALLOTS

The easiest way to make sure you have a continuous supply of cooking onions is to plant sets. Given reasonably fine, crumbly soil at sowing time they can also be grown from seed.

All varieties of onions may be sown to pull young as salad onions, but if you want them specifically for this purpose the special varieties like 'White Lisbon' are best.

There really is no easier crop to grow than onions from sets. Just push these small bulbs into cultivated soil from February to April, hoe occasionally to control weeds and then harvest the bulbs.

Shallots are much larger than onion sets, but they require exactly the same treatment. They store longer than many crops of onions and to the gourmet are the perfect seasoning for many dishes. Each planted shallot will grow and multiply to produce four to eight new shallots.

A well-cultivated garden soil and an open sunny site are required for these crops. The better the soil the bigger the bulbs.

The most popular sowing date for onions is from late February to early April, the right time being when you

155

can rake down the soil and draw out a very shallow drill.

Mid-August is the next sowing time, but for this you must choose the 'overwintering varieties'. These have names like 'Express Yellow', 'Presto', 'Tropic Ace' and 'Sen-shyu'. These varieties produce sturdy plants by the winter and the bulbs are ready to pull in June and early July.

You can also sow ordinary bulb onion varieties out of doors in late September to overwinter on the cropping site. This provides the longest growing season, and gives big bulbs, but the overwintering losses can be quite high. It is usually more acceptable to sow indoors from December to early February for exhibition onions, growing the young seedlings under cold glass and planting them out on the cropping site in March.

Salad onions should be sown in very shallow drills in rows as close as 6 in. (15 cm) once a month from March to September to give salad onions the year round.

Plant onion sets in March. Either draw out a very shallow drill, space the bulbs along it and cover with soil, or push them very gently into the soil until they are just covered. Space the bulbs 6 in. (15 cm) apart and the rows 9–12 in. (23–30 cm) apart.

Shallots should be planted as early as possible, February not being too early in mild weather.

Once seedlings are showing and established, the onions from seed need spacing in two stages to 4–5 in. (10–12·5 cm) apart. Gaps can be filled by transplanting thinned-out plants.

Small maggots attacking the roots of onions are likely to be the larvae of onion fly, a pest which is most prevalent on dry, light soils. Lift and burn any infected plants and treat the seed rows with diazinon granules.

PARSNIPS

Avoid heavily overshadowed sites for parsnips. All ordinary garden soils will produce worthwhile crops, but those which have been well dug in the autumn and have had rotted organic matter added for previous crops are best.

Sow any time from late February to April, when the soil surface is reasonably dry and crumbly. Get good germination by starting the seed into growth indoors on damp tissue. Be sure to sow outside as soon as the tiny roots start to show. Space the rows so that

Lift parsnips in spring before new growth starts and store them in dry peat.

they are 12–15 in. (30–38 cm) apart.

Thin the seedlings in two stages, firstly to 2–3 in. (5–7·5 cm) apart and then, when these are well established, to the final spacing distance of 4–6 in. (10–15 cm). If you want large roots space the rows 15–18 in. (38–45 cm) apart.

PEAS

All garden sites and soils will produce acceptable pea yields. This crop invariably grows well in soil not previously cultivated for vegetables.

For the earliest crops, sow directly into the cropping site, either in late October or early November (in sheltered areas and under cloches) or in early March. Crops from this sowing will be ready for picking in late May or early June. It is more reliable to sow in pots indoors in late January or early February, planting them out under cloches in March to get an early crop. After these sowings, sow successively in the cropping site through the spring and into early summer (see cropping chart for more details).

Sow seeds in a V-shaped drill 2–3 in. (5–7·5 cm) deep. Sow dwarf varieties to give 16 plants per 12 in. (30 cm) of row, spacing the rows the same distance apart as the height of the plant (see seed packet).

It is a good idea to cover the young seedlings of early crops with polythene tunnels or cloches as protection against the weather and birds. When the seedlings are 2–3 in. (5–7·5 cm) high they will need some form of support. The best method is to insert twiggy sticks up both sides of the row.

Tall peas, like the new Sugar Snap which has a very succulent edible pod as well as peas will need nets or sticks 4 ft (1·2 m) high for support.

You may find small maggots, which

Peas raised indoors and planted under cloches give an early crop. Alternatively the seed of suitable varieties can be sown outdoors in late October.

are the larvae of the pea moth in the pods when you are shelling the peas. You can control them by spraying the plants at flowering time, but do this in the evening to reduce the chance of harming bees. A good watering in dry weather after pod formation improves the yield.

POTATOES

All gardens are suitable for potatoes, although crops will be light if grown in heavily shaded spots or where the soil is very light. You will get the heaviest yields from well-cultivated soil with plenty of well-rotted organic matter dug into it.

'Seed potatoes' are not seeds as such, but tubers from the previous year's crop. Ideally they should be about the size of an egg. If your seed potatoes are larger than the ideal you can cut them to make two or more planting pieces as long as every piece has its own shoot.

A good way to increase the yield and get slightly earlier crops is to place the seed potatoes in trays in a temperature of 50°F (10°C) in a light position for six to eight weeks before planting, to produce short dark green shoots. This pre-planting sprouting is called chitting. Whether chitted or not, plant the tubers in rows with a trowel 4–5 in. (10–12·5 cm) deep, 12–15 in. (30–38 cm) apart, with 24 in. (60 cm) between the rows. Begin planting outdoors in late March or early April – or four to five weeks before the last frost is likely to occur.

When the young shoots appear above the ground, draw up soil from between the rows around the stems. This is called 'earthing up'. If young shoots have come through and frosts are still likely, pull the soil right over them to give protection.

Repeat the earthing-up process several times as the crop grows. This operation increases the roots made by the potato stem and increases yield. It also prevents the tubers turning green and becoming inedible.

In very damp conditions in the autumn potato blight can be troublesome. This causes dark spots on the leaves and premature yellowing. You can prevent this by growing early varieties and lifting them early. Alternatively, use a protective copper-based spray in early July.

Pea Cropping Chart							
Type/Variety	**Sowing Date**	**Harvesting**					
		May	Jun	Jul	Aug	Sept	Oct
First Early e.g. Feltham First	Outdoors Oct/Nov Indoors Jan/Feb Outdoors March	●	●●●				
Second Early e.g. Early Onward	March/April			●●●			
Maincrop e.g. Lord Chancellor	April			●●●	●●●		
First Early	mid June					●●●	●●●

Potatoes will yield the heaviest crops on well-cultivated soil that contains plenty of organic matter.

Large seed potatoes can be cut into smaller sections, each with a shoot.

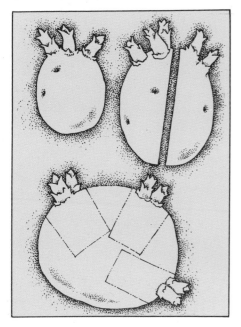

Part of a display of over 40 varieties of radish grown by the author and staged at the Chelsea flower show in 1976.

RADISH

There are two kinds of radish: the ordinary summer radish, which can be cropped from late April to November, and the winter radish (black or red skinned and much larger than the ordinary radish).

Radish will grow anywhere in all reasonably well cultivated soils, from mid-spring to early autumn. The most succulent radish are grown quickly – in four weeks in warm weather – on fertile soil in an open sunny position.

In temperate areas start sowing the ordinary radish as soon as soil conditions allow (you should be able to sow under polythene cloches in February). Draw shallow drills 6 in. (15 cm) apart and sow the seed thinly down the row. Sow in succession every 10–14 days from early spring to September.

Sow winter radish in July, *not before*, in rows 12 in. (30 cm) apart. Thin out the seedlings as they develop, to stand 6–8 in. (15–20 cm) apart.

One possible problem is attack by flea beetles – small shiny black insects which eat neat round holes in the seedling leaves. You can control it by dusting with BHC early in the morning, with the leaves still dewy.

RHUBARB

Rhubarb thrives in any site – however bad – and all reasonably cultivated garden soil will give good results. It is one of the easiest plants to grow and very productive.

Succulent pink stems of forced rhubarb make a good winter sweet.

A popular way to force rhubarb is to cover with straw and an old bucket.

Rhubarb is best propagated from plants of named varieties. Dependable varieties are 'Timperley Early', which is excellent for forcing and general garden use, and 'Victoria'. The latter is a late variety that isn't suitable for forcing, but it yields more stems and crops well into summer.

Use plants that are three to five years old, lift them during the dormant period and chop them with a spade to produce five or six planting pieces.

Each piece, or 'set', must have one rounded pink bud and a fair share of root system.

Dig the soil well and clear it of perennial weeds before planting the sets $2\frac{1}{2}$ ft (75 cm) apart (October and March are good times to plant).

You can get early crops by either covering the plants in the soil with boxes filled with straw, or by lifting the whole crown.

Be careful when lifting not to break off too many thongy roots. Pack damp peat, soil or similar material around the roots, keep them dark and warm, 50–55°F (10–13°C), then forced stems will be ready to pull in about a month.

An alternative method is to place the crowns indoors in a black polythene bag with damp peat.

Do not attempt to harvest a crop the first year. A few stems can be pulled the second year before cropping more heavily and forcing in successive years.

Always try to leave about four good leaves on each plant to continue building up the strength of the plant.

One strong crown should yield 6 lb (3 kg) a year from February to August.

An alternative method is to put lifted crowns in a black polythene bag.

Salsify (left) and scorzonera (right).

Forced stems are ready when the pale lemon leaf colour starts to darken. Try to pull just before this darkening occurs and the leaf edges go brown. Discard the roots after forcing.

Plants to be forced indoors should be lifted and left on the surface exposed to cold temperatures. Mid-November in the north and late November or early December in the south is the very earliest that early varieties should be brought indoors. Late varieties will need more cold.

SALSIFY AND SCORZONERA

These two less common root vegetables are quite easy to grow. They require similar treatment both in the garden and the kitchen, but it is easy to distinguish between the two. Scorzonera roots have a black skin which can be removed by scalding and scraping. Salsify is a similar shape, but the roots are brown, not black.

Sow from March to early May in rows 12–15 in. (30–38 cm) apart. A long growing season is needed.

Thin the seedlings to stand 6–9 in. (15–23 cm) apart in the row when they are big enough to handle. Hoe occasionally to control weeds and water the plants well in dry weather.

SPINACH

'New Zealand Spinach' is not botanically true spinach, but is grown to provide a leaf vegetable. It is therefore usual to consider it together with spinach.

Summer and Winter Spinach

The annual spinach is one of the fastest maturing leaf vegetables and is ideal to grow between slower maturing vegetables such as celery and leeks.

There are two main groups – the round or smooth-seeded summer spinach which includes such varieties as 'Long-Standing Round', and the rough or prickly-seeded winter spinach, such as the variety 'Long-Standing Prickly'. Recently introduced varieties like 'Sigmaleaf' have round seed and can be used for both summer and winter cropping.

Full sun or partial shade are both acceptable and the best soil is a really good moisture-retaining type. Light, dry soils and hot weather make plants run to seed prematurely.

To get continuous cropping, sow summer spinach successively every 14 days from February to July, and winter spinach in August and September. Sow the seed thinly in drills 1 in. (2·5 cm) deep and 12–15 in. (30–38 cm) apart. Thin the seedlings first to stand 3 in. (7·5 cm) apart and then thin again after about a month to 6–12 in. (15–30 cm) apart.

Hoe to control weeds and water well in dry weather. Protect winter spinach from frost by covering with cloches from November.

Summer spinach is a useful crop to grow in fertilized peat-filled bags.

New Zealand Spinach

The spreading plants of New Zealand Spinach are often called 'cut-and-come-again' because they provide a

New Zealand Spinach is a real pick-and-come-again vegetable.

continuous supply of leafy shoots.

Most garden sites and soils will give acceptable results but sunny positions and light well-drained soils are best.

For the earliest crops, sow indoors in pots in late March or early April and plant out, after the possibility of frost, in May or June. Sow the main crop outside in early May. Space the rows 2–2½ ft (60–75 cm) apart and the plants 18–24 in. (45–60 cm) down the row.

Maintain rapid growth by constant watering in dry weather. Pinch out the growing tips, especially those that form early in the season, to encourage the development of side shoots.

Summer spinach is an annual vegetable with a rapid rate of growth.

Swedes have been rather neglected but if harvested before they become too big make a nice vegetable. They are undemanding in their requirements.

touch the top and the possibility of frost has passed. Pollen from the male tassels which form at the top of the plant floats down in the wind to pollinate the female cobs which are formed in a sheath of leaves·lower down the plant. Complete wind pollination is more likely if you grow plants in a block of several rows, rather than in a single row.

TOMATOES

Careful selection of variety is important for outdoor tomatoes, and it is worth studying a seedman's list. One variety you are likely to find is 'Outdoor Girl', the leaves of which look more like potatoes than tomatoes. Equally suitable for outdoor culture, are the bushy multi-stemmed kinds. These include 'Pixie' F_1 (2–2½ ft (60–75 cm); 'Gardener's Delight' sometimes known as 'Sugar Plum' (2 ft (60 cm)); 'Sleaford Abundance' (1½–2 ft (45–60 cm)) and 'Tiny Tim' (15 in. (38 cm)) high, which has very small round fruits and is ideal to grow in a 5-in. (12·5-cm) pot on the windowsill or on a balcony or patio.

Sunshine is the one real requirement for good tomato growing and being tender they need a warm spot in a sheltered garden, such as a south-facing wall or fence. Cloche protection, glass-sided porches, home extensions

SWEDE

Swedes are rather neglected vegetables but are becoming more appreciated now that smaller roots tend to be sold for home use instead of those more suited to cattle food.

Any land that's suitable for turnips will also be right for swedes. Avoid soil infested with club-root or select the disease-resistant variety 'Marian'.

Sow swede in May or June. Space seed rows 15 in. (38 cm) apart and thin seedlings to stand 6–9 in. (15–23 cm) apart in the row. The smaller roots grown at the closer spacing and lifted while young, are the best to eat.

Swedes tend to take care of themselves, though flea beetle may be a problem with young plants – if so simply dust the row with BHC.

SWEET CORN

Select a warm sheltered site for this crop in cooler districts – plenty of sun and well cultivated garden soil are the growing requirements. Add plenty of rotted organic matter to poor soils.

Sow indoors in pots (peat pots are the best) in April. Plant in the cropping site under cloches in mid-May or unprotected when the risk of frost has passed. Alternatively sow directly into the cropping site from mid-May, placing two or three seeds every 12–15 in. (30–38 cm) down the rows,

which should be 15–30 in. (38–75 cm) apart.

Thin seedlings to one, once established. If you are growing them under cloches, remove these when the leaves

Below left: Male and female sweet corn flowers are carried on the same plant.
Below right: Harvest cobs when milky sap flows from the grains when pressed.

Remove side shoots from tomatoes as soon as they appear.

and cold greenhouses will all lengthen the growing and cropping season.

Well-cultivated garden soils improved by the addition of well-rotted manure and other organic materials are required for tomatoes.

Fertilized peat-filled bags are very good for tomatoes, and give heavy crops.

Although seedlings can be raised on the windowsill (the secret is not to sow too early), it is probably easier to buy plants.

Start to liquid feed every 10–14 days when the plants are carrying the first small fruits.

Give the plants a tap on the stem at midday, and syringe with water in sunny conditions to improve pollination and fruit set. Alternatively, spray the flowers with special fruit setting chemical to be sure fruit development will follow.

When the plant has set four or five trusses, remove the growing tip.

Black patches on the base of fruit (blossom end rot) is caused by careless watering. Make sure your plants never suffer from lack of water, especially when they are carrying a heavy crop of fruit.

You can control greenfly and whitefly with resmethrin-based and similar insecticides.

If plants with several trusses of fruit suddenly wilt in hot weather on soil which has produced several crops of tomatoes, they probably have the disease verticilium wilt. A deep mulch of peat or compost around the stem will encourage new roots to form and may salvage some of the crop.

Raise tomato plants in pots to the stage where the first fruits form before planting in fertilized peat-filled growing bags.

TURNIPS

Any garden site is suitable for turnips, but avoid those that are heavily shaded. All well-cultivated garden soils are suitable, but the best shaped roots grow in soil that has been manured and enriched for previous crops.

Sow successively from February under cloches and outside from late March or early April, every three weeks to July. These sowings will mature in about eight to twelve weeks – the warmer the weather the faster the maturity – and the roots should be lifted to eat young and fresh. Late July or early August sowings will provide maincrop roots to lift in November and store for winter use. Sow the seed in rows 12 in. (30 cm) apart and cover very lightly with soil.

As the seedlings produce the first rough leaves, thin them out to stand 4 in. (10 cm) apart along the row. Pull some early roots so that the remainder stand at 8 in. (20 cm) apart. This two-stage harvesting is especially useful with the July sowing. It gives young roots in early autumn, leaving the remainder for maincrop use.

The only likely problem is flea beetle. Signs of attack are neat round holes in the young seedling leaves. BHC dust will control.

Very swollen and distorted roots will be produced on soils infected by club-root disease. If the soil has been proved to contain this disease it is best to avoid growing turnips.

Turnips should be pulled while still young to be eaten at their best.

Herbs

Herbs can make all the difference to a meal, and no garden should be without at least some of the more popular kinds. Usually just one or two plants will provide sufficient seasonings for most families, and there's always space for the smaller-growing species.

A wide range can be grown without even encroaching on the vegetable plot – a number of herbs make very attractive plants in their own right and do not look amiss in shrub and flower borders. The evergreen bay, the powder blue flowers of rosemary, the rich mauve flowers on chives and the ground-covering purple and cream variegated, shrubby sage are good examples.

Many herbs can be grown in containers on the windowsill, on the back step, in small troughs and in hanging plant containers. The perennial kinds like mint, sage and thyme are good for this, and so is parsley. They all respond to regular picking and this prevents indoor plants getting too thin, long and drawn.

An ideal site is one that can offer a well-drained soil in full sun, as good sunlight helps to produce the strongest flavours. This isn't essential, however, as most common herbs will grow satisfactorily in all soils. The only problem is likely to occur on heavy, wet soils, which make for a short life of two or three years in some herbs.

It's sensible to position a herb border near the kitchen door. We only require a small quantity of herbs for flavouring, and it is convenient to nip out and pick a sprig of mint for new potatoes or a sprinkling of chives for cream cheese. If there isn't a suitable bed, a few plants can be grown in pots, tubs or windowboxes placed conveniently close.

Never be afraid to pinch back the shoots of most herbs regularly. Plants such as sage and thyme will grow away again strongly and will produce more compact and bushy plants.

Bay

Although few kitchens are without a few bay leaves, it is grown in comparatively few gardens – which is a pity as it makes quite a pleasant evergreen shrub.

The bay will eventually grow into a small tree, but it also responds to pot culture, either as a low bushy plant, possibly trimmed to a pyramid, or grown on a stem to form the typical standard 'round-headed' plant seen in tubs outside restaurants. It isn't

Bays can be trained in a variety of shapes, and are well suited to pot culture.

difficult to keep plants nicely shaped, but do the trimming with secateurs, not shears as these cut the leaves in half. They will need a trim two or three times a year.

Although it is a hardy evergreen, try to avoid exposure to cold easterly winter winds which burn back the leaves. Plants grown in pots are best taken into a light garage or an outbuilding for protection in the depths of winter.

New plants can be produced by rooting young tips when stems start to harden in July and August. Well rooted cuttings should be grown on in potting compost and then planted out when they are well established. March and April are good times for planting out, as is September later in the year.

Fresh and dried leaves of this herb are used combined with other herbs in

Short rows of chives produce masses of leaves. One plant is often sufficient.

a bouquet garni and on their own to flavour many different dishes.

Leaves can be dried by placing several in a shallow tray in a very cool oven. Dried leaves are likely to have a stronger flavour than fresh leaves.

Chives

Once you have chives established they really look after themselves – and they make a very attractive border with lots of grass-like foliage and masses of mauve flower heads if you allow them to bloom.

Chives flourish in a shaded border and once established should be cut back to the soil regularly to encourage the new growth used for flavouring. Established clumps should be lifted and divided every few years in April or September. If you want fresh supplies all the year, grow a few seed-raised crops indoors.

The grassy foliage is chopped into small pieces which give a delicate onion flavour to salads, egg dishes, cream cheese, soups and sauces. The bright green colour is lost if the leaves are dried, so it is better to keep supplies of fresh leaves coming along (or you can put some into the freezer).

Dandelion

It is debatable whether the dandelion should be classed as a herb or a vegetable, as the leaves are sometimes eaten raw in salads (special large-leaved varieties are available from specialist seedsmen), cooked like spinach or used as a flavouring for soups. Equally it can be regarded as a culinary herb, for its roots may be roasted and ground to make a coffee substitute or additive. Unlike most other herbs, however, it likes a shady spot and a moist, fertile soil if it is to produce large leaves.

April is a good time to sow dandelion, preferably in small groups. Thin the plants so they are eventually 6 in. (15 cm) apart.

If you want blanched leaves for salads, cover the plants with an up-turned pot or box the following spring. After blanching and picking the leaves, give the plants a rest to rebuild their vigour before blanching a few more leaves.

Dandelion roots can be harvested any time after the growth has begun to slow down in the autumn. For the biggest, most succulent roots, it is best to wait until October or November when the foliage has really stopped growing.

Dill

Dill is one of the annual herbs, which means fresh plants have to be raised each year. But it makes up for that by growing quite vigorously, and its thin feathery foliage will grow to about 3 ft (90 cm) in height. If you are growing several plants you can space them 9–12 in. (23–30 cm) apart.

Both leaves and seeds are used, and they have a flavour akin to caraway and aniseed; but use them sparingly for the flavour is quite strong. Chopped leaves can be used to flavour soups, sauces and savoury stews. Seeds can be added to vinegar to produce dill vinegar for pickled gherkins. To give cucumber sandwiches a new tang, try sprinkling the slices with a little dill seed.

The feathery foliage of dill is attractive as well as being useful in the kitchen.

Fennel

There are two plants called 'fennel' – common fennel, *Foeniculum vulgare*, a perennial herb and Florence fennel or finocchio, *Foeniculum vulgare dulce*. This has similar feather foliage but is also grown for its swollen leaf bases.

Common fennel can be sown from March to May, in rows 15 in. (38 cm) apart, but if you want seed heads to develop sow early. Thin the seedlings to 12 in. (30 cm) apart. Old plants can be divided in spring.

As the leaves do not store easily, it is a matter of freezing some for winter use or potting up a few plants to grow indoors.

Cut seed heads in September and October and hang them upside down in paper bags to dry. Seeds soaked in water are said to make a good soothing liquid for stomach ache.

Florence fennel is best sown in April in rows 20 in. (50 cm) apart and thinned to 9–12 in. (23–30 cm) apart. This plant needs a warm, well-drained

The popular Florence fennel is an attractive plant in the garden. Draw soil around the base of the plant to blanch the swollen leaf bases.

soil in a sunny position in the garden.

As the leaf bases of Florence fennel start to swell, hoe soil up around them to give the blanched white colour. These are eaten raw in salads or cooked to flavour stews.

Garlic

As everyone knows, garlic is a very pungent herb, but one that is justifiably popular with cooks.

It is a member of the onion family and can be grown in just the same way as shallots and onion sets. Divide a bought bulb into cloves and plant these 6 in. (15 cm) apart in rows 12 in. (30 cm) apart.

The cloves can be planted in October for harvestable bulbs in July and August, or in March for bulbs ready in October. Lift when the leaves start to yellow, then put them in trays to dry.

Polythene tunnel cloches will produce bulbs of much better quality.

Horseradish

Horseradish is probably better known in a sauce than in the garden, but there

is every reason to find room for a few plants.

Plant sparingly, however, because once established the deep searching thongy roots soon become very invasive and take some digging out. The leaves will grow 2 ft (60 cm) or so high. Although any small piece of root will grow, the top crown-shoot part (which

Grow garlic under cloches to produce nice smooth white-skinned bulbs.

163

Horseradish root cuttings. Slant the base to ensure planting the right way.

is no use for culinary purposes anyway) is best. Plant in spring, 18 in. (45 cm) apart.

Lift the roots in November or December and store in sand and peat for use when the soil is frozen.

Shredded slivers from the white cylindrical roots used fresh in cream sauces provide the traditional, hot mustardy flavoured relish to go with roast beef. Fresh root scrapings can also be used to flavour fish and other dishes to give a pungent flavour.

Marjoram

Sweet marjoram *(Origanum marjorana)* is actually a perennial, but in Britain it is best treated as an annual as it can die outdoors in winter in all but the more sheltered spots.

The seed should be sown under glass in March and the seedlings planted out in late May or early June, 9–12 in. (23–30 cm) apart. Alternatively they

Several low-growing herbs, such as marjoram, make good ground-cover plants.

can be sown direct into the cropping position in mid-April. In either case they need a warm, sunny position.

Gather the leaves as they get large enough and before the plant develops flower heads. Chop them for use fresh and dry some for winter supplies. They are a useful ingredient in mixed herbs, or as a substitute for thyme.

For a stronger flavour and to provide fresh leaves in winter, it is best to grow pot marjoram, *Origanum onites.* There are two types of this plant – a green-stemmed, white-flowered form, and a purple-stemmed and flowered form. There is also a golden-leaved marjoram, *Origanum aureum.* Pot marjoram is a hardy perennial but it needs a warm position if grown in the garden. The seed can be sown in April or September, in drills 12 in. (30 cm) apart. The seedlings can be thinned or transplanted to stations 12 in. (30 cm) apart.

Mint

Mint is a plant often taken for granted, yet there are many kinds and most are worth cultivating.

The common mint, *Mentha spicata,* or spearmint is the species most frequently found in gardens and is most recommended for mint sauce. Another type worthy of note is *Mentha rotundifolia,* the round-leaved or apple mint, a type not affected by rust disease. Many claim this is the best mint to use with new potatoes. There is a very attractive white variegated form of apple mint.

You are unlikely to have any difficulty growing mint – it usually

needs restraining rather than encouraging. A good tip is to plant the pieces of root, from which new plants are grown, in an old plastic bucket (or similar container) with a hole in the base. Bury this in the garden up to 2 in. (5 cm) of the rim and fill it with soil. The mint roots will be contained and not spread all over the garden.

It's a good idea to lift some roots in the autumn and grow them in pots indoors to supply young sprigs through the winter.

Parsley

This is one of those herbs that grows like a weed when allowed to self seed. It is not quite so easy when we try to raise plenty in the garden.

The main difficulty usually lies in getting the seed to germinate. It is a slow germinator, and the old cottage gardener's tip of pouring boiling water along the drill sometimes speeds things along. Be sure to use fresh seed and sow indoors in pots of seed compost for certain success.

Sow in rows 9–12 in. (23–30 cm) apart in spring for summer and autumn use, and late July or early August for winter use. Thin to 6–12 in. apart (15–30 cm).

Parsley is a biennial which will produce leaves for several seasons if the flowering stems are cut before they fully develop. It will stand some shade and produces a lot more leaf if it is given an occasional liquid feed.

One of the most useful herbs, parsley is ideal for garnishing, or in sauces and stuffings, and as a constituent of bouquet garni. Fresh leaves are by far

There are many species of mint. All need the root run restricted.

Parsley seedlings can be transplanted into pots for indoor cultivation.

its attractive greyish-green leaves, there are purple-green and cream, and pink and green variegated forms.

The best flavoured foliage comes from young plants grown in well-drained soil in a warm, sunny site.

All species can be raised easily from seed sown from March to June. Alternatively they can be propagated from cuttings rooted in sandy compost in September.

Trim off the purple flowers before they open, and cut plants back to get a harvest of shoots and also to encourage more basal growth and foliage.

It takes some time to dry the rather thick leaves and woody stems, and they need a warm, airy place. Once dry, just rub the leaves in your hands to break them up, then store in an airtight jar.

Thyme

The common garden thyme (*Thymus vulgaris*) is a really attractive low-growing decorative shrub. Planted close to a path or near the back door, you will be aware of the delicious fragrance every time you brush by. If the young shoots are not cut for drying, the 8–12 in. (20–30 cm) plants are covered with pretty purple flowers in June.

Among the many thymes is a golden-leaved form, *Thymus vulgaris* 'Aureus'. Another particularly attractive type is the lemon thyme, *Thymus × citriodorus*, which has silver and golden-leaved forms.

Thyme needs a sunny site and light, sandy soil. You can propagate by cuttings taken with a heel in May or June, or raise common thyme from seed sown any time from March to July. Once established, put out young plants 9–12 in. (23–30 cm) apart.

the best, but you can ensure additional winter supplies by air-drying bunches of foliage in summer and rubbing it down before storing in sealed jars. To retain the colour, dip fresh leaves in boiling water for a minute or so, shake dry and then dry in a cooling oven.

Rosemary

This is a plant that grows quite large and it looks well towards the front of a small shrub border. If kept trimmed back each spring it will not reach more than 2–3 ft (60–90 cm) high. The very attractive gold and silver variegated forms look nice but are not as strong growing as the green types.

Rosemary also responds well to being grown in a pot.

Plants can be raised from seed sown in spring and summer, or from cuttings taken in August, September or October. Light soils suit the plant best. Although it is virtually hardy very severe frost and cold, or easterly winds will destroy the branches. New growth will often come through again from the base where the plants have been damaged by frost.

Sage

Sage is another shrubby herb, and the various species make attractive ground covers. As well as the true species with

Rosemary is an attractive flowering shrub as well as a popular herb.

Sage and thyme are two popular shrubby herbs, and make a good planting combination.

Protected Cropping

Greenhouses are not the panacea to all garden problems and you will achieve greater success if they are viewed as an extension to the outdoor growing season. Enclosing an atmosphere with glass or polythene does keep out wind and rain, and some of the larger pests can also be kept out, but we need to be at hand to control moisture and temperature.

Higher average temperatures under cover mean more rapid growth, not only of plants but also of diseases and multiplication of pests, so protected crops need more frequent attention.

Automatic systems for heating, ventilating and watering make things much easier for us, especially for those gardeners not at home in the day to operate ventilators, adjust heaters and do the watering. Even so, I advise the progression slowly; gain experience first by gardening outdoors and on the windowsill, then use frames and cloches before adding first a cold greenhouse and finally heating the house.

The margins for error are much wider where the plants are growing in the open with a large volume of soil in which to spread roots. Restrict the roots in small pots and checks to growth are more likely because of dryness, fluctuating temperatures and excessive feeding.

These warning remarks must, of course, be treated only as sensible caution, for greenhouses really can give tremendous satisfaction. They protect us from the cold weather to make gardening more comfortable and allow an even greater variety of plants to be grown. The smell on a warm day when the paths are damped down and a whole range of plants are growing strongly really can't be described. It is the breath of life to true gardeners. But like all pieces of equipment greenhouses need handling properly and the instructions carefully followed.

Careful siting of greenhouses and frames is important, to capture the most light.

Where the spare-time gardener leads a busy life frames and cloches will be more easily handled. They give protection from the weather, bring crops forward a few weeks and ventilation is more crudely provided.

Once some experience is gained then all these protective structures can be used in association with one another. Many seedlings and cuttings raised in heated greenhouses and small propagators need to be moved to a cold greenhouse or frame to harden off before planting outside.

Where space is very limited a specialist interest like orchids, carnations, cacti and tropical plants may demand just one small heated house. A small cold greenhouse is ideal for alpines and here the less energetic and physically disabled gardener can get much pleasure at little cost.

The cheapest way to get a heated greenhouse is to build a lean-to on to the side of the house and draw warmth from the house heating system. Ideally build on the south-facing wall, or west-facing for second choice.

Commercial growers make good use of polythene-covered houses and I see these structures being used increasingly in gardens. They do not have the disadvantage of glass which seems to tempt balls where there are children in the family! Ventilation systems are crude, rather like frames, and they prove ideal for the simple and yet so popular and practical cropping plan of winter and spring lettuce, followed by summer tomatoes and then autumn chrysanthemums.

The polythene house would make the perfect winter cover for a sandpit where there are small children!

Plastic tunnel cloches are inexpensive and can amply repay their cost in the vegetable garden by advancing and extending the cropping season.

CLOCHES

There are three main choices of material for cloche construction. The cheapest in the long run and the material which best retains heat is glass. Panes of glass held on galvanised frames are the most practical but it takes careful handling and some knack to use over a number of years without breaking the glass.

Be careful in handling glass cloches in cold weather when they are so much more brittle. Where the lower panes are frozen into the soil they are especially vulnerable.

Rigid, clear corrugated plastic is also brittle in cold weather but very much easier to handle and the better materials carry a 10-year guarantee

against breaking. Beware of cheap, light clear plastic which will fracture in the cold and when exposed to strong sunlight. The small lightweight plastic cloches with poor anchorage also blow away in strong winds.

Thin polythene film is the cheapest material and, used to cover tunnel cloches, is very adaptable. Select film which has been ultra-violet light inhibited, usually marked U.V.I. on the packs. This film will last two full winters and one summer before disintegrating. Where the sheet is stored out of sunlight in summer it will last three or more seasons.

Be sure to anchor both ends of the polythene sheet over tunnel cloche hoops very securely before fastening

each top tensioning wire. Set the wire hoops out first, bury one end of the sheet, unroll over the hoops, pull tight and then bury the second end. Finally fix the tensioning wire. In very exposed positions it is worth pulling a little soil up over the two edges of the polythene to give even greater anchorage.

PROTECTED CROPPING

There are several forms of polythene sheets with slits and perforations which can be used to cover soil once crops are sown and planted. Then as the crop develops it lifts the film, forming its own support. Potatoes, lettuce, radish and hardy annual flowers have all responded well to this treatment. The slits allow irrigation and rainwater through so quite a wide bed can be covered. A good system for short period cover but not very adaptable.

Cloche Cropping

A cropping plan is advisable if full value is to be gained from the cloche investment. Where glass cloches are used the planning is all the more important if movement is to be kept to a minimum. Where the glass needs no more than lifting from one row to the next, the chance of breakage is much reduced.

There are several absolute musts for cloches, and lettuce is first and foremost. Sown in late September or early October outside and covered with cloches, beautiful hearted lettuce can be cut in April and May.

Strawberries are the second choice, with cloches protecting the flowers from frost and the fruit from wet and birds, apart from the earlier fruiting.

Anemones flowering into the winter and cucumbers, melons and sweetcorn given an early start into growth are other priorities.

Tie one end of the polythene to a stake or bury it.

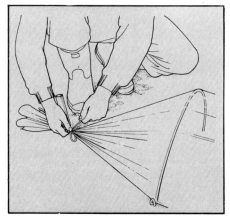

When both ends are secured, adjust the tensioning wires to hold the polythene.

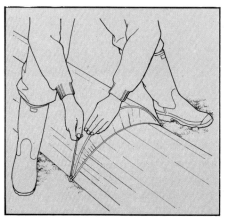

To weed or tend crops, simply slide the polythene back over the wires.

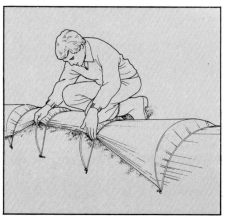

Clocne-grown autumn-sown lettuce, Sweet Peas and Larkspur in early spring.

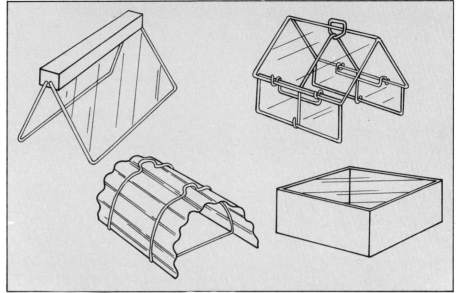

There are many kinds of cloche, but the principal types are tent (t.l.), barn (t.r.) and tunnel (b.l.). Even a box with a glass top can be used.

Think of the cloche cropping year in four parts. The autumn-sown over-wintered crops like salad onions, cabbage, lettuce, Sweet Peas and other hardy annuals.

Over-winter protection will extend cropping quite considerably and a late September sowing of calabrese will overwinter well to crop in May. Cabbage, cauliflower and calabrese seedlings can also be overwintered in this way and transplanted outside in spring to give early crops. Transplanting will delay the harvest by 2–4 weeks to help achieve succession.

The second period is spring, where cloche-warmed soil can be used for earlier sowing and planting. Often one row of cloches can be used for two crops. Early round-seeded peas, carrots, turnip and broad beans first, then over potatoes and French beans.

The third period is summer when they can be used to cover tender crops and bush tomatoes very successfully when planted out. A May sowing indoors will give plants to put out in June and fruit will start to ripen in August. Earlier sowing will give earlier ripening but the cloches may still be needed in early June to cover French beans. A clear example of the need for a little planning.

Fourth comes the autumn cropping which is really an extension of the outdoor summer fruit and vegetables. August-sown lettuce given protection can be cut right into November and radish sown in succession will crop till Christmas. Cloches used to cover strawberries from February to June and tomatoes through the summer can be moved over perpetual-fruiting strawberries to fruit from September to November.

Autumn protection given to parsley, spinach and anemones again provides pickings to Christmas.

Care needs to be taken from May to August when the sun can be very hot and scorching may occur where leaves touch the cloche. Painting over with greenhouse shade materials or a lime wash reduces this problem. Summer crops like courgette, cucumber, marrow and melon will need masses of water in hot weather.

Grow the outdoor ridge type cucumber and the earliest melons like F_1 hybrid 'Sweetheart'. See that the soil has plenty of well-rotted compost mixed into it for all these plants. Lifting the cloches up on sunny days and syringing will improve growth and allow entry for pollinating insects.

Some rigid cloches can be stood on end in pairs to form a tube around single tomato plants tied up a cane or stake. The cheap way to achieve this summer protection is to push in three or four canes and pull a clear polythene bag, with the base slit open, over them.

While cultivation for crops under cloches is much the same as for the open ground there are one or two significant points. At first sight it appears that crops will be very short of water. In practice the surface soil under cover remains dry but water running over the cloche and in from both sides keeps the sub-soil nicely damp.

Excepting mid-summer, even in hot weather running the hose over the outside of the cloche gives the plants underneath all they need. If you really want to cosset plants like melons and tomatoes run a length of 2 in. (5 cm) wide black polythene tube, with tiny holes punched every 8 in. (20 cm), alongside the plants and drip water through this.

Although the surface of the soil beneath cloches often appears dry, the roots of crops penetrate to the moister soil beneath, dampened by run-off water.

FRAMES AND PROPAGATORS
Frames

Although cloches are moved to the crops, frames are usually sited permanently, often close to the greenhouse where they are used to harden off plants – that is acclimatize them to colder conditions – before transplanting outside.

There are, however, two types of frame that are moved. One is the simplest of frames, constructed from a bottomless box with a pane of glass over the top, and this type can be moved to shelter tender rock plants and other single plants. The other movable kind is the original single or double Dutch light frame, (see illustration).

The single Dutch light system is easily moved from one crop to another. The front and back boards are held in place by driving stakes into the ground on both sides of the board.

A good cropping plan for Dutch light frames is lettuce sown in late September and under-sown with carrot seed very early in spring. Cauliflower plants can be set among the lettuce as they start to heart. Then when the lettuce are cut and the carrots and cauliflower well established the whole frame can be moved to cover melons or courgettes.

Much more common are the traditional English frames with high backboard and lower front board, the glass sloping to the south to catch all possible light and warmth. There are many types made of wood, metal and plastic.

If you are buying one or making your own see that it is a good size, 4 ft × 6 ft (1·3 m × 2 m), at least, so that it holds a good volume of air. Tiny frames will heat up furiously, and having little

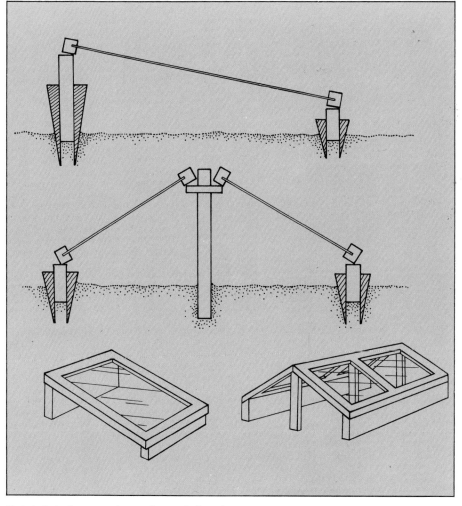

Dutch light frames, a large sheet of glass framed with wood, are supported on two boards for a single span frame. Double spans are made with two low edge boards and ridge board supported on stakes. Edge boards are held between short stakes.

volume of soil to hold the warmth will cool down quickly.

Before the days of electricity, old gardeners built 'hot beds' of rotting manure. The heat from the decomposition was used to raise early crops.

A pit is dug first, the fresh manure stacked in it, firming and adding leaves to extend the period over which heat is released. The manure is covered by several inches of soil and the frame stood on the soil.

Straw bales are an alternative, preferably wheat or oats rather than barley, which is softer and rots down more quickly. Chop into the unstrung sides of a 56 lb (25 kg) bale with a spade. Water well and wash in 16 oz (450 g) Nitro-chalk, 10 oz (280 g) triple superphosphate and 18 oz (500 g) potassium nitrate. Straight chemicals like these are available from specialist garden retailers.

Warmth is needed to get the rotting process under way – ideally a temperature of 50°F (10°C). Once the heat has started it will be self-generating. Expect a high temperature for four weeks and then a steady fall over eight to ten weeks. If a hot bed is started in late February, for example, it will give heat to late April, or early May when the weather is getting warmer.

Soil-warming cables make it possible to raise many seedlings and cuttings that require a high temperature. Lay the cables in parallel lines.

Raise the soil temperature just a few degrees and get early harvesting of crops such as lettuce, carrots, radish, turnips and spring onions. Even if you're not too successful with the heating, the rotted straw is beautiful stuff to improve soil in frames, greenhouses and outside.

If you want to grow tomatoes and similar crops in the rotting straw then add 4 oz (100 g) of magnesium sulphate (Epsom salt) and 3 oz (75 g) of sulphate of iron to each bale at the outset.

Electric soil warming cables are the modern-day equivalent to the old hot bed. Mains electric supply must be professionally fitted and then cables buried 4–5 in. (10–12 cm) deep to warm the soil and nicely raise the temperature in the frame.

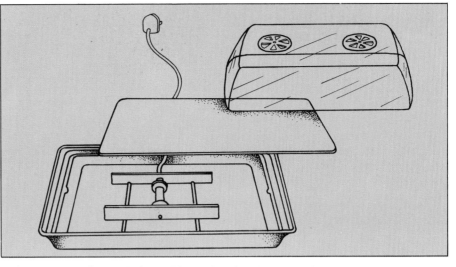

A shallow tray of water is heated by sealed electric tropical fish tank heater for this seed and cutting raiser.

Propagators

Soil-warming cables are a common heat source for small propagators and for seed and mist propagating benches in greenhouses. When the cable is sold it has a watt loading to give heat output. Input needs to be 4 watts per 1 sq ft (77 sq cm) for a cold frame, 8 watts for a propagating frame, and 16–18 watts for a mist propagator where bottom heat to 75°F (24°C) is required.

Experimental work has proved that crops in warm soil can be grown satisfactorily in an air temperature 3°C lower than normally recommended. The use of soil cables therefore allows earlier planting in cold-frames and greenhouses.

The most even distribution of heat across the soil occurs when the cables are spaced a distance equal to the depth to which they are buried. A good rod thermostat in the soil is needed to control the temperature; bury this just 1 in. (2·5 cm) deep at right angles to the wires. Cables are usually buried in sand for seed and mist propagators. See they are put down in parallel lines with the ends gently curved.

Several other heating methods are used to warm small propagators. One simple homemade system uses a 40 watt light bulb, and a low-priced proprietary single seedtray propagator has a sealed heat pad. Small tropical fish tank heaters are also used to heat water under other seed propagators.

Where there is no mains electricity then small paraffin heated propagators can be used. I cannot emphasise enough the need for care where electricity is used to ensure there are no shorts. Professional wiring and great care to avoid piercing the covering on 240-volt soil-warming cables when cultivating crops are essential.

Where cold-frames are not large enough to hold the small propagators either bring them indoors or, much better, use them in a cold greenhouse where any heat lost from the propagator helps to warm the greenhouse.

If sunlight has to pass through a window to reach one side of the propagator and then pass through the propagator hood before reaching the seedlings, very soft, light green and drawn growth results.

Put one of the large proprietary propagators, with automatic misting nozzles and heating cables, in any greenhouse and the gardener's scope to raise many kinds of seedlings and cuttings is greatly enlarged. Exercise a little control in the numbers of young plants raised early in the year if the heated area you have to move these young plants into is limited.

Bottom heat and automatic misting really makes rooting soft cuttings child's play. Watch the automatic leaf, two electrodes in a plastic block, which allows current to flow when wet. When dry the contact is broken and the misting valve is opened. A piece of cutting over the 'leaf' or hardness from water continually drying will interfere with this control.

Mist propagators can be used the whole year round, using them for slow

There are many types of proprietary propagators available, but it is also possible to make one by using a 40-watt light bulb as a heat source.

Although there are clear pros and cons for metal or wood greenhouses, many gardeners have a clear preference for the aesthetic qualities of one or the other.

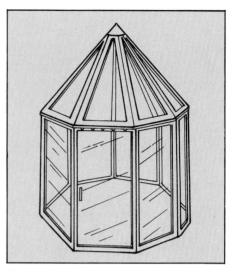

There are more decorative greenhouse shapes, such as this octagonal type.

rooting evergreens, such as *Chamaecyparis* and ×*Cupressocyparis*, in the autumn and winter.

GREENHOUSES
Choosing the structure

Glass Modern, well-designed aluminium structures are best because the lightweight glazing bars cast least shadow, the metal needs no preserving treatment and glazing seals are very good. These houses did have the difficulty of fixing crop support wires, but now special bolts with split rings are available. Two flat sides are filed on the bolt head to fit into the extruded channel in all glazing bars.

Designs are so carefully made that all the metal is packed in a large cardboard box and easily transported. When buying such a house check that the price includes glass, which is often delivered home a few days after purchasing the structure.

Next choice is Western Red Cedar (wood from *Thuya plicata*) which usually comes treated to improve the waterproofing and give a nice natural reddish look. While regular maintenance is not required, treating the wood occasionally with preservative oil will extend its life.

Where white painted timber is required for the sake of visual appearance, it is quite satisfactory but the need to paint regularly is expensive. Finally, galvanized steel and concrete

structures have been used in the past but they are not satisfactory.

After deciding type of structure look next at the shape and ventilation. Freestanding and lean-to houses can have either glass to the ground, preferably where crops like tomato are to be grown in or on the border soil, or low brick wall and timber-clad bases where staging is to be installed for pot plant growing at waist height.

There are also semi-globular and octagonal shapes which can look attractive in the overall garden design. The outside surface area on these is big in comparison with cubic capacity, however; a factor which increases heating costs.

Where the glasshouse has a low brick wall base it is no bad idea to construct either cold-frames or rock garden with second retaining wall against it to retain heat.

Adequate ventilation is essential and very small houses desperately need big vents. The rule of thumb figure is window openings to an area one-sixth of the floor area. The greenhouse door may well provide ventilation, and on

Three traditional types. A lean-to (top) is easy to heat; brick-based (left) is good for pot plants; Dutch type (right) is good for crops grown in the border.

172

small lean-to houses it would be wise to try to fit automatic ventilators on the door.

Sliding doors are generally preferable to hinged doors because they are less likely to be caught by the wind when people go in and out. It can be a distinct advantage to have a door which will slide open sufficiently to get a wheelbarrow through.

If a greenhouse has insufficient ventilation one improvement is the installation of an electric fan. Fit the fan in the top of one end of the house and then fit a louvred ventilator in the base of the opposite end. The fan will be switched on and off easily with a thermostat to control the temperature.

Polythene and plastic houses

Corrugated rigid clear plastic sheet on a timber framework makes a reasonable greenhouse and in a very small garden doubles nicely as a storage shed.

Polythene can be used to produce a very cheap house but has the disadvantage that heat is lost through polythene more quickly than glass and plastic.

One complete sheet of polythene does not have the draughts which pass between sheets of glass and it is excellent for cold house crops.

There are a number of polythene house designs but for me the half circular 'tunnels' with polythene skirt buried for anchorage are preferable. Light polythene structures really do gather up the wind and secure anchorage is essential.

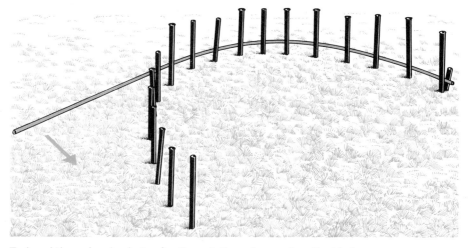

To bend the galvanized pipe for the polythene house described below, use posts driven into the ground. An extra post at the end is needed to hold the pipe.

Whether you buy a polythene house or build your own the ventilation again is critical. All houses must have ventilation both ends. If the ventilation is by a door at one end only the wind will blow in and literally blow the house away. Allowing the wind to blow through releases the destructive force.

Cheapest and simplest are roll-down polythene doors. Roll *down* because where just a little ventilation is needed hot air can be let out of the top of the house and there is not a cold draught whistling across at floor level.

Building a polythene tunnel house is quite simple for a DIY enthusiast.

The instructions below are for the construction of a polythene-covered house, which would completely cover a 10 ft × 12 ft (3 m × 4 m) plot. If you reduce the height, the width and the area of soil cover will be correspondingly increased.

The materials needed are:

3 × 21 ft (6·4 m) lengths ½ in. (1 cm) bore galvanized water pipe (for hoops)

2 × 5 ft (1·5 m) lengths ½ in. (1 cm) bore galvanized pipe (for ridge pieces)

6 × 2 ft (60 cm) lengths 1 in. (2·5 m) bore galvanized pipe (for foundation stakes)

1 × 20 ft (6 m) length of 10-gauge galvanized fencing wire

4 × 8 ft (2·4 m) lengths of 2 in. × 1 in. (5 cm × 5 cm) timber (lintels for doors)

2 × 4 ft (1·2 m) lengths of 2 in. × 2 in. (5 cm × 5 cm) timber (lintels for doors)

4 × 6 ft (1·8 m) lengths of 2 in. × 1 in. (5 cm × 2·5 cm) timber★

2 × 4 ft (1·2 m) lengths of 2 in. × 1 in. (5 cm × 2·5 cm) timber★

Quantity of laths for roller blind door

Quantity of nails

★*Any thin lath wood; alternatively staples and wire can be used.*

The framework of the polythene house described above, ready for construction of the doorway and eventual covering.

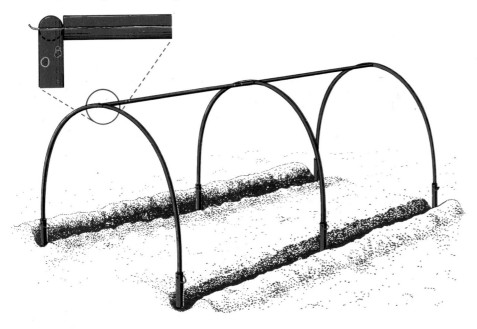

The door frame in position (see finished house on next page).

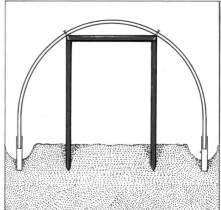

Polythene houses can be very successful for crops like tomatoes and lettuce, and can be moved every couple of years.

Drive a series of short posts into the ground and bend the three 21 ft (6·4 m) lengths of pipe round them to form a semi-circular hoop 12 ft (4 m) in diameter (see illustration). Then measure the site to mark out a 10 ft × 12 ft (3 m × 4 m) area. Take out a trench 10 in. (25 cm) wide and 12 in. (30 cm) deep around the outside, 2 in. (5 cm) out from the marked plot. Throw the excavated soil out of the area, *not* into it. Drive the 2 ft (60 cm) foundation stakes firmly into the ground, positioning one at each corner and one in the centre of each side. Leave 6–9 in. (15–23 cm) protruding above ground.

Drill a hole through the foundation stakes and the end of each hoop and place the hoops in the foundation stakes to erect the main structure. Secure by putting a short piece of wire or bolt through both holes you have drilled.

If the polythene cover ever becomes slack you can lift up the hoop a fraction, drill another hole and secure in the same way to take up the slack.

Drill a hole horizontally through the top of each hoop, but make sure it is in the top and centre. Thread wire through the hole in an end hoop, then the length of one ridge piece, through the centre hoop, then the next ridge pipe and finally through the other end hoop. Secure both ends of the wire to form a rigid structure.

Bury the base of the 8 ft (2·4 m) long 2 in. × 2 in. (5 cm × 5 cm) wooden uprights 4 ft (1·2 m) apart into the soil to construct the door lintels. Drive nails through holes in the hoops, through the cross-pieces and into the uprights, to hold the 4 ft (1·2 m) cross-timbers in place. (Alternatively use thick strips of rubber over the pipes and nail them to the cross-pieces and uprights.)

All rough or sharp edges should be covered with insulating tape or strips of polythene, then the structure can be covered with the polythene sheet.

Use 500-gauge (125 micron) polythene film 24 ft × 24 ft (7·3 m × 7·3 m). Be sure it is ultra-violet inhibited (UVI). The sheet must fit firmly to give the whole structure strength and wind resistance. Fit the cover in warm weather because as the film cools it will shrink and tighten further.

Make sure the 'skirt' around the base is the same length all the way round, then fill in the trenches with soil – firming it to tighten the film.

Cut out the polythene inside the lintels and fold the edge around the lintels, nailing it securely with timber laths and nails. Make the doors either as lift-up blinds or a polythene-covered frames secured as sliding doors. (Both doors must be open to ventilate the structure adequately.)

Wood-framed doors on hinges are tidier and easier to get in and out. The polythene doesn't keep flapping in the wind if stretched over timber. Leave

Primula malacoides is a good plant to grow in a cool greenhouse.

174

the top square of a wood-framed door clear of polythene and cover with plastic net for ventilation. At night and in the winter small polythene blinds can be used to cover the net.

Polythene does attract more condensation than glass inside but the top ventilation soon dries it out. A film of moisture helps retain heat in cold weather when the house is closed.

Siting a greenhouse

All greenhouses need to be sheltered from the wind and away from trees and buildings which cast a shadow and reduce light.

Timber structures will cast much more shadow than the thin aluminium glazing bars. It is important, therefore, to see that wooden glasshouses are sited east-west, then the heavy timbering on the end doesn't block valuable light entering from the south.

Where the wooden end and door does face south some 60 per cent of light can be obstructed in the winter compared to a 30 per cent obstruction with an east-west house.

COLD GREENHOUSE CROPS

Where tomatoes are the main summer crop, late April or early May is usually the safe time to plant. It is much better to delay planting and have the plants grow away quickly. Plant too early and the leaves go pale yellow, even bluish in colour. Should this happen it is better to replace the checked plants because they seldom fully recover.

Cucumbers and melons are even more tender and mid to late May is soon enough to plant. Once the summer crops are finishing in the autumn, clear the house, wash down the superstructure and house pot-grown autumn chrysanthemums.

Lettuce is a very worthwhile cold greenhouse crop.

A cold greenhouse with ample ventilation is an ideal environment for alpine plants and spring-flowering bulbs.

Chrysanthemums are then cut by November and lettuce can take their place to heart in April and complete the cropping sequence.

Many variations can be added to this basic scheme. Pot-grown shrubs like forsythia and camellias can be brought inside in mid-winter for protected early flowering. All the spring-flowering bulbs can be given the same treatment.

Pot-grown peaches can be brought in once the flower buds show colour, to protect them from the frost. Take them out once the fruits have set and the weather is warming.

Bring in pot-grown strawberries and roses in February to fruit and flower in May. Grape vines like 'Black Hamburg' can be grown in the house; the vine is either planted in the border soil or outside with the rod trained through a small hole in the wall or glass.

Hardy annuals can be sown in early autumn and grown both in the border soil or in 5–7 in. (12–18 cm) diameter pots to flower April or May. Good varieties for this are calendulas, East Lothian Stocks, antirrhinums (sown in July or August) and myosotis (sown in May or June). Sweet Peas are a good

cut flower to grow in the border soil and train, cordon-fashion, up strings.

Dahlia tubers can be planted in April to give early summer flowers but choose the dwarf-growing varieties.

Many of the seed-raised pot plants like coleus, celosia, browallia, exacum, and impatiens will grow well and decorate the cold greenhouse in summer, but the seedlings need heat.

Begonias, pelargoniums and fuchsias can be given similar treatment, raised from seed or cuttings in heat and then grown in the cold greenhouse through the summer.

You will find the cold greenhouse useful to carry chrysanthemum stools through the winter. Given a mild winter, with no more than a few degrees of frost in the house, fuchsia and Geraniums can be overwintered in pots if the soil is kept on the dry side and old yellowing leaves cleaned off.

Herbs grown in pots will continue to provide fresh leaves well into winter and from early spring, given cold glasshouse protection. Parsley, mint, sage and chives in pots are good examples.

Cucumbers, peppers and tomatoes are all likely to be infected by soil-

Stocks are very rewarding plants for a cold greenhouse, making ideal cut flowers, but buy types where you can select double seedlings.

borne diseases where they are grown for several years in the same soil. Even where tomatoes and cucumbers are alternated the disease verticilium wilt is likely to occur. After no more than two years' cropping in the border soil it is advisable to change to fertilized peat-filled growing bags. Polythene greenhouses really come into their own here because when the polythene cover needs changing at the end of the second year the house is easily moved to a fresh site and the old site exposed to the weather and given a rotation of crops.

HEATING A GREENHOUSE
Some control of ventilation is essential for all home greenhouses. There are a variety of automatic controls where paraffin wax and similar materials expand in a cylinder as the temperature rises and a piston pushes open the ventilators. Once you have the facility to cool houses in hot, sunny weather then a little heat can be introduced to increase the range of plants to grow in autumn, winter and spring.

Consider the energy source and heat output required when purchasing a greenhouse heater. The first thing to remember is that each 5°F (3°C) lift in temperature between inside and outside will double the heat requirement. A good thermostat sited out of direct sunlight and away from the heat source will give accurate heat control and avoid wasting fuel.

Set the thermostat so that the heating cuts off well before the automatic ventilators start to open.

Electricity is the easiest heat source to operate but remember the cost of bringing a cable to the house and wiring up the heater. Electric fan heaters give air movement which can help to reduce botrytis and other fungal diseases in crops like tomatoes and chrysanthemums.

Gas heaters need pipe installation where mains supply is used, and if bottle gas is used the price of two gas containing bottles should be included in the cost comparison. An automatic changeover from one bottle as it empties to another may be needed.

Portable paraffin heaters are the cheapest to install and often the cheapest to run but they are not as safe to leave untended for long periods. There are automatic controls to some models to raise and lower oil consumption as the temperature varies in the house.

Both gas and paraffin release water vapour when burnt and it may be necessary to ventilate more to reduce condensation where these fuels are used. Burning gas fiercely over a long period in a small heater also releases nitrogen oxides into the atmosphere which causes leaf scorch on tender plants. Again some ventilation may be needed to prevent the oxide build-up and this means increased heating cost.

Always buy a heater with much greater heat output than you anticipate needing. Every now and then a very cold spell will occur and the extra heat output will be invaluable. In many cases more efficient use of fuel is gained where the heater is gently ticking over, rather than always burning fiercely.

Two figures are needed to find the size of heater for any greenhouse. First is the temperature lift. Where the coldest winter temperature you are likely to get is 20°F (−7°C) and you just wish to hold an inside temperature of 40°F (5°C) then a 20°F (12°C) temperature lift is needed.

Next to be calculated is heat loss; some materials hold warmth better than others. Heat loss is usually described in 'U' values, the higher the number, the greater the loss. Some examples are glass 1, asbestos 0·8, brick 4½ in. (11 cm) thick 0·6, 500 gauge polythene sheet 1·4, rigid clear plastic 1, glass lined with polythene 0·5.

If you calculate the surface area and multiply by 1·4 this covers all surfaces and gives some spare. Multiply the total heat loss figure by the degree lift to get the Btu rating and the heater required. Convert the Btu figure to kilowatts for electrical heaters by dividing by 3,412.

COOL GREENHOUSE CROPS
Given a frost-free atmosphere the year round, the range of plants which can be grown is again expanded. There are very many seed-raised winter-flowering pot plants which will survive in a 45°F (7°C) minimum temperature.

Calceolarias, cinerarias and freesias from seed sown in April and corms planted in September, cyclamen, primulas (*P. malacoides*, *P. obconica*, *P. sinensis*) and schizanthus are the most

Columnea is a spectacular hanging basket subject for a warm greenhouse.

Make use of all space in a greenhouse.

Increase the heat and you increase the cropping period and yield of tomatoes like this tasty 'Gardener's Delight' and sweet and hot peppers.

popular. Wash the glass regularly in the winter so that these plants get all possible available light, then very sturdy plants will develop in the cool conditions. Where the temperature is down to 45°F (7°C) and even lower on occasions be very careful with the watering. It is better to keep a little on the dry side rather than risk botrytis and other wet rots.

Greenfly also welcome the winter protection so spray or fumigate regularly, especially if calceolarias or cinerarias are grown.

Given a little heat, lettuce can be cut almost all the year round, and all summer fruiting plants can be planted a few weeks earlier to give a longer harvest period and a heavier crop.

Cacti need to be rested through the winter. Kept frost-free and dry they will shrivel back naturally before swelling up and bursting into growth with more warmth and moisture in April and May.

All plants recommended for the cold house can be grown in a frost-free atmosphere. Column Stocks grow well in these conditions. Buy types where you can select doubles and raise the seedlings indoors or in a heated propagator. Once up, move to the cool greenhouse and all the double flowering forms will turn yellow. Save these and throw away the dark green healthy looking singles! 'Column' and 'Beauty of Nice' stocks can be grown in the border soil to cut or in 5–7 in. (12–18 cm) pots. The bigger the pot and wider the spacing in the border, the larger the flower spikes will be.

Arum lilies are another good pot plant for a cool house. Pot up the rhizomes (swollen root bases) in 6–10 in. (15–25 cm) pots of a good loam-based potting compost and bring

under glass in early autumn. They will grow strongly through the winter and early spring, demanding plenty of water. Dry off after flowering.

Where a little heat is used to bring pot roses into early flowering the bushes need potting up in good time and the new roots established before forcing into growth. By potting one bush into an 8–10 in. (20–25 cm) pot of a good loam-based potting compost in early October, it can be gently forced from the following February. Rested in autumn and early winter, the bush can be forced for several years with just a little fresh compost added to the top of the pot. Have a second batch of potted roses to flower up to Christmas. These bushes are rested from mid-winter to early spring out of doors, and dried off a little before putting them out. Grow them outdoors all summer and house with pot chrysanthemums in September. Select glasshouse cut flower varieties of rose for this treatment; 'Sweet Promise' (also known as 'Sonia') is recommended for this.

A number of perennial foliage plants can also be used to decorate the cool greenhouse the year round. Several raised from seed such as *Asparagus sprengeri*, *A. plumosus* and *Grevillea robusta* can be recommended. Climbing *Passiflora caerulea* is also seed-

Automatic ventilators prevent the greenhouse overheating while unattended.

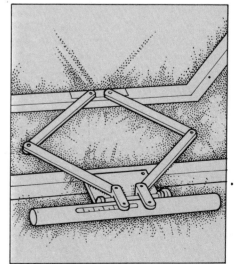

Different varieties of cinerarias will give a range of height and flower size. Sow in several batches from July to August for a succession of flowers.

raised and flowers well under cool glass. Cut it back in spring and grow it in a pot to restrain the growth.

HEATED GREENHOUSES

If you can hold a minimum temperature of 50 F (10 C) in a greenhouse year-round it will be possible to grow semi-tropical plants. Take the temperature up to 60 F (15 C) and the tropical plants, including quite demanding cultivars of croton, ferns and orchids, often described as stove-house plants, can be accommodated.

There is no need for propagators in these temperatures. Seed pans and trays of cuttings placed over the heat source will be kept quite warm enough to give good germination and rooting.

Many plants attractive in summer outside can be kept in good form the year round given the extra heat. Coleus is a good example. Tender evergreen climbers such as *Hoya carnosa*, *Jasminum polyanthum* and *Stephanotis floribunda* can be trained over roof wires to fill the house with flower, fragrance and foliage. Most tender climbers, but not hoya, are best cut back in early spring when they have outgrown the space available to them.

High temperatures will really push up the fuel bills in cold weather and constructing a polythene tent within a greenhouse is one way of reducing the cost and housing a smaller quantity of plants within the tent at the higher minimum temperature.

Strong winds blowing over a glass or polythene house can increase heat loss by 15–20 per cent, so a sheltered site is essential. Lining the inside of the house with polythene sheet to give a double glazed effect does save heat. It also causes a loss of light in winter when the light levels are already very low.

Lining the whole house reduces light by 35 per cent and I would prefer to line just the north-facing side to save heat and reduce light by no more than 18 per cent.

Where warmth comes from soil cables within the greenhouse a polythene tent over the crops in and on the heated area will reduce heating costs by 16–20 per cent. By using cloth rather than polythene to cover only during darkness can achieve a 22–24 per cent heat saving.

Border soil needs preparing well if plants are grown directly in it. Start with the best available garden soil – old turf stacked for a season and then chopped down with a spade is best. Mix seven parts of soil with three parts of peat and two parts grit or coarse sand to make a good compost.

Perennial plants will grow well for many years in such well prepared soil. Annual plants are better either rotated with other kinds or given fresh soil. It is possible to remove all the soil to two spades' depth, wash down with a soil sterilizer and refill with a new soil mix to crop repeatedly with tomatoes and Carnations. A tiny piece of infected soil can quickly reinfect the whole area, however, and I prefer either rotation or the switch to fertilized peat-filled growing bags and similar container growing methods.

At least two thorough cleanings right

Heavy crops of aubergines are possible in a heated greenhouse.

TEMPERATURE CHART

Inside Temperature	Glass to Ground	Brick to Bench Height	Polythene House	Lean-to Glass to Ground
4°C (38°F) just frost free	1·5 kw	1·25 kw	1·75 kw	1·25 kw
7°C (45°F) cool greenhouse	2 kw	2 kw		1·75 kw
10°C (50°F) temperate house	2·5 kw	2·5 kw		2 kw
15°C (60°F) store house	3·5 kw	3 kw		2·75 kw

Guide to heat input for 20°F heat lift in 1·8 m × 2·4 m (6 ft × 8 ft) greenhouse.

Vine weevil grubs eating a primula root. Other crops are also affected.

through the greenhouse will be necessary, especially where the house is heated and kept filled the year round. Early spring and autumn are the ideal times. Clear a section at a time, wash down the glass inside and out, scrub the superstructure, then freshen up the benches and all pot-grown plants.

Constant moving of plants is also necessary, rearranging to give more space as each plant develops. Rake over gravel or expanded clay granules on the bench, wash capillary watering mats and keep everything fresh and clean.

Watering
A watering can with a long spout is sufficient for small greenhouse purposes, although a switch to hose saves time in hot weather and where the house is quite large. Damping down the path and base of the house in hot weather will give a good growing atmosphere.

Keeping the can filled with water on the path allows warm watering of very succulent plants like saintpaulias. Apart from this exception tap water temperature is quite acceptable for most plants.

There are a variety of capillary watering systems which are invaluable to greenhouse owners away in the daytime. Simplest of all is a polythene-lined bench covered with 1 in. (2·5 cm) of fine sand. The sand is kept wet and the plants draw up what moisture they need from the sand. After settling pots on the sand, water once from above to set up capillary water movement.

More sophisticated are the sand beds and areas of proprietary capillary mat which are kept wet automatically. There are several systems where water

is released either when the reservoir level falls or when the mats dry.

Commerial growers also use systems with a separate drip or trickle nozzle to each plant. One or two of these are now available in smaller sizes to suit garden greenhouses. Even the fertilized peat-filled growing bags can be stood over a water-holding tray and the peat kept damp via capillary wicks.

Plant growth is much improved where checks from water shortage are avoided. In cool and cold greenhouses, however, be sure to reduce watering in winter. Where plants are just kept alive over the winter in cool temperatures, wet compost can bring death.

Fumigation
Although pests and diseases can multiply and spread rapidly in the warm confines of a greenhouse, they can be controlled with fumigants and smokes. Choose a still evening after the sun has lost its strength for greatest effect. Strong winds will speed the removal of the fumigant from the house and some chemicals can scorch the plants in hot sun.

Once the smokes are lit beat a hasty retreat and shut the door. Any big smoke leaks from the house should be noted because heat is likely to be lost continuously from these spaces.

Ventilate well before working again in the house. Check the instructions on all containers and follow to the letter. Ferns, for example, are damaged by several chemicals and will need removing from the house before fumigating.

Fruit trees in pots
Apricots, peaches, nectarines, grapes and figs are all possibles for pot cultivation. All these fruits can be grown in the border and trained against the wall of a lean-to greenhouse. They take up rather a lot of room however, and pot culture allows more plants to be given protection, even if the yield from the pots is considerably lower.

Keep the stone fruits outside all winter and bring under cold glass just as the buds begin to burst. This protects the flowers from frost and gives a good set if the blooms are dusted over with a brush at midday. Once fruit has set, is swelling nicely and the chance of frost has passed, the potted trees can be moved outside for the fruit to develop fully and ripen.

Plunging the pots in soil reduces the need to water, which will be twice a day in hot weather. Pots from 12–18 in. (30–45 cm) diameter are required. Pot the trees up in proprietary potting compost and replace the top few inches of compost each year.

Watering is sometimes a problem with peat-filled bags in a greenhouse, but special trays are now available which maintain moisture by capillary wicks, seen here in the inverted bag.

179

Calendar of Work
WINTER November-January

There is no substitute for the weathering of freshly cultivated land to produce easily worked crumbly soil in spring. Cultivate a little at a time to ensure all bare soil is cleared and cultivated by the end of this period. Mechanical rotary cultivators are best *not* used at this time, especially if the soil is heavy.

Dig the vegetable plot over one spade's depth, mixing in well-rotted compost as you go. In rose beds, shrub borders, in the fruit garden, under hedges and in perennial flower borders just skim the surface. Use the spade almost horizontally to cut off and invert the surface inch or two of soil. This disturbs the roots as little as possible and yet leaves a clean weed-free surface. Hoeing this crumbly surface soil in spring and summer will then be easy.

Woody plants ordered by mail often arrive at this time. If the soil is too wet to plant, dig out a trench and cover the roots with soil or damp peat until conditions improve. If it is too frosty even to do this, then cover with damp peat in a shed.

Lawns

Rake of all leaves and debris to keep the sward tidy; where the weather is mild and grass continues to grow it can be cut. Choose dry weather for the occasional cut and see that the mower blades are set high.

If a heavy snowfall occurs it is better not to heap cleared snow on the lawn because the grass will yellow if thawing is slow.

Ornamental garden

A good period to construct new features; paved areas, rock garden, walls and flower beds. Roses and other bare-root woody ornamentals can be planted when the soil is frost-free.

Protect tender plants like fuchias and Passion Flowers by mounding dry peat or strawy material around the base. Netting and hessian over hydrangeas will protect flower buds from frost. Knock heavy accumulations of snow from evergreens.

Rake away fallen leaves from rock plants, herbaceous borders and anywhere slugs are likely to lurk.

This is a good time to move large deciduous trees and shrubs which have out-grown their space.

Vegetables

Check the alkalinity of cultivated soil and where it is acid lime can be dusted over the surface. Choose a frosty morning when the dug surface is frozen to do this.

Give lettuce and cauliflowers under frames and cloches extra protection with old curtains or similar material when frost is very severe.

Place seed potatoes in a single layer in a light frost-free place to start sprouting. Onions like 'Ailsa Craig', early cauliflower, lettuce, cabbage, broad beans and peas can be sown indoors as spring approaches.

Fruit

Check ties are secure to stakes. Spray trees with tar oil – doing stone fruits first (these need spraying by the end of the year). Net trees if birds are pecking fruit buds.

Prune deciduous trees when the wood isn't frozen. Autumn-planted cane fruits can also be cut back now. If you want to try your hand at grafting new fruit varieties on to your trees, now is the time to cut scion wood and store it by just pushing the end into the soil.

Greenhouse

Bring in bulbs, rhubarb crowns and chicory roots a few at a time to force. Wash down the glass and clean the structure thoroughly.

EARLY SPRING February-March

All bare root perennials must be planted now; left any longer the chances of failure increase. Although a few sunny days can really bring new spring growth, be careful. Weather changes can be treacherous at this time and while the sooner every job is done in the garden the better a sudden return to hard frost can damage new plantings.

Lawns
Where raking the surface to remove debris, moss and old grass was not completed last autumn there is a chance to do this now. Once complete, early spring is a good time to apply lawn sand to kill moss and broad-leaved weeds as well.

Once the likelihood of severe frost has passed, edges can be cut and turf repairs undertaken.

Ornamental garden
Just as soon as the surface soil starts to dry, hardy border plants can be transplanted. This is a good time to split Michaelmas daisies, *Chrysanthemum maximum* and similar perennials. Pansies and other bedding plants over-wintered in frames can be planted outside.

Prune hard back all bush, standard and perpetual climbing roses at the end of this period. Late summer and early autumn flowering shrubs like buddleia, caryopteris, and large-flowered clematis can also be cut back hard.

If you did not transplant lilies in the autumn get them in now to develop a strong root system.

Established rock plants will benefit from some new compost worked in around them. Prune back heathers and mulch them with damp peat.

Vegetables
Use all the cloches you have available to cover soil. This dries the surface and warms the soil. Once covered for a week or two hardy vegetables like peas, broad beans, cabbages, radish and round-seeded spinach can be sown. Indoor-raised vegetables can also be planted out under cover.

General fertilizer can be spread over dry land and cultivated into the surface in preparation for spring planting. Shallots, onion sets and Jerusalem artichokes can be planted.

Lift parsnips and any other root vegetables before they make new leaf growth and the roots shrivel. Once lifted store in damp peat in a cool place.

Fruit
Apply a general fertilizer around all fruit – early in the season if the plants are in grass, later if in open cultivated soil. Once the fertilizer has been worked into the surface mulch under trees and bushes with well-rotted compost to retain moisture and smother weeds. Where spring frosts are a problem, damaging blossom, delay mulching until after the fruit has set because the bare soil radiates warmth and reduces frost damage.

Complete all pruning, especially where gooseberries were left to reduce the effect of bird damage to buds. Prune all autumn-fruiting raspberries hard back. The tips of summer-fruiting kinds can also be cut back to remove dead tips and tidy the canes.

Greenhouse
The busiest season in the greenhouse starts now. Small heated propagators can be filled with the hardier annual flower seeds. Cuttings need to be taken from geraniums, fuchsias, chrysanthemums and other summer-flowering plants. The cuttings will need warmth to root.

Pot-grown roses and strawberries can be brought in for early crops. Over-wintered lettuce and salad onions will be ready to harvest.

Try some peas and potatoes in pots for early crops.

Once new shoots come from grape rods they can be tied up on to the roof wires.

SPRING March - April

This is the big seed-sowing, propagating and planting period. Plants established now will have the whole summer growing period before them. Once the surface soil starts to dry get the hoe working in all parts of the garden with bare soil. A large area can be covered in a little time where the soil is crumbly and there are no weeds, I like to hoe right through the garden at least once a fortnight if not once a week. No weed, however deep-rooted, can withstand being sliced through every week.

Lawns

Sow grass seed on well-prepared soil for new lawns and re-seed bare patches once the surface has been scratched over and a little fresh soil worked into the area.

A general lawn fertilizer should be evenly spread at this time.

Ornamental garden

Evergreens can be transplanted in showery weather. Move as big a root and soil-ball as possible to reduce the check to growth, and syringe over regularly with water to reduce moisture loss.

Prune back frost damage on shrubs like hebes, fuchsias and tender evergreens. Plant galdioli and other summer-flowering bulbs. A start can be made planting dahlia tubers towards the end of this period.

Hardy annual flowers need to be sown outdoors now for masses of summer colour. At the end of the period some half-hardy annuals like Asters can also be sown where they are to flower.

Prune shrubs like forsythia and Flowering Currants after flowering. Just cut out some of the flowered branches to retain shape and size.

Vegetables

This is the time to sow very many of the vegetables. It is worth spacing the sowings out to get a succession of crops. A few lettuces sown every 2–3 weeks for example. See there is at least three weeks of *warm* weather between sowings of peas for succession; if the weather is cold delay the next sowing. This is important even when early and main-crop varieties are used.

Plant potatoes, onion sets, asparagus and all the indoor-raised hardy vegetable plants.

Thin out seedlings down the row once they are well established, remembering to leave enough carrots, turnips and similar root vegetables to pull young ones to eat while leaving alternate plants to develop fully.

Work a high-nitrogen fertilizer around spring cabbages to speed growth. Sprouting broccoli needs picking regularly if a succession of shoots are to be gathered.

Fruit

Watch all fruits for signs of pests and diseases. Follow the fruit spray charts on pages 132 and 139, to be sure of good growth and clean fruit.

Tie in the new growth on trained trees, especially peaches, cherries and plums, as it develops. Young shoots growing in the wrong direction are best rubbed out.

Remove flowers from perpetual-fruiting strawberries and late planted runners where the strength of the plant needs to be built for heavy crops in the future.

Greenhouse

Sow a variety of seeds, from half-hardy annuals, sweetcorn and tomatoes for outdoors, to summer-flowering pot plants and French beans for cold glass cropping. Pot up rooted cuttings of chrysanthemums and fuchsias, and once well established move to cold-frames and cloches before putting outside.

Make up hanging baskets. Keep the side shoots trimmed from tomatoes.

LATE SPRING May - June

Warm sunny weather brings tremendous speed of growth. Late frosts are still a possibility until well into this period, so be prepared with large sheets of newspaper. Put these over tender plants and hold the paper in position with stones to give protection to bedding plants, strawberry flowers and emerging potato shoots when the skies are clear at night and frost is forecast.

Sunny weather and rapid growth means heavy demand for water. Watch evergreens in tubs – they will need daily watering in hot weather. Established plants are better watered twice to ensure the compost is wetted throughout.

Lawns

When weeds are growing rapidly is a good time to apply selective weed-killers. If a fertilizer is used at the same time, use a soluble one or water the lawn a day or so after applying dry powders in the absence of rain.

Rapid growth demands regular mowing for the best lawns. Grass underplanted with bulbs and left uncut can be mown at the end of this period.

Ornamental garden

The tender summer-flowering subjects need planting now, and very tender subjects like zinnias can be sown where required to flower. This is the time to sow many biennials and perennials.

Spring-flowering primulas can also be sown, and *P.* 'Wanda' and *P. rosea* can be lifted after flowering, split up and transplanted.

Spray Roses where mildew, blackspot and greenfly are seen.

Put in support for tall-growing herbaceous plants and see that cordon-grown Sweet Peas are tied in weekly.

Vegetables

Keep up the successional seed sowing of salads and root crops. All the French and runner beans can be sown now, along with all the winter green vegetables such as kale, savoy and winter cabbage, sprouting broccoli and spring cauliflower.

Towards the end of the period plant out courgettes, cucumbers, marrows and outdoor tomatoes.

Keep up the hoeing until complete leaf cover reduces the need for weekly cultivation. Pull soil up around potatoes as the tops develop.

Fruit

Maintain the pest and disease sprays; several are timed after petal fall because it is necessary to avoid spraying when bees are pollinating the flowers. If you have been troubled with small maggots in raspberries then two sprays with derris at 10-day intervals will prevent this.

Developing strawberry fruits need lifting from the soil on to straw or polythene to prevent mud splashes.

Red blistered leaves on peaches are caused by peach leaf curl and can be picked off, but spraying to control is done at bud burst and leaf fall.

Melons can be planted now but keep them warm for the best results.

Greenhouse

Glasshouses can be filled to capacity at this time. Shade the glass in hot weather and dampen the paths at midday if possible. Tomatoes in heated glasshouses will be growing strongly, and those under cold glass can be planted from the beginning of this period. If the tomatoes have the first tiny fruits set before planting out cropping will be earlier.

Houseplants and all pot plants growing strongly can be moved up into larger pots. Use the richer J.I. Potting No. 2 and 3 or similar composts for big plants.

All softwood cuttings will root quickly in the warmth.

SUMMER June-August

This is the time to enjoy the results of earlier activities. Warm dry weather slows the speed of grass growth and dry surface soil reduces weeds so there is time to enjoy the flowers, fruits and vegetables.

Water the outdoor garden well and mulch areas with well rotted compost to control weeds and retain moisture if you are going away for a week or two. Set up capillary watering systems for container plants either automatically wetted or easily kept moist by a neighbour.

Try to visit garden centres, nurseries, flower shows and well-maintained parks to pick out other good plants for your garden.

Lawns
Water very well in dry weather. Selective weedkillers can still be applied to kill weeds. It is better to use liquid fertilizers if you want to green the grass up in summer.

Ornamental garden
Summer months are ideal for putting down paving if winter frosts prevented construction work of this kind. Hedges will need trimming if new growth is to cover the cuts by winter. Keep the garden tidy by cutting off all dead flower heads. Where plants like delphiniums are cut back hard another flush of flower will be produced in the autumn.

Transplant seedling biennials to produce bushy specimens. Take cuttings from pinks and rock plants like helianthemum. Chrysanthemum and dahlia flower stems will need disbudding to produce large flowers on a single stem. Propagate iris by division and shrubs like hydrangeas from softwood cuttings.

Prune shrubs like Lilac, philadelphus, spiraea and weigela after flowering.

Vegetables
Try sowing swede seed in early summer if you have had difficulty growing good roots. There is still time to sow salads, beetroot, spinach and carrots. Spring-maturing cabbages need sowing at the end of this period.

Plant out the winter greens as soon as possible and see that they are well watered to get them growing well. Watch for grey and white aphis curling the leaves; early sprays with greenfly killers will knock them out.

Pinch the growing tips from broad beans at the first sign of blackfly. Also pinch out the growing tip of outdoor tomatoes once four trusses of fruit have set.

Plenty of water and liquid fertilizer applied to runner beans, tomatoes, celery and onions will increase the yields considerably.

Fruit
Water applied in dry weather to fruit trees and bushes will increase this year's yield and help build up reserves for next year's crop. Prune out all the fruited canes from summer raspberries once picking is complete.

Tie in the fast-growing new shoots on loganberries and blackberries to ensure a good crop next summer.

Thin out the fruit on apples, pears and plums where the fruit set is heavy. One apple every 6 in. (15 cm) of branch is usually ample.

Greenhouse
Vines, melons and other fruits under glass will also need plenty of water and liquid feeds. Where the tops of tomatoes are tightly curled and dark green they have plenty of food, but if the top of the plant has a thin stem and widely spaced poor leaves more tomato food is needed.

Sow winter-flowering pot plants such as cyclamen, primulas, calceolaria and cineraria.

AUTUMN September - October

Harvest time, the big clean up and a start on the new gardening year. Spread the well-rotted compost from your heap over the soil to be winter dug. This gives plenty of space to fill with leaves and all the old plant remains as flower and vegetable beds are cleared.

Shorter days will mean slower growth and more time for the reconstruction of garden features, whether from living plants or hard landscape materials.

Lawns
Sow seed in early autumn or turf later for the best results. Mow the lawns less regularly as the speed of growth slows until it is too wet to mow.

Ornamental garden
All the summer bedding plants must be cleared as they finish flowering. It is better to sacrifice a few flowers and get the new planting established before winter. Plant all the biennial flowers and inter-plant with bulbs. See that the small bulbs are planted in early autumn to reduce the chance of shrivelling while out of the soil.

Lift early-flowering chrysanthemum stools and over-winter in frames. Hardy annual flowers can be sown outdoors and antirrhinums and Stocks can be sown in frames and cold greenhouses for early flowering next year.

A fine net placed on canes over ornamental ponds will catch falling leaves and stop them fouling the water.

Vegetables
Once the tops have fallen naturally, onions can be lifted and dried for winter storage. Lift potatoes and store in strong, multi-walled brown paper sacks or cardboard boxes. Be sure they are kept out of the light to prevent them going green.

Plant spring-maturing cabbages, and spray all brassicas to prevent caterpillar damage. Start to blanch endive for fresh salads. Lift chicory roots, screw off the tops and store in peat to force in the winter.

Sow hardy lettuce varieties to over-winter under cloches.

Fruit
When picking apples and pears keep the early ripening varieties away from the late keepers. The release of ethylene gas from ripe fruit speeds the ripening and decay of fruit nearby.

Choose a cool, slightly damp atmosphere for apple and pear storage. If the atmosphere is dry the fruits tend to shrivel.

Spray trees subject to peach leaf curl with liquid copper as leaves fall. Take hardwood cuttings of soft fruit bushes. Gooseberries root better if the cuttings still carry a few leaves.

Prune plums and damsons immediately after the fruit is picked. This usually means no more than the removal of unwanted branches.

Greenhouse
Plant up bulbs to force into early flowering but do not house until well rooted. House pot-grown chrysanthemums and freesias. Also bring in specimen fuchsias in pots and tubs to overwinter.

Clean down the superstructure and wash the glass to gain all possible light.

Ventilate freely on sunny days to reduce the chance of mildew on grapes, chrysanthemums and other crops.

Pot up seedlings of winter-flowering primulas, schizanthus and similar plants.

Pests and Diseases

Well-tended plants growing strongly are less likely to be infected by pests and diseases, and good cultivation is the first step to keeping these problems at bay. Garden hygiene is the next most important defence. Pests like mice, slugs, woodlice and vine weevil love to hide in old leaves and accumulated garden rubbish. Many diseases too are carried over from one year to another on old leaves, stems and infected fruits and roots.

After hygiene comes an alert eye; control measures taken at the first sign of attack are more effective and less damage is done to the host plant.

Chemicals to control pests fall into three main groups: those which kill by direct contact with the pests; stomach poisons which fall on the leaf, are eaten by the pest and kill from the inside; and systemic insecticides which are absorbed by the plant sap and kill both by contact and by insects sucking the sap.

Many fungicides, especially those we have used for a number of years, are protective. A coating of fungicide protects the leaves from infection by mildew, botrytis soft rots, rusts, blackspot, scab and similar fungal diseases. Modern systemic fungicides, however, are absorbed into the plant sap, transmitted through the plant and kill the disease as well as affording protection for the next two or three weeks.

Chemicals which can be diluted in water and sprayed on to the plants are the most commonly used, and are often the cheapest to apply. Aerosol canisters are easy and handy for spot application, especially to houseplants. Smokes and fumigants are very effective in the greenhouse. Dust can be applied to plants but it is difficult to achieve an even distribution. If applied when the plants are covered in dew the dusts will stick more effectively to the leaves. Dusts and granular preparations are generally best used as soil treatments.

It is important that sprays are evenly distributed over stems and leaves. The sprays easily cover the upper surface but it is difficult to cover the undersides of leaves, which is where many pests live and multiply. Systemic materials really come into their own for this underside control.

While good cultivation and physical means of control (such as covering a row of carrot or cabbage seedlings with muslin to prevent rootfly attack) is to be preferred, I have no hesitation in using chemicals to keep plants healthy. It is essential, however, to follow the

Red spider mite can be especially troublesome in a hot dry atmosphere. The webbing develops with very heavy infestations.

makers' instructions to the letter. Higher rates do not improve the kill, and the stated time must be left between spraying and harvest of fruit and vegetables.

Bees will also be killed by *some* insecticides, so choose carefully when spraying plants in flower, and even when spraying plants surrounded by flowering weeds.

Where pests and diseases occur repeatedly year after year it may well be necessary to apply a regular protective spray programme. If you do use repeated chemical application, ring the changes with choice of material. This prevents the build-up of strains resistant to one specific control.

There are several biological methods of pest control. There are bacteria which just kill caterpillars, and there are insect parasites of aphis, whitefly and red spider. Such insect parasites need to be used with understanding, however, for they seldom work if introduced when the pests have already reached epidemic proportions.

PROBLEMS AND SOLUTIONS

Aphids are more commonly called greenfly, but cover blackfly, grey mealy cabbage aphis, rose aphis, and several more. Some have wings and some are wingless – all multiply at an alarming rate.

The old-fashioned remedy was to spray with soapy water, which washes the pests off. I prefer very swift chemicals like bioresmethrin, formothion and malathion. If you want to destroy greenfly and leave ladybirds and lacewings (which eat aphids) and bees unharmed, then use pirimicarb.

Aphids, in the form of greenfly and blackfly are known to most gardeners.

Birds, cats, rabbits and squirrels can all be a nuisance. Galvanized wire netting with a small mesh is the only sure way to keep out all these pests. Try to use weathered netting, however, as the run-off from new galvanized wire can kill susceptible plants such as raspberries. Plastic netting does not have this problem, but squirrels will bite through it.

Strands of black cotton will keep off birds, but do not use black nylon thread as this can get wound around feet and wings. Soft fillis twine soaked in tar or creosote stretched in a single strand 6 in. (15 cm) from the ground will keep off rabbits. Pepper dust applied repeatedly is the next best to netting to keep cats away from finely cultivated soil.

Leaf miner are little maggots tunnelling between the upper and lower

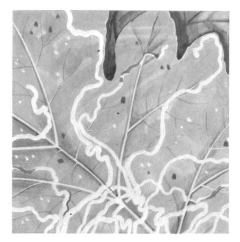

The tunnels made by leaf miners are unmistakeable and disfiguring.

surfaces of leaves. The grubs can be pinched with the thumbnail, but if this does not appeal, partially systemic chemicals like malathion also give control. Chrysanthemums, cinerarias, hollies and celery are all susceptible to this pest.

Leatherjackets can be a problem on heavy wet soils and in herbaceous borders. Roots are eaten by this greyish-brown larva, which is 1–1½ in. (2·5–4 cm) long. Methiocarb used to control slugs will also kill this pest.

Mice and moles are sometimes troublesome. Mouse bait in jars or flower pots on their sides is the sure way to control mice. The containers keep the bait dry and away from pets and birds. Mechanical traps can be used for mice and moles, while smokes

Leaf mottling may be one of the first signs of red spider mite attack.

placed in the underground tunnels will also deter moles.

Red spider mite are tiny spider-like creatures. There are two kinds; the fruit tree red spider mite is seen on strawberries, peaches, apples, pears and other broad-leaved trees and shrubs in hot dry weather; indoor red spider mite attacks many houseplants. Symptoms of both kinds are the same, a bronzing of the leaves, and cob-webbed leaves with heavy infestations. Spray with derris, dimethoate or malathion; several sprays may be needed to achieve control. Syringe regularly with water as this also helps to reduce attack.

Scale insects are tiny shell-like creatures that cling to the stems of plants. They can be removed from woody deciduous plants by spraying with tar oil. Evergreens and green plants are best sprayed with malathion in May.

Slugs and snails are well known, but can be controlled quite easily.

Slugs, snails, woodlice are best controlled with methiocarb.

Whitefly can be very persistent pests on indoor plants such as fuchsia, impatiens and tomatoes. It is necessary to spray once every three days for at least 14 days with either bioresmethrin or resmethrin to gain control. Encarsia is a parasite which can be introduced into a greenhouse, but a minimum temperature of 50°F (10°C) and long daylight hours are needed.

Botrytis, which is also known as grey mould, can be particularly trouble-some on soft fruit and greenhouse

Whitefly are tiny insects, often found on the undersides of leaves.

plants. Winter lettuce also tend to fall victim. This fungus disease shows itself as a fluffy grey mould that develops on soft brown areas. Control is usually possible with dusts and sprays containing benlate or thiram.

Bulb and corm rots are sometimes troublesome. Dipping many bulbs and corms in a benomyl solution before planting will help reduce such diseases as freesia fusarium, botrytis of gladioli, freesia, narcissus and tulip fire, and scab and core rot of gladioli.

Damping off is caused by several fungus diseases which attack developing seedlings. Typical symptoms are apparently healthy seedlings falling over in a patch. The stem at ground level goes to a black thread. Use clean containers, new sterile potting compost and clean water to avoid this disease. Infected seedlings can be watered with Cheshunt compound.

GARDEN CHEMICALS

Garden chemicals often have complicated-sounding names, but there are also proprietary names for the same substance. These are usually easier to pronounce, but there can be several proprietary names for the same active ingredient. To confuse matters still further, some chemicals also have common names. The chart below will guide you through this name maze, and enable you to shop easily in Britain for any of the more common chemicals.

Active Chemical	Common Name	Proprietary Names
Pesticides		
bioresmethrin		Combat Vegetable Insecticide (Fisons), Combat Whitefly (Fisons)
BHC (now HCH)	lindane	Lindex (Murphy), also in Hexyl Plus (PBI), Abol X (ICI), Combat Garden Insecticide (Fisons)
bromophos		Bromophos (PBI)
carbaryl		Sevin (Murphy)
diazinon		Gesal Garden Insecticide (Airwick UK), Combat Soil Insecticide (Fisons)
dicofol		In Combined Pest and Disease Spray (Murphy)
dimethoate	rogor	In Combat Garden Insecticide (Fisons) Systemic Insecticide (Murphy)
fenitrothion		Fenitrothion (PBI), Fentro (Murphy)
formothion		Systemic Liquid (PBI)
malathion		Malathion Greenfly Killer (PBI), Liquid Malathion (Murphy), in Combat Garden and Vegetable Insecticide (Fison)
menazon		Abol-X (ICI)
mercurous chloride	calomel	Calomel Dust (Boots, PBI, Murphy)
metaldehyde	slug bait	Many brands
methiocarb		Draza (May and Baker), Slug Guard (PBI)
–	nicotine	XL-ALL (Synchemicals)
oxydemeton-methyl	metasystox	Greenfly (Aphid) Gun (May and Baker)
pirimicarb		Rapid (ICI)
pirimiphos-methyl		Sybol 2 (ICI)
–	pyrethrum	Plant Pestkiller (Synchemicals)
resmethrin		Sprayday (PBI)
rotenone	derris	Abol Derris Dust (ICI), Liquid Derris (PBI)
sodium tetraborate	borax	Panant (PBI), Nippon (Synchemicals)
tar distillate	tar oil	Mortegg (Murphy)
trichlorphon		Dipterex (May and Baker), Kilsect (PBI)
Fungicides		
benomyl	benlate	Benlate (PBI)
bupirimate and triforine		Nimrod T (ICI)
captan		Orthocide (Murphy)
carbendazim		(with Maneb) Combat Rose Fungicide (Fisons)
copper		Liquid Copper Fungicide (Murphy)
dichlofluanid		Elvaron (May and Baker)
dinocap		Dinocap Mildew Fungicide (Murphy)
dithiocarbamate type	thiram	Garden Fungicide (ICI), in Hexyl Plus (PBI)
DNOC/petroleum oil		Ovamort Special (Murphy)
lime sulphur		Lime Sulphur (Murphys)
mercurous chloride	calomel	Calomel Dust (Boots, PBI, Murphy)
thiophanate-methyl		Systemic Fungicide (Murphy)
zineb	dithane	Dithane (PBI)
Other Chemicals		
betanaphthoxy-acetic acid	fruit set chemical	Betapal (Synchemicals)
indolylbutyric acid	hormone rooting agent	Seradix (Murphy)
anthraquinone	bird repellant	Morkit (May and Baker)
Wound Paint		
	bitumen	Arbrex (PBI)

ALWAYS FOLLOW THE MANUFACTURER'S INSTRUCTIONS TO THE LETTER. Used as instructed all these chemicals will be quite safe, but some can be dangerous if not mixed and used properly. Before buying or using any garden chemical check on the label that it is safe for the plant you wish to use it on (certain chemicals may damage some species or varieties and this will be indicated). If you are using chemicals on food plants, be careful to note the time lapse between applying them and the crop being safe to eat. Remember also that some chemicals can be harmful to fish and pets. Most will also harm beneficial insects such as bees, though some such as pirimicarb are harmless to lacewings, ladybirds and bees.

Index

Acknowledgements

We are indebted to the following for
permission to reproduce photographs:
Michael Warren
Bernard Alfieri
Peter McHoy
Pat Brindley
Kenneth Scowen
Floraprint Ltd (copyright I.G.A.)

192

Climbing Plants . Kenneth A. Beckett . Timber Press. (£ 8.95)
u.k.

Climbing Plants . Kenneth A. Beckett . Timber Press. (£ 8.95)
u.k.